THE MAKING OF
Alternative Cinema

THE MAKING OF
Alternative Cinema

VOLUME 2

Beyond the Frame: Dialogues
with World Filmmakers

Liza Béar

Foreword by Laurence A. Kardish

Westport, Connecticut
London

Library of Congress Cataloging-in-Publication Data

Falsetto, Mario.
The making of alternative cinema / Mario Falsetto and Liza Béar.
    p. cm.
  Includes bibliographical references and index.
  ISBN 978–0–275–99941–4 (set : alk. paper)
  ISBN 978–0–275–99463–1 (volume 1 : alk. paper)
  ISBN 978–0–275–99665–9 (volume 2 : alk. paper)
1. Motion picture producers and directors—Interviews. 2. Independent
filmmakers—Interviews. I. Béar, Liza. II. Title.
PN1998.2.F34 2008
791.4302′330922—dc22   2007037156
[B]

British Library Cataloguing in Publication Data is available.

Library of Congress Catalog Card Number: 2007037156
ISBN: 978–0–275–99941–4 (set)
     978–0–275–99665–9 (vol. 2)
     978–0–275–99667–3 (pbk.)

First published in 2008

Praeger Publishers, 88 Post Road West, Westport, CT 06881
An imprint of Greenwood Publishing Group, Inc.
www.praeger.com

Printed in the United States of America

The paper used in this book complies with the
Permanent Paper Standard issued by the National
Information Standards Organization (Z39.48–1984).

10   9   8   7   6   5   4   3   2   1

For Sebastian

CONTENTS

FOREWORD

Liza Béar is always a pleasure to read. Her conversations with filmmakers are so natural and easy that I wish I could have had these illuminating dialogues with the artists myself.

Béar disarms her subjects into candor. As a filmmaker she appreciates the process of filmmaking and as a critic the history of the art. Her meetings are relaxed, and I imagine when the film artist begins speaking it is with the smile of recognition of a fellow traveler. She sets the stage describing the site of the interview, elicits the personal information pertinent to the filmmaker's specific work, and proceeds with a dialogue about the film and its public reception. Her interviews move like pithy scripts: she sculpts away from improvisation by the precision of her questions and the editing she does before publication. Her subjects casually reveal the stories behind their films and her readers are enjoyably educated.

Movies may be seen and dismissed, but cinema is another matter. Cinema is part of culture, and cinema requires that the movies are only the beginning. Cinema is the argument that films elicit. Cinema is the thinking, the writing, and the full appreciation of film. Cinema requires that one film have several contexts: with other films, with other artworks, within a community, and in the individual biographies of its audience. Cinema recognizes social consequence and the influence films have on behavior, good and bad, in audiences. Béar appreciates the broad nature of cinema, and the filmmakers with whom she chooses to chat also understand that their work exists within several substantial frameworks. Because the director's work is significant it raises questions—both interviewer and interviewee know this—and Béar comes equipped with the right questions. The filmmakers, without didacticism or cant, speak—often with a wry humor—about motives and methods, and enrich the public understanding of their rather private work.

Béar appears indefatigable. She has been interviewing important filmmakers for over 15 years and has not lost her enthusiasm. She continues to write today for magazines and the Internet, but when she began her series of interviews the distribution of foreign films in America was indeed a paltry effort. Following her discussions throughout the book, readers will sense the waves and movements of international cinema as they appeared on American screens over the past 30 years: from the Western European and Soviet films of the 1970s, to the continual development of the American independent movement and the brief appearance of an African cinema (whose promise was unfortunately not sustained) in the 1980s, and the triumphal emergence of filmmakers from Iran and the three Chinas—Hong Kong, Taiwan, and the People's Republic. This is an oversimplification of modern film history but it does reflect the trajectory of critical reception to non-mainstream cinema in the United States.

It is just as well Béar continues to write. The demand for "product" in multiplexes and "software" for the channels on digital television is too great for the idiocies of Hollywood to sate: more foreign-language films are being released in America today than in any time since the explosion of the art film in the 1960s. Although their exhibitors are not representing these films as being in a language other than English, they must be viewed with a different set of expectations than those movies that require neither digestion nor reflection. Béar's pleasant and incisive questioning of filmmakers provides a blueprint for the appreciation of these foreign-language films. Her interrogations of past films suggest ways of looking at new films, but I hope she will find a few more interesting emerging filmmakers with whom to share a table and a microphone. I look forward to reading these in a second volume.

Laurence A. Kardish
Senior Curator, Film Department
The Museum of Modern Art, New York

PREFACE

A testament to the vitality of contemporary cinema in far-flung corners of the globe, this book is essentially a collection of previously published interviews with award-winning filmmakers about the making of their films. I've selected them from several hundred done as a freelance writer on my own recognizance between 1987 and 2004. That period saw increased output abroad and mounting interest in world cinema in the United States. Ranging in age from 18-year-old Samira Makhmalbaf to 93-year-old Manoel de Oliveira, the filmmakers are from 23 countries in Africa, Asia, Australia, Europe, Latin and North America, the Middle East, and the former USSR (see Appendix 1).

My interests are particular rather than general, so the dialogues explore in detail the sources of the scripts, story settings, modus operandi of the directors and, when possible, the cultural and political context for the films. About a third of the book is devoted to first-time feature directors, for whom the creative and logistical challenges are the greatest, which should make the book of especial interest to aspiring filmmakers.

In fact, the early *Bomb* interviews, between 1987 and 1992, took place while I was completing my own first feature (*Force of Circumstance* [1990], a political thriller) and then teaching directing workshops at Columbia and New York University graduate film schools. Interviewing and teaching were an exciting mix, and the dialogues were in part fuelled by my own experience and by the needs of filmmaking students. It really all started when I saw Gleb Panfilov's hilarious film *Tema* at the New York Film Festival, in which a Moscow writer searching for his muse at a country retreat finds that everyone there is a writer too.

As well as outstanding first-time directors (at the time of the interview), also represented here with one or more films are master directors such as Zhang Yimou from China, Hong Kong's Wong Kar-wai, Taiwan's Tsai Ming-liang, Abbas Kiarostami and Mohsen Makhmalbaf from Iran, France's Jacques Rivette and Agnès Varda, Lucian Pintilié from Romania, Jim Jarmusch and Milos Forman from the United States, the United Kingdom's Michael Winterbottom, and the late Ousmane Sembène from Senegal.

Given the mostly spontaneous, open-ended nature of dialogue, the text tends to be analytical detective work rather than theoretical in bias, and hopefully will be fun and inspiring to read for filmmakers and film buffs alike.

Almost all the stories were published to coincide with the theatrical release of a particular film (a sine qua non of assignment in the mainstream media),[1] sometimes as long as 18 months after the film's festival première and the original interview. For every story included, there are half a dozen tapes in a shoebox for films that regrettably didn't get U.S. theatrical distribution or were not assigned for publication.

Because this is a chronological sequence of single articles rather than an academic treatise, I have no axe to grind and no desire to engage in any kind of polemic. What others may consider offbeat I consider natural. But there tends to be an organic progression from one interview to the next, shaped in part by my own interests and by the thrill of recognition when these resonate in superbly crafted films; films that transcend or reflect the current zeitgeist and miraculously just popped up at Cannes, Sundance, or the New York Film Festival.

It's not my aim to persuade aficionados of big budget, special-effect action movies that there is much to be gained—aesthetic delight, wisdom, humor, suspense, nuanced political and psychological insights—from low-budget, satirical, or minimalist films from places such as Israel, Taiwan, Mexico, Portugal, Palestine, or downtown New York. Obviously, I think there is. Rather, my aim is to add to the understanding of the filmmaking process and to urge readers to see the films for themselves.

In popular parlance and reflecting an ambivalence in the national psyche (are we part of planet earth or not?)—as opposed to the well-established nomenclature of film historians or film festival programmers—"world cinema" sometimes denotes "the world outside the United States." Such a U.S.-centric view—which I don't share—seems inappropriate for an art form that continues to transcend national borders, both in coproduction deals and at its aesthetic core.[2] The interviews in this book with U.S. independent filmmakers reveal that, while distinct, their approach to filmmaking, what they set out to do, their resources, and their sensibilities have more in common with filmmakers from other countries than they do with studio films. In the current political climate, reaffirming the humanist values of the filmmakers I have chosen to profile takes on a special significance, whether intended or not. Readers may draw their own conclusions. That said, it's the individuality and uniqueness of each film, and of each filmmaker's context and concerns, that I have sought to bring out.

Liza Béar
New York, September 14, 2002–July 5, 2007
http://lizabearmakingbook.blogspot.com

---

[1] The initial selection of which films to screen, and which filmmakers to interview, was mine.

[2] While the filmmakers in this book are identified by nationality, by far the majority of their films were made through intricate coproduction deals, which fall outside the scope of this book.

ACKNOWLEDGMENTS

I'd like to thank the featured filmmakers—directors, screenwriters, and actors—for their frankness in sharing insights about wonderful films; the Film Society of Lincoln Center,[1] which programmed many of these films at the New York Film Festival and New Directors/New Films; the Festival de Cannes (which I attended for four years); the Festival of New Latin American Cinema, Havana (three years); the French Film Office[2]; the Montreal Film Festival; the Sundance Film Festival; and the Venice Biennale.

The longer dialogues were first published in *Bomb*; thanks to editor Betsy Sussler for enthusiastically backing my choices and championing the integrity of the dialogue process.

The shorter feature stories, the format favored by the mass media, first appeared in *The New York Times, Newsday, the Star Ledger, The Village Voice, Ms., Elle, Salon.com, Time Out New York, The Boston Globe, The So. Florida Sun-Sentinel, The Christian Science Monitor, indiewire.com,* and the New York *Daily News.* Thanks to the assignment editors for battling to make space for profiles of foreign filmmakers, especially post-9/11.

For crucial support of various kinds while writing and assembling the book, thanks to the Author's Guild, the Author's League Fund, Charles Béar QC, Pierre Béar, Sebastian Bear-McClard, Stewart Cauley, Susan Ensley, Coleen Fitzgibbon, Dee Dee Halleck, Peter Hargrove, Jonathan C. Howard, Stephen Kaldon, Livia Kamberos, Michael McClard, Eric Mitchell, Tom Otterness, Howard Seligman, and Celia Wyndham.

[1] The Film Society of Lincoln Center sponsors the New York Film Festival and cosponsors New Directors/New Films with the Museum of Modern Art.

[2] The French Film Office programs Rendez-Vous du Cinema Français at Lincoln Center each Spring.

Thanks to S. Victor Burgos of PhotoFest and The Kobal Collection for invaluable research and assistance with the photographs, and to Milestone Films, Miramax Films, New Yorker Films, Chris Chang, Robin Holland, Gary Indiana, Joanna Ney, Laurie Simmons, and Zeitgeist Films for facilitating or supplying other photographs.

Thanks to Robin Andersen for initiating the deal with Praeger and for writing the perspicacious introduction; to Anthony Chiffolo at Praeger for clinching the deal; and to Laurence A. Kardish, whose expertise and passion for world cinema is revealed annually in the New Directors/New Films series at MoMA, for writing the foreword.

And thanks to my editor, Dan Harmon, for his stamina, good humor, and skill in fielding a sticky wicket.

—Liza Béar

INTRODUCTION

My biggest fear when I'm making a film is whether or not the contrivance calls attention to itself and distances you from the suspension of disbelief.

Atom Egoyan

Atom Egoyan, Toronto-based director of the intriguing postmodern film, *Speaking Parts*, in which all the characters communicate via video, seems to discover his own attitudes toward filmmaking while talking to Liza Béar. He understands the power of image creation and the possible artistic hazards such as voyeurism, which may result when "the image is of a reality that is desired and not attainable." It is no accident that these personal and creative insights would emerge during a conversation with the author of *Beyond the Frame: Dialogues with World Filmmakers*.

Liza Béar reinvented the art interview in the pages of *Avalanche,* an avant-garde magazine she cofounded with Willoughby Sharp in 1970.[1] Published until 1976, its 13 issues were dedicated to sculpture and conceptual and performance art. With its focus on the artist, the magazine took a documentary approach to then-emerging art forms through probing interviews, extensive photographic coverage, and innovative design.

A decade or so later, she turned her attention to first-time directors and screenwriters of international cinema, and writing for the cultural quarterly *Bomb*, she was able to further explore and develop her unique dialogic approach to the world of art-house films.[2]

---

[1] It is hard to overestimate the impact that *Avalanche* had on the art community at the time. As a sui generis publication, it has become an eagerly sought collector's item and an invaluable resource for scholars. For one discussion of *Avalanche's* attitude toward the art interview, including photographs and examples of interviews, see Gwen Allen, "Against Criticism: The Artist Interview in *Avalanche* Magazine, 1970–76," *Art Journal* 64, no. 3 (Fall 2005): 50–61.

[2] In addition to the interviews, *Bomb* also published short stories written by Liza Béar.

One of the most engaging dimensions of the conversations presented in this book, and the thing that accounts for their edginess and anticipation, is the author's understanding of the creative process and how it might be nurtured and expressed. The questions and interactions are clearly informed by her own work in the field of experimental narrative film and video, and as a writer of short stories.[3]

In these pages the wealth of discussion on the topic of creativity, approached from a multitude of angles, is enthralling. French director François Ozon incorporates the enigma of creativity into the plot of his Hitchcockian thriller, *Swimming Pool*, and tells Béar, "creativity is not something that just happens, that falls on you from the sky, but something very concrete." Yet long-time director Agnès Varda, with five decades of experience, found her initial inspiration for the documentary *Gleaners and I* in a chance encounter that sensitized her to a woman's plight: "That was the emotion that launched the film."

These interviews are extraordinary works of art in themselves. As dialogue, the interview is developed into a literary art form in its own right. A question leads to a series of thoughts, and the musings that emerge between the participants bear little resemblance to the staccato, pre-determined serial questions of conventional interview practice. Indeed, at times the flow reverses, and questions and answers change voices. Nor do these conversations remotely approach the cult of celebrity.

Artists are truly present in these interactions, generous with their words, and often deeply introspective. Through the discursive process some become intent on arriving at a mutual understanding of cinema, art, and interpretation. In these cases the conversation moves into theoretical terrain about the meaning of representation, and the fluid nature of image construction and filmic reality. Such feats of communication only occur in the heady atmospheres that coalesce out of trust, wit, confidence, and experience.

An interview that truly engages the artist, engages the reader as well, and stays in the imagination in much the same way that the characters of an exceptional film or novel remain in one's thoughts for days afterward. I recall the young Iranian director, Samira Makhmalbaf, chasing the fog through the mountains of Kurdistan to get the right shot. These discussions are so captivating, and the result a set of recollections so vivid, I have to remember at times that I wasn't there.

Many of these conversations are grounded in a sense of place. An interview is set up: a hotel, a park bench, a restaurant. We move easily through the different worlds of film locations: a dining-room table, a city street, the icy gray of a Russian winter. We also move through time in the interview: the weather changes, the waiter comes, someone answers the phone.

When voice is committed to print, another layer of expertise is involved. Moments of film sequences, character, and plot are cut in, carefully crafted through structure and pace.

---

[3] Liza Béar's feature film *Force of Circumstance* was shown at the Museum of Modern Art in 1990. Her earlier short film *Oued Nefifik: A Foreign Movie* (1982, Super 8, 27 min.), shot in Morocco, was also shown at MoMA in 1999 at an exhibition of Super 8 films titled "Big as Life."

These directors find their homes in 23 different countries, and with these interchanges the reader is guided through a rich global tapestry of human cultures and sensibilities.

From a magic carpet in rural Iran, a life-affirming fable *Gabbeh,* is woven out of a director's struggle against oppression and ultimate rejection of war and violence. For Mohsen Makhmalbaf, color becomes the visual metaphor for love and life, and his palette is pulled from the sky, the fields and flowers, and transfixed into the carpets that tell the stories of the nomadic clan he follows. Like the carpets, he says of his film: it is "nature inspiring art."

We also meet Samira, Mohsen Makhmalbaf's eldest daughter, who began watching her father make films when she was eight years old. He let her quit Islamic high school at the age of 15, taught her filmmaking, and helped her make two award-winning features by the time she was 21. Samira's second film, *Blackboards,* follows itinerant schoolteachers who carry their blackboards on their backs as they hunt for students in villages through the mountains of Iranian Kurdistan. Working primarily with nonprofessionals, she incorporates the many, often deadly hazards of their lives into the film, and the blackboards take on new practical survival functions beyond their role as a visual metaphor. Though quite distinct, we find shared narrative and visual qualities between the film making styles of this Iranian father and daughter.

Can a locale be melancholy? In *Love Serenade* we find that the answer is yes. Australian director Shirley Barrett explains that quality is why she picked a small town in the country's south, called in the film, Sun Ray. The film moves through the stark openness of empty, fenced yards, and the town's bleak spaces make the towering silos, the setting for the film's finish, all the more surprising. In this story of youthful passions and middle-aged dalliance, Barrett's characters embody the tension of the place. *Serenade* offers a sensibility as fresh as the two young women whose actions seem to spring from the landscape itself. But speaking to the author, Barrett reveals intimate details of the film's considerable autobiographical content as well, with some lines based on actual entries from her teenage diaries. The conversation seems to allow Barrett to find the humor in, as she says, being "pathetically deluded" by love at an impressionable age.

Love Serenade is produced by Jan Chapman, who also produced *The Last Days of Chez Nous,* a Gillian Armstrong film. Barrett graduated from the Australian Film and Television School where directors Jane Campion and Armstrong also received their degrees. All were part of the exciting period when Australia experienced a film renaissance, and through these interviews we find traces of the influences and aesthetic explorations that connect Australian Cinema. Their characters are often moving in a dance between art and life, as depicted but also experienced by the filmmakers themselves.

The selections and groupings in this collection expand our views of the filmmaking process in ways that delight and surprise, illuminating a world of interconnections that offer their own insights.

So many of the compound relationships involved in collaborative filmmaking are discovered here. In *A World Apart,* the story of South African apartheid is told from the perspective of a 13-year-old girl. We hear from the screenwriter Shawn Slovo, who as a child was forced to share her parent's love with their struggle for justice and equality.[4] She explains why it was so difficult to be her mother's daughter in the escalating repression of 1963, and how her mother's death in 1982 left their relationship unresolved. Moving from the writer's struggle to create a work of fiction from childhood memories, the book presents another view of the film's creation through the eyes of director Chris Menges. His interest in this story was sparked by the anger he felt experiencing apartheid while shooting a program in South Africa for British television. Working closely on the set with Slovo, he explains how he shaped scenes and dialogue to foreground the politics while maintaining the power of the personal.

Exploring the parameters of collaboration and creativity, we discover shared partnerships that resonate and develop among actors, directors, crews, and producers, but at times we are surprisingly confronted by a question answered frankly that reveals the limits of collaboration. Such was that case with Brigitte Rouan, actress turned director, who candidly recounts lengthy arguments with cameramen who struggled against her vision. They could not see the film through her eyes. And then after shooting, she was drained by the grueling pace of postproduction, a schedule set not by her but by her editor, who was at the time, her husband.

This book also represents the art of selection. Over the years, the writers, directors, and actors Béar has chosen to talk to and write about culminate here in a body of work with vision and coherence. In addition to interviews, this book contains shorter feature stories, writing that demonstrates the author's versatility and recognizable expertise.[5] *La Vie De Bohème,* the story of struggling artists in Paris, is a quintessential art-house film by Finnish director Aki Kaurismaki, and a fine sample of Béar's film interpretations. Altogether, the writings in this book would first appear in 20 different publications.

Liza Béar's film writings demonstrate a sensibility that seeks to foreground the profoundly social nature of the human condition, one that reveals the interconnected tangle of relationships among sisters, brothers, mothers and daughters, fathers and sons, gang members, estranged neighbors, teachers and students, and star-crossed lovers. Characters fall in love with dancing, bondage, images, a bicycle, peace, unemployment, the quest, a cat, the idea of suicide, and each other. But the longings of the human heart and the passions that bind one to another are always tied to a sense of place and history with a profound acknowledgment that what it means to be human is not shaped in a void. A love story in Mexico City is retrieved from the brutality of dog fighting. As characters move through history their actions have context and consequences. They are caught within declining empires, economic dislocations, repressive governments, class conflict, dangerous urban environments, the middle-class, the wrong gender. They are hungry, rich, poor, artists, writers, and

---

[4] Slovo is the daughter of Joe Slovo and Ruth First, members of the African National Congress (ANC) active at the height of South African apartheid.

[5] The feature story is a distinct form of journalism with precise strictures. Quotes are folded into the text, and usually provide the conclusion.

petty swindlers. Ultimately, these films tell their stories from a deeply humanitarian perspective. As American Indian author Sherman Alexie, writer of *Smoke Signals*, put it: "I'm a member of a tribe and proud of that. Every moment that can be found in Shakespeare's tragedies and comedies can be found on my little reservation. Hamlet lives there. King Lear lives there. And so do Romeo and Juliet."

It should come as no surprise that these conversations would also touch on heated controversies. What do directors think about and how do they respond to audiences and criticisms? Some disparage scenes in *A World Apart* for the depiction of laughter and happiness at a dinner in the meager home of poor black Africans. Do scenes of joy and dancing belong in stories of pain and tragedy? Directors also recount the hardships suffered through the course of making their films; the practical obstacles and the financial barriers they were forced to overcome. In the face of adversity, many astounding works of art were created with little money, at times using nonprofessional crews and actors, some shot in remote, rural villages, others set in dangerous, unprotected urban neighborhoods. From the gritty streets of Mexico City, director Alejandro Iñárritu turned threatening conditions to his advantage by employing young gang members to protect the equipment while he made *Amores Perros*.

A film's production can also take an unexpected turn, but not necessarily in the wrong direction. Wong Kar-wai, director of *In the Mood for Love*, from Hong Kong, learned more about camera style and filmic content having to frame his own shots in the absence of his legendary cinematographer, Chris Doyle.

Global cinema has also been the subject and target of censorship. In *Beijing Bicycle*, the theft of a mountain bike sets in motion a contemporary tale of class conflict and social dislocation; significantly, in the new China not one of the five feature films by director Wang Xiaoshuai was theatrically released. There are few discussions of censorship more cogent and relevant than the one that takes place between Béar and Milos Forman, as he explains his reasons for making *The People vs. Larry Flynt*, and the dangers posed to democracy by right-wing ideologues who would control the speech and art of others. Romanian filmmaker Lucian Pintilié was forced into exile in 1972 because he refused to submit his art to the "small, necessary, capricious demands of the system." He told Béar, "Political dictates are always capricious. One day they want one thing, the next day something else." After the fall of the Ceaucescu government, Pintilié returned to his country and directed *The Oak*, a scathing social satire that portrays "people who gradually get used to monstrosity, for whom evil becomes banal."

Another side of censorship is personal and self-imposed, and as we find in these interviews, it is not always about the failure to express a political opinion but also occurs when a person fails to express an emotion. In this case, as Canadian filmmaker Denys Arcand explains, "Films are made also to repair the past. In this film, [*Barbarian Invasions*] I could make the son say that he loved . . . his father."

Mohsen Makhmalbaf tells Béar about the economic constraints of filmmaking imposed in Iran under the Shah, a less direct form of censorship, but a stifling of expression nonetheless. After the revolution he visited his grandmother's grave to tell her about the changes in Iran, from a "kind of Hollywood cinema" that was "close to hell" into a humanist one where people no longer made "movies solely to make money." That change led to the flowering of Iran's new-wave cinema, which in the years that followed enjoyed international acclaim. Although today in Iran filmmakers must work under the eyes of government censors, the U.S. State Department makes it difficult for filmmakers from certain countries to obtain visas to accompany screenings of their films. When he was invited to show his groundbreaking film *Ten* at the New York Film Festival in 2002, Abbas Kiarostami's visa was famously denied by the U.S. government.[6]

In these pages, Béar chronicles a period of filmmaking that spans over 15 years and brings to life a golden age of mostly pre-9/11 international cinema. By 2007, global cinema' s enduring value and essential qualities had been acknowledged by the mainstream. Three of the five films nominated for an Academy Award for best director were made by foreign filmmakers,[7] and many films that won Oscars included international participation.

Indeed, as budgets and box- office returns continue to be the measure of success in Hollywood, the once most dominant of the American popular arts continues its downward spiral. As this book goes to print, movie attendance in America has reached its lowest point in 10 years. The two most-cited reasons for staying home were rising ticket prices and the quality of the films.[8] As Hollywood features lost their magic and imagination to marketing demands and bottom lines, going to the movies lost its fascination. In the pages of this book, we find another, very different world of cinema, one where directors, actors, and screenwriters value the art of film. In the hands of these filmmakers, the inspiration for and practices of making movies are decidedly varied, and usually quite distinct from commercial motivations.

This book offers its readers a rare view of filmmakers and their art, one that provides a gripping combination of films, interactions, collaborations, and explorations into the creative process. As such, it is a solid work of scholarship, and will remain an invaluable resource to film students as a seminal work on the aesthetics and themes of global cinema.

With these interviews, Liza Béar has made a substantial contribution to the international art community and to all those who continue to be captivated and enriched by global cinema.

Robin Andersen
Author of *A Century of Media, A Century of War*
Director of the Peace and Justice Program
Fordham University

---

[6] Kiarostami was granted a visa—though at the last minute—to be present for his recent retrospective at the Museum of Modern Art, in 2007.

[7] "Oscars Go Global," *The Sydney Morning Herald,* January 24, 2007, http://www.smh.com.au/articles/2007/01/24/1169594339263.html.

[8] Neal Gabler, "The Movie Magic Is Gone: Hollywood, Which Once Captured the Nerve Center of American Life, Doesn't Matter Much Anymore?" *Los Angeles Times,* February 25, 2007, http://www.latimes.com/news/opinion/commentary/la-op-gabler25feb25,0,4482096.story.

GLEB PANFILOV

Tema

A famous writer not satisfied with himself, who understands that he has lied to himself, he has not lived the right . . . Whereas characters like Sasha and Chizhikov are very hardworking, idealistic people who don't compromise . . . who don't do things for money—that notion was very urgent at the time. It's still very much to the point right now, it always will be.

Gleb Panfilov, 1987

New York, September 30, 1987. 11 A.M. sharp.

Location: The 27th floor of the St. Moritz Hotel, overlooking the dense green rectangle and the brackish waters of Central Park. On the horizon, a yellow-grey bank of polluted air caps the foliage. Gleb Panfilov, Soviet director, and Inna Churikova, leading actress, are in town for the New York Film Festival screening of *Tema* (Theme). This is their first visit to the United States.

Also present: a Russian interpreter from the Soviet Mission to the U.N. and an escort from Suzanne Salter Public Relations, to make sure we stick to our tight schedule. A representative of IFEX, chief distributor of Soviet films for the past 25 years, leaves as I arrive with Jimmy de Sana.

Panfilov, in a red and blue checked flannel shirt, sleeves rolled up, is on the phone. Inna Churikova, warm and gracious, radiant in a deep blue silk dress with red polka dots, motions us to the salon area: a couch along the wall, a small glass table and two napoleonic chauffeuses. The interpreter and I sink into the upholstery. Inna offers us a drink; we exchange some social French. Jimmy takes her portrait by the window while someone struggles with the Perrier bottle caps; they are not twist-off tops. Panfilov produces his own bottle opener, everyone is relieved, good, that one works. I watch his capable hands.

Out of the comer of my eye, I catch the upward movement of an arm towards a face. It's the PR person checking her watch. Instinctively I check mine. Panfilov, whose birthplace was Magnitogorsk in the Ural Mountains, was an engineer before

Portrait of Inna Churikova by Jimmy de Sana, 1987. Courtesy of Jimmy de Sana Trust.

he decided to make films in the early sixties, during the Khrushchev era. I don't mention it, though. No time to get too biographical. This meeting is more of a salutation, an act of recognition, some shared time . . .

I show them a copy of the last issue of *Bomb,* they like the scale. In the Soviet Union, Gleb says, the photo magazines would be in color. He is intrigued by the vodka ad on the back cover, wants to know the caption for a Duane Michals photograph.

I check the recording. There's a weird click at regular intervals, it's probably just the tape.

The interpreter's voice is smooth, cadenced, neither sinister nor ingratiating, and yet, there is an inflection, there's a trace of . . . I can't quite decipher the emphasis. I try to read Panfilov's expression instead. He has a great face too, Jimmy and I agree, in complete contrast to the pale luminous oval symmetry of Churikova's, friendly, a craggy furrowed brow with dark-bright deepset eyes and thick, triangular eyebrows that protrude. His hands are shapely and assertive, his gestures controlled.

I make my first serve.

With this film, it's as if a cold, strong, immensely refreshing wind blows into Lincoln Center from the Soviet landmass, dusting out the corners, temporarily releasing little points of fun.

"Are all the films as funny as *Tema*," I ask, hoping to elicit a comparison.

Tema follows the fortunes of a famous playwright, Kim Yesenin, on his arrival at a small country retreat some distance from Moscow. It's a bleak, deserted, wintry landscape, obviously freezing cold, and the place has the hush of deep snow. The locations are final repositories (a museum and a cemetery) but the film is nothing if not alive and passionate, acute in its details.

The interpreter converts my words into his, English into Russian and back; God knows what happens in the process. The question is scooped up with alacrity. I beg Valeriy not to do diplomat-style simultaneous translation for the sake of the recording. English-Russian-Russian-English, it feels more like a relay race.

The answer is circumspect; the ball goes into the net.

"There is an element of comedy in all his films," the interpreter returns politely, "He cannot do without it."

I raise my eyebrows. Not accustomed to this particular linguistic ballpark, we switch from first to third person without standing on ceremony.

"He says humor helps the Soviet people a lot, they know how to be humorous and they like it, it's their way of life. One cannot live without humor."

I think of the laughter in the auditorium on Monday night, laughter of delight and recognition, giving the lie to Panfilov's remark at the press screening that his film came with an address, wasn't intended for an American audience. A scene with a literate and resolute traffic cop who resists being upstaged by a literary lion has got to appeal to the entire motorized world.

"Was he surprised at the reaction of the New York public?"

"Oh yes, pleasantly surprised. But he thinks it was just a coincidence. He thinks that Tuesday's audience will react differently. That's his opinion."

Inna Churikova, who has been following this exchange closely, expresses some concern:

"Modesty is a good trait of character, but not to that degree!" Panfilov smiles skeptically.

I wanted to know how they met.

Twenty years ago, when he was looking for an actress for his first feature, *No Crossing in the Fire,* a film about a soldier . . .

"I wanted someone a little bit strange-looking, with big eyes like Inna has . . . I saw her on TV, but I couldn't figure out her name because I missed the credits, I just caught the end of the program. I spent three months, no, even longer, trying to track her down. Then I found her."

I turn to Inna. "Is Gleb a good director?"

Some of the Russian gets submerged in the mirth that ensues. Inna, who had already starred in eight features and many television shows, has had the lead in the six films that Gleb has directed since they met in 1968. That's a long period of collaborative time and she believes in him, she trusts him. But also it's difficult sometimes for her to work with other directors when she's always working with her husband.

Her husband reminds her of a film she just starred in Hungary, *The Messenger Boys,* by Karen Shakhnazarov. That was definitely not his film.

Later, at home, I do some contextual research. The USSR has fifteen republics; each has one production studio for feature films, and others for documentaries, specialized films. Soviet industry manufactures all the line items in the supplies and materials category of a film budget, raw stock, cameras, lights, lenses, tripods, et cetera. This tends to limit the number of films that can be produced per year to between 130 and 145. Film attendance in the USSR is still at the level it was at in the thirties and forties in this country; the Soviets see fifteen times as many films as the U.S. public, and ticket prices are the equivalent of $2 or may even be as low as 35 cents per show. Consequently, according to my source, box office profits from the Soviet film industry are able to pay for the entire costs of running Soviet television. Directors and major players receive a salary from one of the studios and also a percentage of royalties from box office revenue.

"How hard is it to get a film started in the Soviet Union?"

"Financially, we do not face any great difficulties because GOSKINO, the state film committee, gives out the money."

GOSKINO is the highest-ranking film bureaucracy in the Soviet Union. It controls (or did, pre-Glasnost), the Soviet film industry. It allocates the funds for production and then decides on distribution.

"Yes, but when you have an idea for a film, how difficult is it to persuade the authorities to let you make it?"

> "I believed in my film. But I also understood that at that moment,
> I was . . . ahead of my time, beyond the frame of the permissible."

"Well, of course that is the main task, to persuade GOSKINO that your idea, your concept, is right, is a good one for a film. This is usually done verbally first. Then, if they agree it's a good idea, you present a scenario and they make a production schedule."

Tema was made eight years ago, in 1979. Made but not released. Did GOSKINO read the script, I wonder. If they disapproved, why was the film produced?

"What bothered GOSKINO about the film?"

"They didn't like the way I'd done some scenes. They asked me to redo them another way, but I wouldn't. I wouldn't change anything. It would have been a different film if I had. For this reason the film stayed on the shelf."

Along with quite a few others, including several works by Kita Muratova, recently shown at the Montreal Film Festival.

"The scene where the Jewish writer says, here everything's a lie, he wants to leave the country?"

"Yes, yes, especially that scene."

"Was this the main reason?"

"It was one of the main reasons. But there was another. The main character, Kim Yesenin, believes that his life has been in vain, that he hasn't lived in the right way, that he has lied to himself. That was also a serious matter. The leadership of the secretariat of the Writers' Union couldn't take that."

"Couldn't take what?"

"This kind of self-doubt in the portrayal of a writer."

Kim Yesenin, powerfully played by Mikhail Ulyanov, is named after the Russian poet Sergei Yesenin, who committed suicide because he wouldn't compromise on his work. Kim is trying to write a new play but he is not at peace with himself. His fame has been won at a price: for ten years he has tethered his subject matter to official requirements, he has traded in his artistic autonomy. In other words, he played safe. Now he feels bad about it and worse, he has lost touch with his real intuitions, or he is afraid he has.

"Where was it shot?"

"The film was shot in Susdal, near Vladimir, about 200 kilometers from Moscow."

"Are most of your films shot outside Moscow?"

"No, mostly the films are devoted to urban life, like *I Wish to Speak*, which is about the mayoress of a small town, and *Vassa*, based on the play by Gorki."

Right from the start Kim is tense and quarrelsome. He picks a fight with his friend Igor over the choice of radio music—a somber Schubert piece versus something more cheery. In his first brush with the law at the entrance to the town, Kim switches gears and turns on the charm. He has no scruples about using his social connections as a famous playwright to intimidate the young traffic cop who tries to serve them a ticket. The ubiquitous junior lieutenant (Sergei Nikonenko)—he turns up in almost every scene—is also a compulsive scribe and Shasha's unsuccessful suitor.

"How tight was your shooting schedule for *Tema?*"

"February, March . . . it must have taken three months to shoot. It was wintertime."

"In some scenes there was a blizzard, it was snowing really hard."

"Yes. There was not much time to shoot each day because the days were so short."

Tema wasn't taken off the shelf until after filmmaker Elem Klimov was elected president of the Soviet Filmmakers Union in May 1986. According to a source, Klimov is the David Putnam of the Soviet film industry. One of his first acts was to create a "conflicts" commission for the release of previously censored films. It was first shown in Europe at this year's Berlin Film Festival, where it won the Golden Bear and IFEX picked it up for North American distribution.

"Did you lose a lot of shooting days because of the weather?"

"There were some delays due to the weather conditions. Sometimes, though, we needed bad weather for the story. The weather was really an essential part of it."

I mention the virtual absence of primary colors in the film.

"Sharp colors are not characteristic of the Russian winter—at least of the Russian landscape. What you get is a more diffused kind of light. But of course clothes played an important role in the portrayal of Sasha's character."

Kim is first attracted to Sasha when he notices her at the local museum where she is acting as a tour guide for some French tourists. Sasha is much too perceptive to fall prey to his advances or his designs on her. It doesn't seem that she wants to be his muse or his confidante either. She has quite enough relationships and projects of her own, and if she got them out of the way, then maybe they could get together but her presence makes it clear this would be on her terms. However, the attention she pays to Kim is enough to send his current lady-friend scuttling back to Moscow in tears, so something is up. Clear-headed though she is, the film hints that she might become a victim of her own compassionate nature. "To you, everyone is lonely and unhappy," her departing lover tells her. And, after all, despite his anxiety, Kim is still quite a charismatic fellow, he hasn't totally lost his touch. However, he is on a collision course with himself and, in the dinner scene, Sasha acts as a spur to his self-interrogation. To the dismay of his flattering dinner companions, she confirms his self-doubts, his estimate of his earlier plays. Paradoxically, in so doing, she doesn't alienate herself from him, far from it. Lucidity itself, she becomes identified with his state of mind and as such, is assured a place in his emotional pantheon.

"Did Inna pick her own clothes?"

"Yes, I had to because at first they picked clothes for me that were too modern."

"You know, what was important for me," Panfilov is saying, "was the mood created by the white, the black, the grey, the paleness of the grey [skies], the passage to the interesting light of her face, her eyes, as if it was [a natural extension of], was reflected from the snow . . . I didn't need any active colors, because that would have disturbed the effect. . . . The red telephone, in the scene where Kim calls his ex-wife, was a foreign object. Apart from that, it's only at the very end of the film that you see different reddish colors. It's to increase the tension . . . [leading up to] . . . the explosion of Kim's car."

If he were a painter, he says, he would represent the film by a single image. Against a vast snowy backdrop, he would show a small car stranded in the snow with tiny figures of men and women against a grey sky. Looking down from the grey sky at this road would be Sasha and Chizhikov . . . Chizhikov the peasant poet, the "poor spirit" of the film . . . that is his vision of a painting that would symbolize the film.

"You've made about seven films with Inna since 1968, including *Tema*, two before, and several after . . . "

"Six."

"Six. Is *Tema* the most risky film that you have made?"
Panfilov and the interpreter confer in Russian at some length.

Towards the end of Tema Kim, having made his way to Sasha's apartment, is forced to hide in her kitchen when he hears her return with someone else. Terrified that he will be discovered and made a fool of, Kim immobilizes himself next to the refrigerator while Sasha pleads with her boy-friend (a dissident writer who earns his living as a gravedigger) not to leave for Israel. A hungry cat wanders back and forth from the arguing couple in the doorway to the kitchen, nearly giving Kim away. It's an intense, poignant and yet hilarious scene which is underscored by the precariousness of Kim's situation. It's also an ingenious use of off-camera to integrate a sub-plot, a sub-plot that serves to heighten Kim's own dilemma.

Finally the interpreter is saying something I can understand.
"And what would be the risk," he asks.
I return to the St. Moritz. I'm not just thinking about the dissident writer's complaints. *Tema* is a very introspective film. There's a lot of tricky stuff to deal with, aside from references to the regime.
"The risk of having, for instance, a main character who thinks aloud, who talks to himself all the time. That's a hard thing to pull off. Of quoting poetry." It's a big challenge to deal with other art forms in film.
Panfilov smiles.
"Well, you are supposed to take risks."
"I agree, but I was wondering how the script got past the authorities."
"You hand in a blank sheet of paper if you don't want to risk anything. Of course, if you have an exciting, fast story, the risk is less. With this kind of scenario, though, I could have ended up with a very mediocre picture, I could have made it too thin."
"Were you walking on ice?"
Panfilov is amused at my insistence. After all, in '79 he'd already made quite a few films. He has a sure touch. And the best actors, Mikhail Ulyanov, Inna Churikova.
"I'm a good skater," he says. "Good at keeping balance."
"When they . . . they . . . the big guys . . . stopped *Tema* from being released, you had to wait seven years. . . . I know you made two other films, *Vassa* and *Valentino*, but what happened to you during that waiting period?"
"Do you mean, did I regret having shot the film?"
"No! No, not at all. I just wondered how it felt, waiting for it to be released." Did patience turn into frustration, frustration into anger?
"I believed in my film. But I also understood that at that moment, the film just would not fit into the predetermined frame, the . . . [mindset] of the society. I understood that I was beyond the . . . "
" . . . ahead of your time."
"Ahead of my time, beyond the frame of the permissible. So I accepted it, the official decision."

Panfilov is animated. He wants to continue. In *Tema* he was sure that he was saying something new.

I know what he means. The film is as much about self-critique as a critique of the system. He's dealing with artistic integrity, with autonomy, with sources, with the whole complex dynamic of what makes a writer get going, bring a work into being. With the relationship of individual to social values, this being different there from here, where we could use some model citizens, if it's not too late.

It's a sobering fact to Kim that the tracking of his thoughts, his own internal dialogue throughout the film intersects with the literary activity of his host/friend/rival Igor who, busy at the only typewriter in the house, has already fictionalized their trip into a short story. It also intersects with the quite genuine dilemmas of Kim's provincial compatriots and, in a sense, co-writers. He probably doesn't think of them as his peers because first of all they are a lot younger and secondly they are not Muscovites. Less famous and of unequal talents but maybe equally deserving.

Panfilov is still on track. He's talking about his version of Gorki's *Vassa,* and *Hamlet,* which will be the basis for his next film. He's trying to do something that hasn't been done before in film. He has seen something new in these plays, a completely new reading, something that no other filmmaker has seen.

I tend to believe him.

In the graveyard scene, where Sasha extols the virtues of Chizhikov, a peasant poet who died in obscurity and about whom she's writing a book, Kim's reaction is immediately one of appropriation, he seizes on it as a potential theme for his next play.

"If I see no connection, no association with everyday life, it's not interesting for me to make a film. There were many new things in *Tema* when it was made . . . A famous writer not satisfied with himself, who understands that he has lied to himself, he has not lived the right . . . Whereas characters like Sasha and Chizhikov are very hardworking, idealistic people who don't compromise . . . who don't do things for money—that notion was very urgent at the time. It's still very much to the point right now, it always will be."

"What sort of budget are the films made with?"

"*Tema* was made with 400,000 rubles. That's maybe $450,000."

"How involved does the production studio get once you have shot the film with the editing and the final cut?"

"At the beginning of my career, of course, the studio tried to poke its nose into my affairs more often, to [have their say] in the final editing. But later on when I became more famous and experienced, they believed and trusted me more and did not trample on my art ideas. Besides, I think it's okay when the studio is involved in who to choose for the cast, because the studio finances the film and they are also interested in the success of the film."

"The financial success."

He thinks it's the same in the United States. He feels obliged to show people [at the studio] the material that's already been shot to find out their reaction.

"To show the work-in-progress?"

"Yes, before the final cut."

"Are the films widely shown in the Soviet Union?"

"There is a special committee which determines the value of a particular film and decides how many prints should be struck. Then the municipal authorities determine how long the film will run in each town or city."

"So is there a wide audience for your films?"

"It varies from film to film. For the early films it was maybe 20–25 million. *Vassa* was nine million."

"How would you characterize what GOSKINO is after these days, GOSKINO's taste?"

"I don't put in my films the subjects that GOSKINO likes, but those which I like, which are interesting to me. But right now their taste has changed for the better. GOSKINO just doesn't interfere with such things any more. Actually, now they allow all the story ideas that the directors propose. You know, the context for film-making has changed a lot in the Soviet Union in the last few years. That's because the whole political climate has changed."

"In the old days, they always wanted the main character to be a 'positive hero,' a model citizen?"

"Yes."

To positively reflect the values of the state. Happy ending here, positive hero there. The official Soviet version of the feel-good, formula film. However, even prior to Glasnost, according to a recent analysis, rather than being ruled primarily by ideological considerations, the Soviet film industry was an intricate balance of power between political chiefs, GOSKINO, the filmmakers' union, the studios like Mosfilm and Lenfflm, and the movie-going public.

"So there should be more of a range of characters."

"Well, as a matter of fact, it's a paradox but now the problem is more to show a normal, nice person. Today we have a whole slate of black films—with drug addicts, prostitutes, bandits—there is a big lack of simple, honest characters in films. The Soviet film studios have gone to the other extreme."

"GOSKINO today accepts any topic, any scenario, you can bring up anything you want, nothing is taboo?"

"Right now, yes. But it's hard to predict what will happen in a year from now. Let's hope things will still be that way next year."

Originally published in *Bomb*.

Shawn Slovo, Writer

A World Apart

One of my prime motivations for wanting to work in the film industry was to get further away from my parents' area of activity. But I identify very much with the liberation struggle.

Shawn Slovo, 1988

May 9, 1988. The week before Cannes. A grey, misty Monday morning in Central Park, across the street from the Mayflower Hotel. Exiled South African writer Shawn Slovo has just returned from a screening tour of A World Apart. *As we walk down the narrow twisty path, Shawn tells me how responses to the film differed in Los Angeles and San Francisco, and amongst men and women. After a while, we reach a dark green wooden bench overlooking a sandy baseball field where kids are playing. We stop.*

Liza Béar: Is this okay?

Shawn Slovo: Sure. It's nice to be out of the hotel. The only reason I'm staying there is because I used to work for Robert De Niro and he keeps a suite there.

I turn on the machine and pick up the thread.

LB: The events upon which the story is based took place in Johannesburg in 1963. You started writing the screenplay some twenty years later. Was it just the pressure of time passing that made you take the plunge or something specific?

SS: It was my mother's assassination on the seventeenth of August in 1982. She was assassinated by a parcel bomb . . . she was working in Mozambique at the University, as the director of the department of sociology. The parcel bomb came into her office. We'd had quite a volatile and intense relationship, like most mothers and daughters, but we were beginning at this point in both our lives to talk about the past, about the guilt and the anger. And suddenly she wasn't there anymore . . . So that was the main spur. If she was still alive I don't think I would have written this particular script.

LB: Had you done much writing previously?

SS: I'd been working as a story editor and script fixer for about ten years. I'd done a lot of rewriting.

LB: You felt pretty comfortable with the medium.

SS: Yes. When I wanted to write, it was always scripts I wanted to write. I had been preparing myself for quite a long time, learning and reading other scripts.

LB: What made you select this particular time period for the story?

SS: You know, I wanted to tell the story through the eyes of a thirteen-year-old because I thought it would make the situation of apartheid more accessible to Western audiences. A thirteen-year-old can ask the [right] kinds of questions . . . At the same time, 1963 is quite a crucial period because that was when the repression that we have today began. The African National Congress (ANC) became outlawed and banned in the early sixties, the Communist Party

Barbara Hershey and Jodhi May in *A World Apart* (1988, UK) directed by Chris Menges. Courtesy of the Kobal Collection / Working Title / Film Four International.

had been banned, the leaders were arrested and detained, or else went into exile. It's quite a crucial period in South African history. I'm not sure whether I've succeeded . . . I know I haven't succeeded in placing it in its context from the reaction of audiences, but I think if people's curiosity is aroused by the setting, then that goes part way towards what I hope the film will do, which is to focus attention on South Africa.

Molly's attitude to her mother's activism is a mixture of curiosity and resentment. The script uses both these attitudes as vehicles for incidents that trigger the plot. Her desire to know is partly a desire to not feel excluded from her mother's world, even though she cannot really shoulder the consequences of knowing, or the attendant need for secrecy. It's also partly a desire to assert her own developing ego against her mother's. The resentment is created by the effect of the Barbara Hershey character on their relationship. Her mother is too busy to hear her, even when Molly has something politically relevant to relate to her. Molly sees her mother's work as taking precedence. She feels shortchanged when the constant and mounting demands of the struggle reduce their brief snatches of time together to perfunctory conversation.

It's a classic dilemma, not exclusively a filial one. Molly wants attention on her time and on her own terms. But the struggle cannot wait and an activist lives at an accelerated tempo, feels an urgency far removed from the normal routines of domestic life.

Molly wants to know and yet cannot quite assimilate this knowledge into her world of private school and Spanish dance lessons. By the same token, Molly's growing political awareness, which is not acknowledged by her mother, alienates her from the other thirteen-year-olds, supporters of the apartheid status quo. Ironically, as the plot tightens its screws, Molly becomes more and more isolated. Her father's flight from the country and her mother's arrest under the 90-day Detention Act make her the object of ridicule and insults at school, and eventually lead to the loss of her closest school-chum. Yvonne, who had vigorously defended her from her schoolmates' taunts earlier on, now abandons her at the point when her mother is in jail and Molly needs her most. Molly increasingly turns to the housekeeper Elsie for companionship and solace, accompanying her to the township where her family is confined.

LB: The bits of background information that were presented were used very skillfully as plot elements—actually it's one of the reasons I enjoyed the script. It seemed everything was necessary and had a place.

SS: I'm glad to hear you say that. We minorities also need films.

LB: You still think of yourself as a South African?

SS: Well, in my heart, yes. I have British citizenship and I've never been back, but once you're born there . . . it is the most beautiful country in the world . . . And when you have the kind of history that I do, it's hard to detach emotionally from it.

LB: Were you born in Johannesburg?

SS: Yes, in 1950.

LB: So you were probably your mother's age in the film when she was assassinated.

SS: Pretty much, a few years older.

LB: And you were exiled after your mother's release from jail?

SS: My father went underground because the ANC was having to regroup and this was the time that they made the decision to switch over to armed struggle . . . My father went in this capacity to get international support.

LB: Did he support armed struggle?

SS: He does, yes.

LB: He does still.

SS: Yes.

LB: And did your mother?

SS: Well, yes. You know, I mean, it's . . . yes.

Pause.

My father left the country illegally. He went away to do his work, fully intending to come back. While he was away there was the Rivonia raid. They arrested Nelson Mandela and the others . . .

LB: For treason.

SS: . . . and tried them for treason. As [my father] Joe Slovo was part of that group, he became a wanted man. It was purely by coincidence that he was out of the country. And he tells the story that there was a meeting of the [ANC] executive where his leaving the country was an issue. There were seven of them. Three of them said he should go on this particular mission, three of them said he should stay in the country, and Mandela as the chairman-leader cast the vote that sent him out of the country. Otherwise he would have been serving a life sentence. But for him, there was never any choice about what he was going to do for the rest of his life. A lot of South African political exiles went on to build up other kinds of careers, but he has steadfastly committed himself to the African National Congress and to the struggle. And my mother was given the burden of being the breadwinner. But anyway, while he was away they introduced the 90-Day Act, and she was the first white woman to be interned under the Act, and after 117 days when they released her . . . she wrote a book about it called *117 Days* . . . they banned her, which meant she couldn't work as a journalist and be quoted. So she applied for exile and they gave her a one-way exit visa and we joined my father in exile in England.

LB: You were telling me earlier that you really feel men have a different response to the film?

SS: Some do, yes.

LB: In what way?

SS: Some are extremely moved. It depends on their history, I suppose. I think men feel quite uncomfortable, don't know how to relate to the Barbara Hershey figure because she's not the stereotyped . . . It's actually not a film about a woman who wants to get laid. Some of them had a bit of difficulty with that. They find her cold in the first part of the film. I think that shows a lack of understanding of the sorts of pressures that were operating on a woman like my mother, who was not only a mother but a journalist and an activist. It's quite rare to see that portrayed in film.

LB: At one point the interrogator tells her, we saw you, we followed you, you were the only woman there. Was she unique in this respect?

SS: Yes, she was, for those times. The African National Congress was quite a sexist organization. My mother, whose professional name was Ruth First, had difficulty as a woman being in the ANC because a lot of the Black members of the ANC held that tribal traditional view of women walking ten paces behind them. But she was quite unique in the extent and scope of her activity because of the kind of woman that she was. She wasn't the only one . . .

LB: But there were very few.

SS: Uhhuh.

LB: How significant is it that your mother was a member of the Communist Party?

SS: The Communist Party has worked alongside the ANC—it's part of the liberation struggle. My father is now both the Secretary-General of the South African Communist Party and the only white member of the executive of the ANC. He's known as public enemy number one, as a KGB colonel, the bogeyman who gets his orders from Moscow! I don't know if you saw that . . .

LB: No, I didn't.

SS: Oh, you should see it. It was really interesting. One of the things that kept coming up was, "Where'd you get your orders from?"

LB: American paranoia.

SS: And then even they had to admit that a recent CIA-FBI investigation of the Communist role in South Africa concluded that the Eastern European countries are helping the ANC with financing and arms, but there's absolutely no evidence that they are behind or masterminding . . . It's a fabrication by the Bothas and the Thatchers, a conspiracy.

LB: Many events presented in the film are based on memory, but not entirely. Was it a natural transition for you to go from memory to imagination, or was that a struggle?

SS: It was a struggle. The first drafts of the screenplay were kind of therapy. You know, Molly was the victim. It was messy and emotional and self-pitying. That was the struggle within the writing and getting it to some control, some detachment.

LB: How long did that take?

SS: I did it over a period of about 18 months. I wasn't doing it exclusively because I was working at the same time. It took about five drafts before I felt I could show it to the world and then there were major rewrites even after that, once Chris Menges had become attached.

LB: The film was shot in Zimbabwe. Were you involved in choosing the locations?

SS: Oh yes. I had a very unusual experience for a writer. It's partly because the director Chris Menges and Sarah Radclyffe the producer have a lot of respect for writers, partly because it was an autobiographical story. So I was there for every single reccy . . .

LB: What is a reccy? Reconnoiter?

SS: Yeah. And I was there throughout the shooting, both in a consultative and in a writing capacity.

LB: Was there much rewriting done on the set?

SS: Not really. It was ready to shoot by the first day of principal photography. It wasn't that there were problems. It was always a bit too long. But I was there also for the actors who were uncomfortable with certain parts of their roles. And Chris wanted the film to be as authentic as possible, so he cast all those subsidiary roles . . .

LB: He cast them himself?

SS: With Susan Figgis, who's an amazing casting director. They worked very well together. Chris wanted the people from the region who'd had experience in the liberation struggle, not only in South Africa but in Zimbabwe, to be involved, and I think that's what contributes to the emotion and authenticity . . . Linda Mvusi, who played Elsie, is a South African exile who's actually an architect living in Harare. Her brother was murdered by the racist regime. So when her brother Solomon in the film died, the feeling that came up was real.

LB: What do you think of Barbara Hershey's take on the role of Diana Roth?

SS: Without being like my mother, what she's done that's quite extraordinary is that she's created a believable and sympathetic and compassionate portrayal of the character.

LB: Molly's parents in the story had been activists since she was born. Knowing how children imbibe values from their parents, how come Molly didn't take it more for granted, by the age of thirteen, how come she wasn't completely acclimatized . . .

SS: The reason is because of the history of the liberation struggle. During the fifties, when Molly was growing up . . . apart from a period in 1957 and in 1960 when we went into exile, we had quite a normal middle-class upbringing. My parents were arrested for treason in 1957 and held for a week, and then they were acquitted . . .

LB: But otherwise there was no visible disruption of daily routine?

SS: Not really. It was a very different, exciting kind of childhood. My parents were really involved with what they were doing. People like Nelson Mandela would come to the house and visit them . . .

LB: So the threat and the menace and the danger weren't already there . . .

SS: At times, but '63 was the first time I really felt that my world was going to be turned upside down. Also, Molly would have been ten in 1960 and the increasing demand and dissatisfaction and the fear comes with age . . .

LB: Molly feels more comfortable with the maid Elsie than with her mother . . .

SS: Well, her mother tends to be absent, and Elsie's always around.

LB: An activist also has to work under conditions of ironclad secrecy. I like the way the secret drawer in Diana Roth's study functioned in the plot.

SS: Oh yes, [secrecy] was a constant theme. My parents were continually having meetings in cars. Someone would come to the house and then they'd walk out into the street . . . Questions were met with vagueness and evasion.

The early morning mist still has not dissipated. The air feels cool and damp. We relocate to the restaurant.

LB: Have you always seen yourself as an activist in relation to the South African situation?

SS: No . . . in fact, one of my prime motivations for wanting to work in the film industry was to get further away from my parents' area of activity. But I identify very much with the liberation struggle.

LB: As the film clearly shows. But are you interested in the concept of an activist—other than as part of your autobiography or making the screenplay work?

SS: Well, it's something I think about all the time. I'm a member of the African National Congress and I participate as much as I'm able to when I have the time, but I'm certainly what I would describe as an activist. I would like to be able to bring the skills that I've developed in my own life to [the struggle] . . . to somehow tie the two things together. And the film is one way of doing that.

LB: How significant is the ANC now?

SS: It exists only in exile. But all the organizations within South Africa like the UDF, the trade union organizations, have all adopted the ANC charter. They just can't call themselves the ANC. I don't see how anyone could not embrace the Freedom Charter of the ANC.

LB: Does the ANC see divestment as desirable?

SS: Not only desirable, they see it as the only thing to avoid a bloodletting in South Africa. The racist regime will not be able to exist without . . .

LB: The support of the multinationals. So, is it actually making some headway? Because a lot of companies have pulled out.

SS: Yes, but it's got to be total to make any headway. This country [the U.S.] is where the hope of the ANC lies. Margaret Thatcher has such a regressive attitude towards South Africa. Her people, the Foreign Office, have been talking to the ANC because they know the future of British investment in South Africa depends on their forming a relationship with the ANC. Suddenly Margaret Thatcher, who is intent on taking the whole country back to the Middle Ages—anti-gay legislation, by cutting inroads on the Health Service and education—has been branding the ANC as terrorists in public. There's a big contradiction in British policy, a real shortsightedness on their part. The ANC sees a lot of hope in the activism in America, what's happening now in isolated pockets, but it has to be a concerted legislative national effort for it to have impact. Not only in Britain and the US, but also in Germany and France and Japan.

LB: Why did the Abelson father [the father of Molly's best friend] develop such incredible hostility towards Molly after her mother's arrest?

SS: Out of fear. He's a businessman and the people that Diana Roth, the Roth family, represent he regards as a complete threat to the economic order, and [he thinks] after the revolution he'd have to leave. Which is actually a misreading out of ignorance. Because it'll be a mixed economy. The big fear, again out of ignorance, is that it'll be a totalitarian communist dictatorship state. The Botha regime preys on [the fear among white South Africans] that they're going to lose all of it.

Pause.

You know, I'm not under any illusion that this particular film is going to change anything . . .

LB: Well, it's pretty hard to change things . . . but the South Africans are portrayed as warm, humorous, lively, and you feel that in spite of the conditions, they find their own ways to survive and enjoy life, maybe even have fun . . .

SS: It's very interesting you should say that because one of the criticisms I had while I was doing this publicity student tour was, how could I portray black South Africans—you know, that scene where Molly finds a foot in the chicken soup . . .

LB: That's a great scene.

SS: It's my favorite too. And I love the way Chris directed it. It was shot exactly the way I had imagined it when I wrote it. But people said, how can you show happiness, isn't this a kind of Uncle Tom representation. And the answer is, just because people are oppressed, it doesn't mean . . . that's the amazing thing about South Africans, they have the capacity of space and love and warmth and spirit, an indomitable spirit . . .

LB . . . that can't be crushed . . .

SS: . . . no, so victory is certain.

Originally published in *Bomb*.

CHRIS MENGES, DIRECTOR
A World Apart

Directing has to be based on what you as the director feel is the image and the imagination and the magic . . . it's no good just saying, this reads very well and it's very exciting, if you can't personally take it on into your world.

Chris Menges, 1988

June 13, 1988. A World Apart, *which came back from Cannes with two awards, is due to première in New York on June 16th. Chris Menges, the director of the film, won the special jury prize for a first feature. We sit at a black shiny table in the interview suite of a midtown Lexington Avenue hotel with a glass of water. It's early in the morning. Chris Menges is gentle and softspoken.*

Chris Menges: I've sort of gone backwards and forwards from documentaries to cinema films . . .

Liza Béar: You mean, fiction feature films?

CM: Yes.

LB: You call them cinema films?

CM: As opposed to television documentaries, I suppose. I've sort of gone backwards and forwards . . .

LB: Starting about when?

CM: I started as a trainee in 1958 with an American filmmaker who was living in Britain called Alan Forbes. We did a series of documentaries for the cinema and television.

LB: About anything in particular?

CM: One was about street entertainers in London, one was about the second march to Aldermaston.

LB: Oh, I went on that.

CM: It was called *No Place to Hide*. What else did we do? We did a film in Naples about street urchins. And a little fiction story set in the City of London in an area that had been badly blitzed during the war.

LB: Was this a two-man crew type of situation?

CM: I was the trainee. Sometimes I did the sound. He shot, or employed a cameraman. It was just a question of my being taught by Alan. So that's where it started.

LB: Best way to learn, right.

CM: I think so.

LB: On the job.

Pause.

LB: You eventually became a lighting cameraman on big budget feature films.

CM: I've only done two, three big budget films, if you call them big: *The Killing Fields, The Mission* and *Local Hero.* And then lots of films with Stephen Frears.

LB: Oh, really. Which ones?

CM: Not recent ones. *Bloody Kids* was the last one I did with him. And *Gumshoe, Walter, Last Summer*... About six films I did with Stephen. And then I did about six or seven films with Ken Loach starting with *Kes* in 1970. That was my first job as a cameraman though I was operator on his first feature, *Poor Cow*...

LB: Do you feel all this experience really prepared you well to direct your first feature?

CM: Well, I think Ken Loach is probably a terribly good teacher. And lots of Ken's films have got kids in them. He always wants the technical aspect to be played down and the most thought given to the actors. Or, in Ken's case, usually the non-professional actors. He won't dub anything, so the sound's always got to be good. It's got to be real sound. And you've got to very much what I call wing it, catch it. Also, in around 1965,1 worked for a Canadian company called R.N. King Associates. And they made what I called wobblyscope documentaries for ...

LB: Wobblyscope?

CM: Hand-held documentaries for CBC and PBS and companies in Canada and in the States, which were reportages. They were always with a handheld camera and tape recorder, we were always chasing stories. And that also teaches you great disciplines—like it's not always necessary to film the people who are talking but it might also be interesting to film the people who are listening. Silly things like that that are terribly obvious, but probably in the mainstream of being a technician you don't get taught those things, you're not that lucky. I think your teachers are terribly important in shaping your own sensibility.

LB: So did you . . . I mean, your three lead actresses won an award at Cannes, not that awards necessarily . . .

CM: Awards don't really mean anything.

LB: Well, they do. They're good for getting people to see the movie.

CM: Yes. Yes. From that point of view I suppose.

LB: It seemed to me that you were very comfortable with the actors and actresses.

CM: Every once in a while I've gone off to do a documentary film because serving the director as the cameraman all the time is . . . in a sense, you need after a while to make your own mistakes, because when you're shooting for somebody else you have to be terribly aware of the needs of the actors, the needs of the story, the needs of the director . . . And you know how you can structure and stricture and STOP . . .

LB: . . . you can not catch it by structuring it too much.

CM: Absolutely. Absolutely. And so I've always had to sneak off and do documentaries. And in a sense, I suppose *A World Apart* was one of those little journeys off into doing . . . time to do my own thing.

LB: What drew you to the script?

CM: Well, the first job I'd ever done, after I'd worked with Alan Forbes, was in 1963. I was sent to South Africa as a camera assistant by *World in Action*, which is a current affairs program in Britain. I was assistant, but I actually got made up to cameraman on that. My job at 22 was to try to catch apartheid in action. Those early jobs always leave an incredible . . . you could not go to South Africa without feeling great anger, and I felt great anger. And that anger never went away.

LB: Had you been shown other scripts?

CM: I'm always reading scripts. And when the script for *A World Apart* turned up about two years ago, I knew it didn't have a director or a producer. I was asked whether I'd like to shoot it. And I said, oh no, this is much too good for me just to be a cameraman . . . (laughter) I want to OWN this, I want to be possessive about this story . . . I suppose partly because I come from a large family of kids and I've got a lot of kids myself. And because I think I know . . . I do know . . . I do understand . . . the tension within that family. Because it's a very international story. It's not actually a story that's specific to South Africa.

LB: It's not just the children of activist parents, but of working parents . . .

CM: I think the children of working parents can be put through enormous pressures and there are enormous contradictions that the parents have to go through. And often it's quite an enriching experience. It doesn't have to be looked at in negatives. One has to learn to be quite philosophical about it.

LB: Basically it's the pacing that's difficult, isn't it.

CM: Exactly.

LB: Switching from their pace to your pace. That's a world apart too . . . Shawn told me that the script changed a lot when you came on board. How did it change?

CM: We worked on the script together. Shawn was trying to say a lot of things that never even happened to the family—for instance, the scene where Molly says, "You never even told me where Daddy was." This never happened. So there were several things going on at once. Shawn was telling her story as it happened, and things that she wished had happened that never did happen . . . all of which was very intriguing. So there was a lot of discussion and a lot of changes. But also, although it's Shawn's story, I don't think Shawn recognizes herself in the story, which is fair enough.

LB: She's fictionalized it beyond the particulars of her situation.

CM: Exactly. When you read a script, you obviously do visualize what you think the script's about, and then you try and gently cajole the writer into . . .

LB: . . . shaping it in that direction.

CM: Right. For me it was very important that the politics didn't somehow get lost, and I thought it would be very easy for the politics to get lost.

LB: Really. But aren't the politics the source of the dramatic tension?

CM: They are. But many people could have let the politics slide away, and I think most people would have.

LB: But you made sure right from the very first scene . . .

CM: Yes, the politics were built up.

LB: . . . when Molly's father is saying goodbye, he makes that gesture for silencing Molly's questions—"I can't talk about it"—which immediately sets the tone for a climate of fear.

CM: If you're taking on a story to tell, the most important thing is you must visualize it, you cannot leave anything to chance. Shawn's script, the original script that I read, is a superb script. There were things that both Shawn and I, in working together, wanted to direct the film towards.

LB: Like?

CM: Well, the politics. But also the image of the child, the child with her mother, the child with her sister . . .

LB: Her world.

CM: Mmmm . . . it has to be based on what you as the director feel is the image and the imagination and the magic . . . it's no good just saying, this reads very well and it's very exciting, if you can't personally take it on into your world. It's like you'd be working in a vacuum.

LB: So did you do that on paper or after you'd started to find locations?

CM: Both.

LB: Was Zimbabwe an obvious choice for the locations?

CM: On the way out from that shoot for *World in Action* in 1963—which incidentally is the year Shawn's story is set, it's really bizarre—we went up to Bulawayo which was then in Rhodesia . . . it was *World in Action*'s first year, we were buzzing around, having a great time. So I just knew from that trip that, for historical reasons, Bulawayo was a backwater because all the principal energy was in Harare (it's not now). Also it's very very near South Africa and because of that there are many refugees, both black and white living in Bulawayo.

LB: From South Africa.

CM: Mmm, 'cause it's right near the border. You've got a city that hasn't really changed a lot (because of the warring factions, ZANU and ZAPU), since Zimbabwe's independence. So when the film came up I said to Sarah Radclyffe, our very eminent producer—eminent because she did not mess with the script, and so many producers do mess . . . she was very very supportive, very helpful, terrific—I said, it's got to be Bulawayo before we even went. We went and looked and it was. But I also knew, first film, be sensible about this. Choose one small city . . .

LB: . . . that you know . . .

CM: . . . and [make sure] that all the locations are within ten minutes of the hotel.

LB: Really! That's quite a feat in itself.

CM: Yep. [I said to myself] be smart about it. But also, coming from Ken Loach, try to get the accent right, so people aren't worrying about it, try and have people who've actually been involved in the politics, know what it's like to be interned, know what it's like to be beaten up.

LB: Right. Because it's too big a jump for actors to make otherwise.

CM: It's too big a jump for anyone to make because on a film set you have to create the total conditions of the reality. For instance, for the police force we needed, we went to the local rugger teams and told them what we were doing. We got an ex-South African police officer to teach the others . . . The planning of the minutest details has to be perfect. Once you've done that, you're standing on concrete. Then you can go off and create the story. For instance, [the actor who played Solomon], he's been interned. Our technical advisor had been eighteen months in prison. The list goes on endlessly. When you're dealing with non-professional actors, and most of them were non-professional, except for some hardcore that we brought over from Britain, they have to be able to call on real experience. With professional actors there are different problems. Professional actors like to rehearse. And every time they rehearse you see them mentally ticking away, well I did that bit. But of course if you rehearse non-professional actors they only get more confused.

LB: So how did you deal with that one?

CM: I didn't allow any rehearsal! As little as possible. Because even with the professionals, the mistakes are more interesting.

LB: Did you have any fights on the set?

CM: Only with Barbara.

Laughter.

LB: Who was involved in the selection of the leads?

CM: Well, I'd worked with Andre Konchalovsky on *Shy People*. I could see that Andre and Barbara were shouting at each other a lot and it's quite clear that Barbara is quite an opinionated woman. And she had that steely quality that I was trying to base the character of Diana on from my own experience. It wasn't really a reflection of Shawn's mother. She was my first choice. Then I went off and saw lots and lots of people. I was looking for colonials. I was quite happy to have Americans because in a way they are colonials, you know what I mean? [Laughter] They come from Europe and they live here. I was looking for Australians, anybody who had a colonial history. I wasn't looking for Britons, because Britons don't know anything about living away. So really Barbara was the first and last choice. And she's terribly good.

LB: How about Molly? She must have been difficult to cast. The film hangs on her.

CM: It was difficult. All the kids are non-professionals. They're all Zimbabwean, because the accent's important. I think I lost my balls a bit when it came to the part of Molly, and ended up picking a kid out of a school in North London, Jodhi May . . .

LB: Camden High School, right.

CM: Yes. A kid with all the problems, which meant that when she came to Zimbabwe, she didn't know the accent. She had to stay in the hotel with the crew. Her mother came. But of course, what I'd much rather have done is [have her be] like the other kids, who were all Zimbabwean so they sounded South African and who all went home every night. Because this whole pressure of being an actor is a big number. But Jodhi did very well. Clever kid.

LB: That was a really great performance. You didn't need a lot of takes, right? It looked like Jodhi was totally into the part, she got it right away.

CM: No, no, she got it very quickly. The hardest thing of all, particularly when you're dealing with non-professionals, because you don't have any film to see of them, is choosing people you believe, and then once you've chosen them, knowing when to keep your mouth shut. D'you know what I mean?

LB: Yes!

CM: Because sometimes too many words is confusing. So it's just a question of getting the balance right.

LB: Shawn was with you on the set.

CM: I wanted her with us all the time. Lots of reasons. One is, traditionally writers are given a bum steer. I've worked with eminent directors who've made sure that writers are not around. If you want to change things, you should be able to change them with the writer there. And in my arrogance I was going to sort this one out. But also Shawn was coming to terms with her past through the film, and being there was a part of that. And quite often actors or actresses would say, well that would never happen, and I'd say, "Right Shawn, sort it out." It was a question of making it as fluid as possible. It made it difficult too.

LB: Were you ever up against time pressures?

CM: We had nine weeks which is a long time. And we had 2.6 million pounds, which is a lot of money. Our biggest mistake was that the script was too long. And we wasted time shooting things that we couldn't use. If your film's too long and you have to cut scenes out, it's a bit like taking bricks out of a wall. Before long the wall tends to fall down. So that was our biggest problem.

LB: Were the riot scenes hard to stage? Or had all those people been involved in riots?

CM: You have to remember that in Zimbabwe there was a revolution kicking the Rhodies out, and before that kicking the Brits out. And they got their independence in 1980. So in 1987 most of the people had firsthand knowledge of what it's like to have a war because they were fighting the Rhodesians. You could talk to the militant youth and they'd know what the hell you were talking about. Also I made sure we had an enormous amount of library footage. I made everybody watch that and participate in what they were doing . . . Everyone had to have a point of focus.

LB: Like what?

CM: Well, if you were in a mob scene, what exactly were you doing there? What was your work, what were you carrying, who were your mates. So that people weren't just aimlessly walking down the street. Nothing new, but just important. You can forget so much.

LB: Especially on the set.

CM: It all comes down to planning.

LB: You said earlier you tried very hard to keep the politics central in the film. I think that you succeeded, but are some people saying, it's a mother-daughter story and there's not enough political information?

CM: First of all, this is Shawn's story, and it's her beautiful script, and it is about her life. And I as the director had to respect that. It was important to keep the politics as strong as possible. But this is a film about a white kid. And a lot of people have criticized that it's not a film by a black filmmaker about the struggle in Soweto, it's not a black story. And of course, it isn't. Many black stories have got to come forward and the sooner the better. This is only a part of what's happening, it's not the total. I want to read you something (pulls out newspaper clipping and reads quote from Mandela).

I have cherished the idea of a democratic and free society in which all persons live together in harmony and with equal opportunities. It's an idea which I hope to live for and to achieve, but if needs be, it's an idea for which I am prepared to die.

What people don't understand, even in Britain, and they should perhaps understand more clearly than in the United States, because it's part of their history, is that basically since 1912, the ANC, for nearly fifty years, was going along the peaceful road towards democracy and it got absolutely nowhere. It was only after the Sharpeville massacre and the banning of the ANC that the armed struggle started. You wonder how the United States got its freedom. It got its freedom by taking up armed struggle against the British. Then you get ministers from the Republic of South Africa on the radio saying that the ANC are terrorists. And you wonder how these ministers have the audacity to say this when there are no democratic rights if you're black. First, bring democracy. That's what it's all about. Because of white people needing to protect their wealth, they've oppressed everything that the black people ask for in fighting for their rights. When people in the United States actually have an opinion about this, things will change. And if this film in any way helps people have an opinion about what's happening in South Africa, then it'll have done something. One is affected by everything, by reading books, by reading the newspaper, by going to the theater, by just talking, by listening to music. . . . I think little seeds are planted, and from that things grow.

Originally published in *Bomb*.

ATOM EGOYAN, DIRECTOR, AND ARSINÉE KHANJIAN, ACTOR

Speaking Parts

The way the script started was as a love relationship set in a hotel between two people who worked in the hotel. I'd written that as a play some time ago. It was based very much on a situation I'd encountered delivering laundry.

Atom Egoyan, 1989

Atom Egoyan's third feature, Speaking Parts, *is that rarity: a conceptual breakthrough as well as entertainment of the highest order. A mystery-romance set in a cavernous hotel,* Speaking Parts *combines the sensuality of cinema, the immediacy of video and the binary logic of drama to make a subversive statement about the power of the recorded image. No mean feat: it does this without going into self-destruct. The characters' amorous needs and professional aspirations are wittily served by taped or interactive video, bridging chasms of time and space, the image a wanton substitute for physical presence: Egoyan makes you think as he makes you laugh. Ultimately, through Arsinée Khanjian's Lisa as the emotional driving force of the film, (and the only one who's not part of the image-making machine) the watchful, insidiously pervasive technology is vanquished. In a final ironic twist, fantasy loses its stranglehold, and passion triumphs over opportunity. Aided by a superb Canadian cast and crew, 29-year-old Egoyan brought in the silky production ahead of schedule and under budget.*[1]

211 West Broadway. A table by the window. In town for their New York Film Festival debut, Atom and Arsinée breeze in, windswept and animated. We order, and soon get down to business.

Liza Béar: I suspect you both come out of the Toronto theater scene?

---

[1] Zeitgeist released the film theatrically in New York, San Francisco, Seattle, and Washington in February 1990.

Arsinée Khanjian in *Speaking Parts* (1989, Canada) directed by Atom Egoyan. Courtesy of the Kobal Collection/Ego Films.

Atom Egoyan: Yes . . . Aren't you eating?

LB: I'll have some soup. This deadpan, laconic acting style in your films—is that something you developed in your theater work?

AE: My first theater work all had to do with questions of communication, and people's ability to confront each other—the tendency to overcomplicate our dialogues in order to get to very simple points which everyone is too embarrassed to recognize.

LB: Verbal redundancy.

AE: Right, in some of the plays I've done, the verbosity of the characters is taken to an extreme. That was the theme of one play where three boys are at a beach presumably to look at women, but one character who's very verbose, very nervous is actually a suppressed homosexual. His two friends bring him to the beach to watch him suffer as he spins these incredibly intricate tales which they know are fatuous. It's a very cruel piece. The last play I did, the one I did in residence, which never got produced, was about . . .

LB: Minimal language?

AE: Very minimal language. And at that point I realized I would find better expression for this type of language in film than in theater.

LB: Why?

AE: Well, first of all there was the frustration of getting a play produced. I find that, strangely enough, it was far easier and more tangible for me to go ahead and make a film than to wait for a theater company to option a play.

LB: How did the two of you meet?

Arsinée Khanjian: I was in community theater in Montreal. We were rehearsing *The Mousetrap* in Armenian. Atom was in Montreal looking for an Armenian older couple for *Next of Kin*. He was going around to theatre groups to see who was there. So I got auditioned and a week later he called and said I got the part. I didn't know if I was supposed to accept it or refuse it, but I thought I'd better accept!

LB: Why did she have to be Armenian?

AE: Because the film deals with this Armenian boy who transplants himself. He's very dissatisfied with his English-Canadian family, and they're in therapy because he can't really deal with his own identity. And while he's in video therapy with these people . . .

LB: Oh, so you had already used video in the first film.

AE: Oh yeah. It was the type of therapy where people's conversations are taped and they go back later on and look at their reactions. Through that, perhaps, they come to some sort of revelation about why they're behaving the way they are in their family situation. So one day, by mistake, he sees another family's tape. And this other family is Christian Armenian, immigrants who had to give up their son for adoption when they came to Canada because they couldn't afford to keep him. In the meantime, they'd had a daughter who's grown to reject their very traditional values, which is why they're in therapy.

LB: Arsinée played the daughter?

AE: Yeah. Anyway, while the boy's watching this tape, he gets the idea of tracking down this family and telling them he's their son, using all the information he's gained about these people through the tape. So it's a very . . . odd film.

AK: [To Atom] The funny thing is, you hesitated initially because you didn't at all perceive the character with an accent.

LB: Would you say you'd rejected traditional Armenian values?

AK: [laughing] Oh yes, God knows.

AE: Our meeting was probably the biggest rejection.

LB: Was the family opposed to uh . . .

AK: Well, I had studied theatre in Montreal, classical theatre . . .

LB: Molière, Racine . . .

AK: Oh yes, all of that, but after that I had switched my course of studies to languages, partly because acting was not perceived as a profession.

LB: Is Armenia mostly Moslem or Christian?

AK: Oh, Christian. It's a Soviet republic right now, fairly small. The reason I was born in Lebanon, as were my parents, is because of the Armenian genocide in 1915, in which Turks massacred millions of Armenians in their villages in what is presently Eastern Turkey. So my grandfather left Eastern Turkey and went to the Middle East, and that's how we ended up in Lebanon.

AE: And my people went to Egypt so that's where my roots are.

LB: Believe it or not, one of my grandparents was born in Cairo and another in Turkey. [General laughter.]

AK: Well, here we are.

LB: So how did your collaboration develop?

AE: Well . . . AK: When we met it was . . .

LB: His turn.

AK: Yeah. Good.

Pause.

AE: [slowing down a little] It was a very strange type of meeting . . . Because of Arsinée's social position, the fact that it ended up being a . . . permanent relationship, working and living, actually came as a surprise. It's strange when you're so close to somebody and yet you use them to communicate images, you make images of them. It's a very perverse type of activity to engage in, and yet it's worked out quite well.

AK: It was funny. After we finished shooting *Next of Kin,* Atom was completely out of money. He already didn't have anything. I mean, he shot that film on a $37,000 budget, so . . .

LB: Which you got from the Canada Council?

AE: Yes, but after being rejected a number of times.

AK: . . . so to survive, he went back to this job he'd had for $5 per hour working as a doorman . . .

AE: . . . at a very academic college at the University of Toronto.

AK: And we spent the whole summer at the door of the college, opening it and closing it. It was quite interesting. We were talking earlier, about how you lose that excitement about things . . .

LB: Already?

AK: Yeah. After *Next of Kin* we got small offers. Every time it was a great occasion for happiness, we'd react physically, jump up and down and express it. And now we can choose, which wasn't necessarily the case at the beginning. Things have happened quite fast, too. In five years.

AE: I've always considered my work to be quite marginal in a way . . .

LB: But you choose really major themes, don't you? Love, sex, death, communication aren't marginal themes. They're very central. That's why you get the audience response that you do.

AE: It's funny, I never see it that way: I know those are the themes I'm dealing with, but my approach to them is as oblique as possible . . .

LB: All the same, I don't know if you want to *call* yourself marginal . . .

AE: Because it's like the kiss of death! All right, all right. [Rephrasing] The issues that I'm dealing with are extremely pertinent, have a strong relevance to anyone, but the processes I use to interpret them are very personal and deeply felt and idiosyncratic. It has taken me probably this film to realize there is a large audience for them, and that's something that's come to me very, very slowly.

LB: Between your second feature, *Family Viewing* and *Speaking Parts,* there was only a two-year time span. By U.S. independent standards, that seems remarkably short, and the difference between . . .

Waiter: Are you going to order anything else?

LB: Maybe . . . And the difference between the two is so great that I suspect something quite major must have happened that enabled you to . . . apart from having a much bigger budget.

AE: Not that much bigger.

> "I was torturing myself over, how do you create this moment? And I talked to a friend, a filmmaker, and he said something so simple: ultimately, you have to create a world in which that sort of thing can happen."

LB: Structurally, *Speaking Parts* is much tighter than *Family Viewing.* The art direction . . .

AE: What happened is very simple. After *Family Viewing,* and not because of *Family Viewing,* I was approached to direct a number of programs for two TV series that were shooting primarily in Canada, *Twilight Zone* and *Alfred Hitchcock Presents.* I directed several episodes. Being part of that production machine, I became aware of how to create a certain look.

LB: So you learned under pressure of having to direct at a . . .

AE: Frantic, frantic pace. And I also learned how to create images that are seductive. *In Family Viewing,* the images are meant to be degraded; they're meant to separate you, to an extent. In *Speaking Parts,* since the film is so much about people being seduced by images of each other, it was very important that the images themselves be very seductive, otherwise it wouldn't have worked, I don't think. And what's interesting for most people is that *Speaking Parts* has a look that they associate with a type of film that doesn't require the kind of thought processes that they undergo when they see it . . .

LB: What's great though, is you make them laugh at the same time.

AE: Especially in the English language. I think it's probably quite unusual for people who speak with a North American accent to find themselves in the middle of this beautiful rich film which has very high expectations of its audience, which doesn't ask them to go to sleep for two hours. Usually the production value is used to disguise the fact that you're looking at a film. You're supposed to take yourself to this reality, which is the image, and to forget the fact that you're watching a photographed image, to almost accept it as a sequence of events that's actually happening, that you lose yourself to. And really I'm trying to subvert that sensation.

LB: Hmmmm . . . Well, you can't subvert it totally because you need suspension of disbelief on one level at least. But you do engage on multiple levels. The whole structure of the film is pretty interesting . . . The opening sequence of the film consisted of one-beat scenes. They were also one shot, one unit of . . .

AE: Of information. The film is about dialogue. No more than two characters are ever in a scene together, and whenever there is a third character he's asked to leave. The groom, for instance, in the bridal interview scene . . .

LB: Which is hilarious, by the way.

AE: In a sense, the concerns of one scene are mirrored in the concerns of the next. For instance, Lisa's looking at a videotape of the bride's father while Lance is being auditioned by Clara. Then Lisa goes to the orgy while Lance and Clara are masturbating via video teleconference. And there's the whole wedding sequence when Lisa is behind the camera, while Lance finds out he's got the part that Clara auditioned him for.

LB: So what are you saying, you used intercutting to do what?

AE: To create a dialogue between scenes. Also, because the dramatic impetus for a lot of my films requires people to have knowledge of other characters, it's always important for me to define an environment which will allow that to happen. In *Next of Kin,* there was the video therapy clinic which allowed characters to hop in and find histories of other people. Information about someone is the most difficult thing to gain access to in real life. It's usually held at a great great distance from you.

LB: I liked your new definition of character profiles in the After Dark video store. Eddie draws a character profile of Lisa on the basis of the videos she rents.

AE: Right, right. I'm very interested in what you said, there being problems one has to find a solution to, that really figures in my own thinking dramaturgically. Devices like coincidence . . .

LB: . . . simultaneity . . .

AE: . . . simultaneity, those ideas are very important to me. My biggest fear when I'm making a film is whether or not the contrivance calls attention to itself and distances you from the suspension of disbelief. I remember when I was making my second film, *Family Viewing,* to me the most contrived moment in that was when the two grandmothers were exchanged. I was torturing myself over, how do you create this moment? And I talked to a friend, a filmmaker, and he said something so simple: ultimately, you have to create a world in which that sort of thing can happen. And that is really the greatest challenge . . . through the tone of the piece, through the feel of the piece, you create a world where certain properties can exist. Properties which may be heightened or surreal or totally improbable in our day-to-day lives.

LB: A world in which people go to a special place to watch videotapes of their deceased relatives is already a bit absurd. It makes me think of *Soylent Green.*

AE: It's about five years ahead, I would say. I wouldn't say it's totally a science fiction world. They have them in Japan.

LB: The shot of Clara watching her dead brother in the video mausoleum bothered me.

AE: But you know, we are a culture obsessed with the preservation of image, and perhaps you're not familiar with the fact that people do go to cemeteries and look at tombstones where images are kept.

LB: Well, I'm not. But in that scene, I feel the video is a violation of the human mind.

AE: But that's just it! The whole film is about things being violated. But being violated in such insidious ways that we're not entirely sure who has the right to lay claim to what history. And even in this perverse sort of situation where Clara has made the disastrous mistake of thinking she can create a sacrifice equal to the one her brother made for her with her script . . . Of course, the moment you decide to make an object of something emotional, a feeling, a memory, all of a sudden because it is an object it can be bartered with, it can be taken away from you, it can be changed, it can be manipulated.

LB: There's the artist's dilemma in a nutshell.

AE: The way the script started was as a love relationship set in a hotel between two people who worked in the hotel. I'd written that as a play some time ago. It was based very much on a situation I'd encountered delivering laundry, and that sense of being in a working environment with someone that you adored, and only being able to see them when you had a functional reason to do so. Being too shy to be able to go further than that, and yet going out of your way to provide them with special towels, making sure they were provided for in a special way. The other person of course doesn't care if you give him hand towels when he's run out . . .

LB: Or leave red roses in the dryer . . .

AE: I like that sort of situation, that tension. So that was the point of departure. And also I like the types of relationship that occur during a film production, when people become involved in the creation of illusions, because they're in a very odd frame of mind and it's conducive to romance.

LB: A very intense frame of mind.

AE: Yes, and yet it's also very fragile, very precarious. So the point of departure was the idea of the hotel, the laundry room, the person delivering, the cart in the hallway . . .

LB: That gave you a lot of nice sound cuts, that cart.

AK: A lot of trouble for me too.

LB: You really started with a dramatic premise. What about the video element?

AE: Well, that came very late. To be quite honest, after *Family Viewing* and after *Next of Kin,* those two films which deal so much with the video image, I was very wary of doing it again because I didn't want to repeat myself. And I know with *Family Viewing,* I'd done something quite radical with the video image, inasmuch as I made it part of the form of the film . . .

LB: It allowed you to do a heck of a lot.

AE: And once I said, okay, look, it's stupid pretending I'm not fascinated and obsessive about this image, and I don't really care if I'm called limited, I have to use this, because the type of subject matter I'm dealing with, the whole idea of romantic projection, ideas of representation and presentation, the differences between the two, needed to have a cinematic equivalent. I could not do it literally and do full justice to the complexity of my ideas.

Waiter: Dessert is chocolate pecan pie, chocolate miséricorde, carrot cake, raspberry . . .

LB: What was I going to say . . . real time is in film, right, and . . .

Waiter: . . . French sorbet. Raspberry windsor tart?

LB: Anything that's fantasy is in video. At the end Lisa's imagination takes over.

AE: What's happening there . . . As an actor, Lance wants to be more than an extra, he wants to be singled out. Lisa intuits that, which is why I have her single him out on those close-ups of the videos. And she's able to do that because she is somehow . . .

LB: In tune with his feelings.

AE: Yes. And later what happens is that he beckons her to come towards him. And when she enters that composition, and there's no one there, what she then becomes aware of is the tool which has framed the composition, which she goes forward to touch. That "tool" is her intuitive logic, and as she's touching that, and the image fluctuates between film and video, what's actually happening is there's a fluctuation between the real world and an intuitive order. And of course once you adhere [only] to that intuitive sense, you're mad by normal conventions.

LB: So when she's touching the screen, what is she touching?

AE: She's touching madness.

LB: The image takes over.

AE: The other thing that's just as important to this film as the use of film and video is eye line.

LB: How so?

AE: Well, people on the video screen are always looking directly at camera, and people who are looking at the video screen are always looking off camera.

LB: Oh yes. Well, so they should. Otherwise it'd look like TV.

AE: Yes. Because the video image is the image of "the other," an image of a reality that is desired and not attainable, therefore the point of view, the gaze of the person being adored is being made an icon of. Or the gaze of the person that holds the power of transformation is always very, very direct and somehow confrontational.

LB: [to Arsinée] You played Aline in *Family Viewing*. Lisa was a much more challenging role.

AK: Yes, it was. It required a lot of thinking and recreating the character in my mind. I knew what Aline could be. I had references around me, or in me, for bringing that character into life. But with Lisa, I just didn't know who she was, I just couldn't imagine what she . . .

LB: You'd never been in love that way?

AK: Not in that way, because I'm a very proud lover. If I can't get what I want, I find every sort of way of either getting it or completely forgetting it. So I've never made myself vulnerable to a love story or a love hurt in that sense.

LB: Yet Lisa emerges as the more heroic. Lance comes out as a bit of a slimy character. An opportunist.

AK: Just a bit!

AE: And actually quite stupid, I think. He is not that bright.

LB: Here you are, intimately connected to the director and yet playing the role of a love-smitten lass. Lisa's the only character who's defined by her emotions rather than by her social role. She has other objectives—she wants to learn how to do interviews like Eddie . . .

AK: But the reason she gets involved with that process is that, in her mind, it's another way of getting through to Lance, it's another way of reaching him. She's fascinated by other people's ability to function at the level of images. She herself has absolutely no sense of process or any way of applying that process to her life.

LB: But she doesn't just want the guy, does she? She also wants to enhance her own understanding—of the way things are. Some of the funniest dialogue is between Lisa and Eddie, in the video store.

AK: It's the only human dialogue . . .

LB: Without video intermediary. It also shows her to be sharp, and curious, with almost an Alice in Wonderland . . .

AE: . . . wonder.

LB: The other theater work Arsinée has done I assume is not in this vein—this very terse—do you mind it being called Pinteresque?

AE: Not at all. It's a compliment. He's an idol of mine.

LB: David Mamet is someone else your work makes me think of.

AE: Another idol. I'm really curious, are these questions on this piece of paper?

LB: No, just notes.

AE: Can I have it?

LB: Let me see if it says anything embarrassing. [looks] No, okay, you can have it. Oh, here's a question. What's the key difference between Lance and Lisa?

AE: The key difference?

LB: Yeah.

AE: The main difference is that Lisa . . . in a curious way . . . Lisa is capable of finding her own place in society, and Lance always needs someone else to define his place in society.

LB: How has she found it? Because she's able to adapt to situations?

AE: Because in her own way, marginal and as fragile as she seems, she does not wait for people to make projections onto her.

AK: Because she's not a slave of the image . . .

LB: She takes initiative . . .

AK: Yeah.

AE: Though she's punished for it to an extent, and though she doesn't really become part of the society, she has initiative to find her own place. While Lance is a vessel, really, waits for other people to project things onto him.

LB: In a way, isn't that what an actor is?

AE: She is the classical male, and he is the classical female.

AK: In society, you mean.

LB: Which is why they look androgynous.

Pause.

AE: Liza, tell me about your film.

I turn off the recorder.

Published in *Bomb*.

BRIGITTE ROUAN

Outremer [Overseas]

After the film won prizes everywhere, the family came around. They're not all happy because the image I give of colonialism isn't as rose-tinted as they would have liked.

Brigitte Rouan, 1990

A deftly crafted and mordant social drama set in Algeria during the last years of French Colonialism, Outremer [Overseas], *which actress Brigitte Rouan co-wrote and in which she co-stars with Nicole Garcia and Marianne Basler, marks a debut for Rouan as a director. [It won her an award at the 1990 Cannes Critics' Week.] Using a triple perspective, the film tracks the shared experiences of three bourgeois sisters as they come to grips with conventional expectations of love and marriage against a backdrop of increasing political turmoil. This interview took place during the screening of* Outremer *at the Museum of Modern Art's New Directors New Films series in March 1991; the film was released nationally in the U.S. by Aries Films.*

Liza Béar: How important was it for you, given that you have this background in acting, to not only direct, but star in your film?

Brigitte Rouan: Quite frankly, Isabelle Adjani called me. She was on this panel that gives out advances on box office receipts. She said, "I adore your script, but give me some ammunition because there are three hundred of you tomorrow, and we only back thirty projects. Who are your leads?" I didn't know. "Who's your producer?" I didn't know either. "Where are you shooting?" I'd like to shoot in Algeria, but I'm not sure. Isabelle said, "How come? Every French actress is going to want to play these roles."

LB: What was it like working with three co-screenwriters?

Marianne Basler and Brigitte Rouan in *Outremer* (1990, France) aka *Overseas*, directed by Brigitte Rouan. Courtesy of the Kobal Collection / Canal / LIRA.

BR: Well, I hadn't planned to, but I'd willingly do it again. I had written a play for three women and I wanted to make a film out of it but I didn't have the nerve. Philippe LeGay said, it's a great story, you have to do it. We got together and for a week I talked non-stop about my family and my education.

LB: Your family being French-Algerian.

BR: Algerian, French, Catholic, military, the lot. I talked my head off and Philippe took notes. Then we went to the country for three weeks to write. The first draft was chronological and there were way too many characters. Eventually, the three sisters emerged. Why did that happen? I think it was a completely unconscious decision.

LB: Are there three sisters in your family?

BR: Yes. But the film isn't autobiographical in that sense. I think certain choices are symbolic and they impose themselves on the story. So anyway I thought, the script is too romanesque, it's not cinematic enough, it's tedious. It's what François Truffaut used to call the "seventh reel syndrome." The story takes off, but it doesn't go anywhere. We paced up and down all night and in the morning we both came up with the same idea, that the story had to be told from the point of view of all three sisters. Philippe had to go shoot his own film so I had to find another writer. The screenwriting period was very brief but very intense. We'd work twelve hours a day. The second writer, Christian [Rullier], was very intellectual. He especially helped me with the structure, which was better in the script than in the film, but I didn't have the money to do everything I wanted. The dance scene is the only one that's structured the way I really wanted . . .

LB: There are three versions of that scene.

BR: Right. Ideally, that is what I would have done more often. What if I said, remember that interview we did in the restaurant? And you say, oh yes, it was snowing outside. And I say, no, it wasn't snowing, there was a full moon. Everyone remembers it differently. For one it was sad, the weather was bad, the music was too loud, she had a stomachache. For the other it was a fabulous day, she was wearing a new dress, she was in love. But it's the same event. That's the film I wanted to make.

LB: The film opens with three very quick scenes of Zon, the eldest sister, on the quay waving good-bye to her husband, a navy officer—her change of costume and the number of children with her indicate time passing. On the soundtrack, there's an aria from Glück's *Orpheus and Eurydice,* which serves as a refrain throughout the film—"L'amour est préférable à la liberté."

BR: Which is a joke, of course.

LB: Yeah, I think everyone in the audience got it.

BR: They always get it. Everywhere. The audience is much smarter than money people, bankers and television producers seem to think. This isn't an esoteric film.

LB: The death throes of the French colonial milieu are savagely satirized—I guess that comes from close personal observation. Were you living in Algeria during the period just before independence?

BR: No, because I left at the age of four. At first my family was furious that I was making this film. They saw it as washing dirty linen in public. They wanted to sue me. It was dreadful. Rumors were flying so high that an aunt of mine claimed she'd seen extracts from the film on TV, before we'd even shot a single frame! After the film won prizes everywhere, the family came around. They're not all happy because the image I give of colonialism isn't as rose-tinted as they would have liked. My aunts would say, you were so tiny, how could you remember all those things! A cousin my age told me stuff I'd completely forgotten. I'd only kept a general impression, certain very precise sensations and a few phrases. And out of those, I built a story.

LB: Did you go back to Algeria more recently?

BR: Yes. Since I was planning to shoot there, I went back and forth six times to scout locations. But we ran into censorship problems. We were supposed to shoot in '88, but they had those teenage riots in the streets . . .

LB: That's strange, since the film is so anti-colonial and anti-conventional French.

BR: The censorship committee had my script in front of them when they reviewed my application for a shooting permit and they said that the Arabs in the story were portrayed as rapists, treacherous and lazy. I was seated at the time, fortunately. I said, let's start with the most serious charge. Where do you see a rapist? And they said, on page 78, he taps Gritte in the back. That gesture is known over there as "le sourire Kabyle" (Kabyle's smile). It's what the Kabyles do when they are going to cut someone's throat. But in my film that's not what the man does: they become lovers. Not that I wanted to do *Lady Chatterley's Lover*. She's in the garden after dark in her nightdress. I think that says it.

LB: Okay. So Morocco would be out of the question too. That leaves Tunisia. How long was the shoot?

BR: Very short. Initially we had eleven weeks. The production kept on being scaled back. At the last minute it was down to seven weeks. That was one of the hardest things to do, cut scenes from the script. Three weeks before we went into production my producer's partner, who by the way did nothing for the film, walked into the office and said, that scene with Nicole in the bathroom, it's not doing anything, we can cut it. He started to rip out the page. I said, but sir, there are sexual references. So he said, okay, put it back in.

LB: What was the budget?

BR: Twelve million francs. It should have been twenty million. By the time everyone gets paid off it'll be closer to fourteen million. We all worked for half-pay.

LB: The film is a success so I take it everything went well during production?

BR: Now that it's done I have very good feelings about it but right after we'd finished shooting, I wanted to make a film called, "I Hate Technicians."

Because with the actors, directing was sublime, and with the crew it was incredibly difficult, except for sound and costumes. I had problems with my cameraman.

LB: Did the DP say, "It's my image?"

BR: What he'd say was, "It can't be done, we don't have time, you won't make the day. I don't want to sound like a movie cop but I just want to make sure the entire film gets shot." Let's face it, it was my first feature, and I am a girl, after all . . . For the most part they were really sweet. But because I'm a theatre person they'd think, she doesn't know about film, we'll cover for her. Sometimes my shots would seem abstract to them. For instance, that scene when my character runs along the wine vats, and then I switch to a subjective camera. The camera takes my place in the back of the cave in the darkness. To have them do that shot, I spent all morning arguing. They just didn't get it.

LB: They didn't understand the camera move.

BR: Secondly, they didn't want to shoot in complete darkness. They said, on TV you won't see anything. I tried to explain, to me my grandfather's caves were like the Pantheon in Paris, big black cathedrals. When you're six years old, wine caves are really scary, full of ghosts.

LB: Because of your experience in the theater, it must have been easier for you to direct actors.

BR: I know what it is to be an actor, what an actor's solitude feels like. A highly emotional scene, like Nicole's scene when she cries and says, take my children, that's really hard to do. At the crack of dawn, you're asking someone to lay themselves out, to reopen old wounds, to summon the demons, and then you say, cut. Next scene. The actor's stranded, with no emotional resources to fall back on. I tried never to let that happen. I didn't want my actors to be in pain because I personally have suffered so much on the set. In the process of opening yourself up and releasing all that energy, all that adrenalin, the actor becomes emotionally vulnerable. As an actor, you have to be totally devoid of any hint of tension, of any defensiveness, you have to feel hyper-at-ease. If a director is mean to you just before the first slate, it knocks you off balance, you lose your concentration. But it's the actress who is nervous, not the character. It's very important not to confuse what you're feeling as a person with the emotions your character's portraying.

LB: What have you learnt about directing from other directors?

BR: Nothing. Nothing at all. As an actress, I make no comments during a shoot. I observe. Before I got into directing, I was completely naive. Which is probably why the camera did not favor me greatly.

LB: You weren't conscious of camera placement?

BR: I didn't have that particular sensory awareness. When I was younger, I would regularly fall in love, not with my acting partner, but with the cameraman. It's a very sensual relationship. 'Cause they have their eyes on you eight hours a day. It's almost an umbilical link. Now I'm better in front of the camera. It's exactly the opposite of theater. On the stage you're wide open. In film, it's the reverse. It's like a sponge, you're kind of sucked up by the camera.

> "My family was furious that I was making this film. They saw it as washing dirty linen in public. They wanted to sue me."

LB: The film was edited by Yann Dedet, your husband, who also plays your husband in the film.

BR: Was my husband. It's really marvelous to work with someone you love, but also terribly difficult.

LB: But you're still friends.

BR: We're very, very good friends. He's edited almost all of Truffaut's and Pialet's films. He's a great guy. The problem during the editing was that he became a terrorist, just as my cameraman had been. If we had to work together again, I hope I would have the strength, the self-confidence to just say, very calmly, "No, not exactly. Let's do it like this." It was very complicated because Yann is a workaholic. He'd want me to be there every minute. And I felt completely exhausted and emotionally drained by the production. Now he admits he shouldn't have been so demanding, should have had me come to the editing room only every other day. But I have to admit, if I made this film, it's because of him. He was the one who gave me the confidence to dare make a film.

LB: It's interesting how supportive men can be at times.

BR: Extremely.

LB: I love the particular blend of social satire and melodrama that you have in the film.

BR: If you see an old man slip on a banana peel, it's terribly sad. If you see a fabulously dressed woman slip on the banana, it's comic. There was a line of dialogue in the film that everyone wanted to cut. It's when my character dies. The scene is tragic, but her last words are not "Darling, I'm dying," but "Phone the bank," because they have money problems.

LB: The story begins in '46, but the Algerian revolution took place in 1962.

BR: I didn't want to deal with the return of the pied noirs to France when they were kicked out of Algeria. That wasn't my theme. I didn't experience that particular pain. The only reference to it is Marianne perched on her suitcases being insulted by members of the secret army who were preventing people from leaving.

LB: The film shows how the politics of colonialism go hand in hand with conventional views of love and marriage imposed on women by Catholicism.

BR: Yes, of course. It makes total hysterics out of them.

LB: Is the film still too political for the French? Are they distanced enough from the events?

BR: No. In the south of France, there's an enormous number of pieds noirs. It was quite something when I showed the film there. They cried a lot more, they laughed a lot less. They applauded for a long time. For once, it wasn't a portrait of us eating couscous and speaking French with an accent. But during the Q and A afterwards, people got mad because my point of view of the government is way too far left for those people. They would jump up and say, "But we didn't all have aeroplanes, we weren't all rich, I've never killed an Arab."

LB: Unfortunately the sentiments expressed in the film are all too accurate, even if the details change from one group to the next.

BR: Right. But at one point, before Cannes, I was criticized because in the first part of the film there are practically no Arabs. I'd say, Arabs were servants and they weren't allowed in the house. Only Spaniards were allowed to serve at the table. Arabs were only allowed to do housework. Unfortunately I had to cut those scenes. But in the second part, Malene is working with them. And in the third part, since Gritte the youngest sister has a real life job, she's a nurse, she has some understanding of the social situation. But she doesn't really have any political consciousness. She's aware that something is wrong, that there's a big chasm between the family discourse and reality, but she doesn't have the means, the language with which to express it, so she throws up.

LB: Still, you can see that there's a progression in political awareness from one sister to the next, and as the most aware, Gritte becomes the denouement of the film.

BR: Let's say there's a lot of me in Gritte. Rebelling against the family, understanding that the kind of language that was traded at the table or in offices or living rooms, was not reality. These women had a voice, but they didn't have an idea in their heads. They spoke exactly like their husbands, in place of their husbands. No one ever analyzed anything, except for Algerian intellectuals. So obviously the film is a metaphor. I wasn't old enough to participate in the revolutionary discourse. Even if I had been old enough I don't know whether I would have. Once I said to my mother, if I'd been eighteen, I'm sure I would have done something. And she'd say, sure, hothead that you are, you would have joined the OAS (a right-wing organization) and fought against the Arabs.

LB: The film's dedication to your mother reads "who was pretty, but who could have been beautiful."

BR: Yes. I think she could have been a wonderful person but she didn't have the opportunity.

Originally published in *Bomb*.

GILLIAN ARMSTRONG
The Last Days of Chez Nous

I only do the material that I am personally affected by and that mirrors things that I believe in. I'll find something where already the writer and I are thinking the same way. It's not that I'm out consciously looking for it.

Gillian Armstrong, 1992

"Her legs go up to her bum and they're not for lunch"; the heroine's grandma tartly rebuffs a mesmerized pub customer in Starstruck *(1982), the musical odyssey of an eighteen-year-old singer who's practicing her tightrope act above the counter. Director Gillian Armstrong's films seethe with saucy local idiom, interlacing into the drama a real Australian spunkiness, but their warmth and intimate human quality have a universal appeal that easily transcends the original locale. Armstrong directs with élan in sumptuous landscapes or actively peopled interiors—favoring a dynamic open frame and punctuating fluid camera choreography of sweeping amplitude with decisive point of view shots. No wonder, then, that in 1984 she became the first foreign woman approached by MGM/UA to direct a big-budget feature,* Mrs. Soffel, *starring Diane Keaton and Mel Gibson. The mother of two small girls who has fortunately had "a long happy marriage," Armstrong recently returned to Australia to shoot* The Last Days of Chez Nous, *a tightly drawn study of a successful forty-something author, Beth, who is not so fortunate, walking a proverbial tightrope as she tries to orchestrate maternal, conjugal, filial, and sibling loyalties. Or is she? And how will the arrival of Beth's younger sister rattle her rambunctious Sydney household? This emotionally wrenching drama, which won its lead actress, Lisa Harrow, the 1992 Australian Best Actress award, complements the strong quixotic women portrayed by Judy Davis in Armstrong's earlier films (*A Brilliant Career *[1979] and* High Tide *[1987]), and keeps us on edge. For someone with such an outstanding career (she's been awarded the Order of Australia), Armstrong is inspiringly unassuming, combining one hundred percent focus on the moment with steely authority and a quick sense of humor. I spoke*

to her all too briefly on her way to Sundance for the U.S. premiere of Chez Nous, *which Fine Line will release nationally in March.*

Liza Béar: What I thought was very interesting about *The Last Days of Chez Nous* and also *My Brilliant Career* is that you've picked as one of your central characters a writer. I wonder . . . you don't direct from your own scripts, right?

Gillian Armstrong: I did some of my short films. None of my big films.

LB: Were you drawn to the character of a writer partly because you don't write yourself, as many independent filmmakers do?

GA: No, that had nothing to do with it. *Chez Nous* was written around a writer because the author, Helen Garner, is a novelist—the decision was hers. I was given the script when she'd already done about three drafts, so I had nothing to do with collecting the background to the main character, her profession.

LB: What drew you to that script?

GA: I like the script because it is a very honest study of people in relationships— sisters, father-daughter, husband-wife—a contemporary story that is rarely being done in Sydney.

LB: It's also what I call a democratic film. There are a lot of relationships going on simultaneously.

Gillian Armstrong, director, *The Last Days of Chez Nous* (1992, Australia). Photo: Robert McFarlene. Courtesy of Photofest.

GA: That was actually one of the reasons I was attracted to the script—it studies a situation from several people's point of view. That's rare in a lot of material I'm given, which is much more formula, with the hero or heroine defined in black or white. This is a character study which is quite complicated and it varies throughout the story, who you're with . . . whose point of view you take. And that's part of the richness of the writing. You asked two questions, one was a more practical one.

LB: Yes. I think multi-character films pose special directorial problems—going from one pair of characters to another.

GA: Ultimately, as a director when you go out to shoot you have to make each scene work within itself, day by day. But for the overall balance of the film, that's something I work on—I do work with the writers on all the scripts—for a long period of time beforehand. I must have spent six months to a year on the *Chez Nous* script with Helen Garner. Balance is the key thing to consider.

To go back to your first question, it's never been a problem for me, that I'm not a writer. I have great admiration for writers—I feel I'm a script editor. And every published novelist will tell you the most significant person in their life is their editor. I could see the biggest trap with this kind of film is that the audience may not care about any of the characters. Certainly, in the end, they are meant to care about the female character, Beth. And what I was aware of from the beginning, working with the writer, and then working with the actors, was that we were all treading on fine lines, because a lot of times the characters are being unpleasant and selfish. I had to keep the threads together so that in the end, you still like the key character. You could actually have the audience distanced from them all.

LB: It must have been very different from directing *High Tide* or *My Brilliant Career*.

GA: Shooting so much of the story in one place was a major challenge, both artistically and practically. It could have become tedious and claustrophobic that so much of the story was within four walls. That's something I was aware of and planned very carefully. I also discussed it with the cinematographer and the designer so that we created a very strong mood within the house, reinforcing the dramatic moments of the story. I think we used every corner of the house in the end. There was not a corner left unturned. The house was so small we weren't sure whether it would be possible to shoot a movie in it at all. The rooms look bigger on the screen because we often used wide-angle lenses. I said to the cinematographer "Ultimately, it's your decision." For me there were a whole lot of pluses about the house, particularly the whole exterior with the back staircase and the verandas.

LB: How big was your crew?

GA: It was a full feature film crew. I had Geoffrey Simpson, the director of photography, be the camera operator as well, to cut down on the number of people. It was also a huge problem for sound. They couldn't follow an actor moving from one room to another, because the boom would hit the doorway. You could use any old radio mikes, but both they and I don't think that's the best sound quality. I had a wonderful sound department, a team of three. Sometimes the radio mike might be reinforced by an overhead boom or hidden microphones that were all over the house. It was a very hot summer. We decided in the end it brought us closer together. We had to spend so much of that summer squashed in a corner of the room or standing in sinks, in the bath.

LB: To get back to your principal aim, within this multiple web of relationships, to keep the audience identified with Beth . . .

GA: Ultimately.

LB: Ultimately. Kerry Fox's persona on screen as the younger sister Vicki is absolutely flamboyant. She's completely engaging . . . In that kind of situation— I'm playing devil's advocate—what is going to keep the audience identified with a successful, more demanding older woman who *prima facie* is not a sympathetic role?

GA: Well, there's no simple answer to that. We were just walking a delicate line. It was something I was aware of and in some moments pulled Lisa Harrow back if something went too far. Some people don't like the younger sister. In the end, I'd have to try and keep a balance with all of them—watch for the tone and the performance. It's also what I emphasized in the shooting—whose moment I hang with and whose expression I'm with at the key moments.

LB: You got a screenplay whose approach is more novelistic than throughline drama.

GA: I'd say it's more of a character study than plot driven.

LB: But then all great films are character-driven.

GA: Yes.

LB: The film has a pyramid structure. We got to know the family in such detail, at times I thought you pushed it to the edge. But, by the end of the film, the frustration has a definite pay-off. If you had sown more clues as to the denouement— because there's only one major thing that happens, right?

GA: Yeah.

LB: It's not like there's a succession of plot crises. Had you shown more clues, then the pay-off wouldn't be so great. But when the pay-off came, it was completely heartwrenching. Basically it's a betrayal story. There are a lot of ways to look at it. You could look at it as a successful woman gets her comeuppance. That would be a very traditionalist approach.

GA: It's not meant to be that, no.

LB: You could see it as youth wins out over age, because Beth loses the guy.

GA: If you think Vicki wins out . . .

LB: Or you could see it as Beth winning out because she learns something about herself, and self-awareness has become part of the canon. You can go through anything, as long as you learn something at the end of it, right? It doesn't matter what you seem to be losing, because the gain is greater than the loss.

GA: Uhum.

LB: Then your primary value is knowledge.

GA: Self-knowledge.

LB: So, I wonder, what do you want the audience to be left with?

GA: The last thing you said, not the first two. I've heard a lot of discussions. People are deeply affected by the film and discuss these characters personally as though they're all alive and get quite passionate about them.

LB: Oh, they do. That's a strength of the film. It addresses such central human concerns . . . not at all offbeat. By the way, what was the budget of *Chez Nous*?

GA: Three and a half million.

LB: Is that the level you usually work at?

GA: No, *Chez Nous* was the lowest budget I've had for about five years. *My Brilliant Career,* which was fifteen years ago, was just under one million. But times have changed. People worked for less, the costs of stock and lab have gone up. Today in Australia it would probably have cost eight. But I've done twelve million dollar features like *Mrs. Soffel.* And *High Tide* cost more than *Chez Nous* as well and had a longer shooting schedule. *Chez Nous* was funded from a low-budget fund at $3.2 million (Australian). That was the deal. So everybody worked for less money and it was an eight week instead of a ten week shoot.

LB: To me, it's interesting the way the themes develop in your films. In *My Brilliant Career,* Judy Davis plays a young woman growing up at the turn of the century who wants to be a writer—maybe to you it just symbolized wanting to be an artist of one kind or another. And you leave her at a certain point, where she sees marriage as a threat to what she wants—i.e., to be her own person, and the film comes full circle, because she's been writing the story of that growth. Then, in *High Tide,* it seems like we've skipped a couple of stages. We've got Judy Davis playing a woman who is a performing artist, and not terribly happy about it. She's made some trade offs—she's abandoned her child—I'm simplifying the plot—as a result of the death of her husband—and the whole film is about the recovery of that mother-daughter relationship. Lost and found. We're left on a very upbeat note. She loses a lousy career and finds a wonderful daughter. There it's not really a trade-off between career and relationship because the career's not that great, it's crappy. So there's no ambiguity about how to read this film. Now in *Chez Nous* we go to a woman who's a little older than the Judy Davis character . . .

GA: Oh yes, definitely older.

LB: Mid-forties, which is a very interesting age to take for a woman character in a film, because everyone shuns it like the plague.

GA: They don't exist.

LB: And there you've managed to find a script that's a combination of domestic drama, sibling rivalry, generational conflict, and you've kept up your interest in the art/life conflict. What's fascinating to me is: you don't write these scripts, but you've kept this wonderful continuity of theme, at least in three Australian films, as though you've found screenplays that reflect your own train of thought, your own deepest concerns.

GA: All the screenplays that I choose do, because in between the ones that I choose—right at this very moment there are three in the rubbish bin upstairs (sorry, writers)—I turn down hundreds. I only do the material that I am personally affected by and that mirrors things that I believe in. I'll find something where already the writer and I are thinking the same way. It's not that I'm out consciously looking for it. The writer theme is really coincidental.

LB: Beth could have been a woman doctor or . . .

GA: Yes, she could have. It's been fifteen years between the two films that've had writers.

LB: If you had wanted to make a film about a writer's conflict between the demands of her life and her work, you would set it up very differently. I did wonder how Beth could get anything done in the house where there's no solitude or privacy . . .

GA: Well, actually the house is based on the real writer's house, and a lot of the story is autobiographical. The thing is, in the drama we didn't spend half an hour with Beth sitting alone at the typewriter. But then, this was a story about the domestic part of her life.

Pause.

LB: You didn't study film immediately.

GA: I went to the Swinburne College of Education which is an art school.

LB: Did anything really significant happen there that turned you onto film?

GA: That's where I learned about film.

LB: Oh. Right. But what drew you to film rather than painting or sculpture or conceptual art or performance?

GA: I originally went to art school because I wanted to be a theatre designer, and the only school in my state that had costume design was Swinburne. The idea was you went in the first year and did general art, and then you would major, either in film or graphic art. Or you could transfer to another college and do something else in the arts—painting or whatever. And when I was in the first year I saw all the student films from the film television course and was very intrigued. They made films seem accessible to me, and I saw, for the first time, films that were purely artistic expression, and that's what excited me. They were so different from commercial cinema and television.

LB: Did you get to see Fassbinder, or any European directors?

GA: We saw films from all over the world. But the key thing to me was seeing films made by my peers, contemporaries, that made me feel I could do it. That anybody could. We had no film industry in Australia at that point. We actually had a booming film industry in the Thirties and the Forties, but then the American cinema chains bought up all the theaters and took over and totally dominated our cinema, as they do around the world. So, in the Seventies, when I was a student filmmaker, there was a push from a number of people to set up a film development corporation to encourage a film culture in Australia. It's hard for an American to understand because they grow up in a culture which is full of their own cinema, but the first Australian feature film that I had ever seen was in my final year at art school, and I was embarrassed by hearing Australian accents on the screen. I'd never seen an Australian film at the movies, ever.

LB: What was the film?

GA: It was a film called *Two Thousand Weeks*. It wasn't a bad film, it was just so odd, it didn't seem real. A real film had American accents, that's the cultural imperialism that America's taken around the world. So I was very fortunate that by the time I'd graduated, short and independent films were actually being made in Australia. The film development corporation offered grants, films from two minutes, ten minutes, half an hour, and some directors who'd been doing commercials and documentaries, like Peter Weir, were getting grants to do a half hour drama, and we as students were sometimes attached to them.

LB: What had you done before *My Brilliant Career*?

GA: Film students in Australia all think that I walked straight out of film school and got a feature. What actually happened was, I did four years at art school before I finally decided that film was the thing I liked to do and I did three short films that year, very short, two minutes. The last one was a ten-minute with sound. Then I worked as an assistant editor in a commercial film house for a year. At this point with the government funding, they decided to set up a national film school. There'd never been a proper film school. So I applied to go to the national film school. They chose twelve people from all over Australia the first year—it was just a pilot training scheme—a postgrad director's course.

And in that year we were allowed to make three films with professional crews and cast. They had money to pay actors.

LB: Oh, not student crews?

GA: No. We were really tested as directors. Two of three films that I made won a lot of awards. One of them was sent to an international student film festival, and I went overseas with the film and traveled around for eighteen months.

LB: How did you meet Judy Davis?

GA: Oh, that was years later. I'm still just out of film school—second film school. When I came back I did some low budget documentaries, paid work as a director, and at the same time I worked on some friends' films as art director, which meant I did props, the wardrobe.

LB: So you really got a good grounding.

GA: Then I worked on two low budget features as an art director/designer and then I worked on a much more professional feature being produced by Margaret Fink, who produced *My Brilliant Career,* as a props buyer. She and I got along very well. She was the sort of person who wanted to know about every member of the crew, what they'd done. She asked me to read a book that she had the rights to. At that point she was talking about all sorts of people like Polanski directing it. When I came back to Australia from overseas, I worked at adapting a short story into an original screenplay, which I then made into a fifteen minute 16mm drama, called *The Singer and the Dancer,* which won the Sydney Film Festival short film award. Then Fink came back and asked me whether I would direct the film. So that was about two years later. And five years out of the second film school. That's for all the film students who think you get a feature just like that.

LB: Do you see yourself continuing to make films in Australia?

GA: I'll make a film anywhere if I like the script. It's the material that matters. There are wonderful actors all over the world that I'd love to work with and production designers and composers. The greatest thing about working in America has been the chance to work in an international film community, which has been very exciting and a great honor.

LB: Did you get what you wanted from making *The Last Days of Chez Nous?*

GA: I think most directors would say that they're never ultimately satisfied. There's always part of your film you'd wish you had more time for. I always find it very painful to watch because I see all the flaws, but in the overall sense I was very proud of the cast and the cinematography.

LB: But I meant more in terms of what the film's trying to say.

GA: It does seem to be communicating what we wanted it to say, and affecting people, which is your ultimate aim, both emotionally and intellectually.

LB: That if you're juggling a lot of balls, as Beth is, you're going to drop one once in a while.

GA: Well, Helen Garner's contention is that women in the nineties have been trying to do it all and they can't. They have to kick a couple of balls away, and make choices, and say, "Myself, my personal space and my relationships should take priority." That is her point of view, that you can't be a superwoman and you have to have priorities. Don't be so perfectionist about getting the kitchen bench nice and shiny. Ultimately, with such a deeply human drama, every person in the audience brings their own spirit and background and emotional reaction to situation and characters. What's fascinating is how diverse the reactions have been. People like or love or hate the characters. Overall, the central track that I was taking, most people would go with. But all you can do is trust your own instincts, and hope that there are some people out there that will think the same way as you do. And there are some. I realize that I can't control all their reactions. I have to accept that.

Originally published in *Bomb*.

LUCIAN PINTILIÉ

An Unforgettable Summer

These bureaucrats live in a completely false world. They think that any fragment of text refers to them. So in *The Inspector General,* for instance, if the actor playing the role of mayor limps, they think of Brezhnev's limp, and that for sure we must be making fun of Brezhnev and the former Soviet Union. Ridiculous . . .

Lucian Pintilié, 1994

An Unforgettable Summer, *starring Kristin Scott-Thomas, is the second film by noted theatre and film director Lucian Pintilié, former enfant terrible of Romanian culture, since his return to Bucharest as head of a film production studio in 1990. A vivid, stylized adaptation of the short story "La Salade" by Petru Dimitriu, the film is a suspenseful moral drama set in a remote military garrison in the 1920s that parallels the mood of the new Romania. It features superb performances, stunning mise-en-scène and savage satirical bite. I spoke to the impassioned director prior to the film's release by MK2 Productions USA in November.*

Liza Béar: This isn't your first trip to New York.

Lucian Pintilié: No. I've made several because I've staged at least seven or eight plays here in the United States, in Washington and Minneapolis while I was in exile.

LB: In 1972 the Ceaucescu government forbade you to work in Romania, your native country. Under what circumstances?

LP: I was supposed to direct Gogol's *The Inspector General.* All the eyes of the regime were fixed on me because this was the third or fourth time that my work had drawn a big wave of protest . . .

LB: Why was that?

Kristin Scott-Thomas creates turmoil in a military garrison in Lucian Pintilié's *An Unforgettable Summer* (1994, Romania). Photo: MK2 Productions, courtesy of Photofest.

LP: Because, both in the theatre and the cinema, I had practiced my art freely. I had refused to submit myself to the small, necessary, capricious demands of the system. Political dictates are always capricious. One day they want one thing, the next day something else. Two or three times in the past, I had agreed to make modifications. To my great regret.

LB: Textual modifications.

LP: Textual or even directorial.

LB: For instance?

LP: These bureaucrats live in a completely false world. They think that any fragment of text refers to them. So in *The Inspector General,* for instance, if the actor playing the role of mayor limps, they think of Brezhnev's limp, and that for sure we must be making fun of Brezhnev and the former Soviet Union. Ridiculous—the merit of my plays is not derived from political allusions. However, the real trouble was that *The Inspector General* is a play about bureaucratic folly. I figured it would be easier to stand firm and to defend my work than to agree to any textual changes. If you give these people an inch, they want a mile. So I went on a hunger strike. It was the shortest hunger strike in the world history of hunger strikes, it only lasted four hours. The authorities immediately gave in and they didn't touch the play. They allowed one more performance. There was an enormous crowd, it was a big hit—the theatre was surrounded by a militia on horseback—but they banned any further performances. And then I understood the difference between someone who has no political power because he's free, and the authorities that have political power but are enslaved by petty concerns. I felt empowered for the first time in my life. They called me to the Central Party Headquarters and said, "Comrade Pintilié, unless you change your world view you can no longer work in Romania."

LB: You went to live in France.

LP: Yes. I survived because I was able to direct theatre and opera all over the world.

LB: You couldn't make films in France?

LP: It's not that simple. Jack Lang, the then minister of culture, had invited me. At the time, I'd only made one television film, *Sunday at Six,* and two other films, *The Reconstitution* and a Chekhov adaptation which showed in Cannes. When I got to France at the age of 39, I felt I had to do something that would create an immediate buzz. So I did a production of *Turandot* with 18 dwarves at the Théatre National Populaire. It was a huge success. After that, everything went on automatic pilot. I received offers to direct plays in England, the U.S. and Canada. Growing up in a socialist country, I'd had no financial problems. I was used to not lifting a little finger. At the same time, I suffered enormously because I didn't know how to struggle to make films.

LB: What were your directorial aims in *An Unforgettable Summer*? The mise-en-scène is very different from *The Oak,* which must have been a seminal film for you since it marked your return to Romania after the fall of Ceaucescu.

LP: *The Oak* was made in a fit of rage, with great energy and violence and gaiety. I wanted to portray people who gradually get used to monstrosity, for whom evil becomes banal. So I saw the film as a burlesque, and I used this crazy comedic rhythm from the '30s as a way to show the daily apocalypse. In

An Unforgettable Summer, I had a completely different take on evil, I was less involved. So I changed the point of view. I wanted to show a world which gets used to crime much more coldly, to have a much more contemplative approach to the subject matter and a classical dramatic structure.

LB: Also the story is set in the '20s.

LP: Exactly. In cinematic terms, this translated into more formal cinematography and storyboarded camera moves with fixed start and end points. To sustain this kind of geometric composition, you need physical situations you can control. The whole film was shot on sets by the Danube delta. That mountain in the opening shot is a little hill of 200 metres. We did have to wait for the sheep, the crows and the seagulls.

LB: You found Kristin Scott-Thomas in Polanski's *Bitter Moon*?

LP: Yes. I cast her within five minutes. I changed the role of the heroine in my film to take advantage of the fact that she's English and speaks French very well. I wanted to recreate a character that's completely disappeared—the mittel European.

LB: With a touch of Garbo.

LP: Yes, in the sense of mysterious beauty. But beyond that, on a cultural level. For instance, in my wife the actress Claudie Bertolli's family (she's half-Italian), everyone speaks three or four languages fluently. So I made Marie-Thérèse, the Kristin Scott-Thomas character, half-Hungarian and half-Romanian, and she speaks English because her father is a diplomat. At the age of 22, her future husband, a Romanian, saves her from rape in the Budapest subway. She is so grateful that she becomes a fierce patriot. She embellishes everything that's Romanian. To her, the little hill is more beautiful than Fujiyama. She has a Mozartian nature.

LB: *The Magic Flute* is on the soundtrack.

LP: Yes. In my opinion, there's something very dangerous in a character who ascribes all the qualities of the world to one country. Her husband is mediocre, no one special. So if the husband and the country don't correspond to her Utopian ideals, she feels betrayed and withdraws her love. This is exactly what happened to Romania after the fall of Ceaucescu. For five, six days, all the TVs of the world talked about this fantastic revolution that was taking place and when they discovered things weren't so fabulous after all, they abruptly and definitively withdrew their interest. Bye bye forever. Just like the character of Marie-Thérèse.

LB: You were invited by the new régime to be head of a Romanian production studio. How does that work?

LP: Of the five studios that they set up, the only one that's viable is mine because I understood right away that the only chance of survival is to do co-productions with other European countries. If you make films just for the Romanian public, you get nowhere. The other four studios are always changing their structure, whereas I don't change mine. I have very little money, enough to make about one-third of a very modestly budgeted film. But that's not what counts. What's more important is to be able to contact Western Europeans who are potential partners in some official capacity. That gives the studio some clout as do my name and the script quality of young Romanians who want to make films. So far I've done five films with France and Germany and I have two more in development. Next door to me is a really unusual phenomenon, an independent producer who was my line producer when I made *Scenes of Carnival,* which was originally banned in Romania. He has fallen artistically in love with me, and only makes his films at my side.

LB: So are things a little better than before?

LP: They're very different. There's no longer a problem about artistic freedom in the sense of freedom of speech. You're free to do what you want if you have the means. On that level, it's an enormous difference. A thousand times better. The new government is neo-communist, with a tendency towards a kind of wanton, unfettered capitalism. Which is very convenient for me.

Published in *The Film Journal.*

CHANTAL AKERMAN
On the Set in Brooklyn

BERLIN TO PARIS, WITH A STOPOVER IN BROOKLYN

July 9, 1995[1]—William Hurt is in Brooklyn again, but he's not playing the cigar aficionado he portrayed in *Smoke*. On a warm evening at the end of May on St. James Place in Fort Greene, a crew member is hosing down the sidewalk for another take of a scene from Chantal Akerman's forthcoming film, *A Couch in New York*.

The romantic comedy, written by the Belgian Ms. Akerman and the French screenwriter Jean-Louis Benoît, stars Mr. Hurt as a psychoanalyst who trades his Manhattan high tech apartment for a bohemian abode in Paris. The apartment belongs to a young French dancer played by Juliette Binoche. After 8 weeks of shooting interiors in Berlin, the production moved to New York for 15 days (three of them in Brooklyn) and from there will go to Paris.

"The story's about how two people from totally different worlds can meet," said Régine Konckier of Films Balenciaga, the co-producer with Jean-Luc Ormières. "The psychoanalyst discovers the dancer's world through her apartment. She arrives in New York and takes up his practice. Not intentionally, but because people are unhappy and she wants to help."

In the scene being shot this particular day, Mr. Hurt's character, unable to cope with his new apartment in Paris, has returned with his golden retriever to the Brooklyn neighborhood where he grew up, so he can stay with a childhood friend.

"Ms. Akerman chose Brooklyn," Konckier said, "because she wanted a mixed neighborhood" an area in which different ethnic groups co-exist. Mr. Ormieres added, "As a European, Brooklyn existed in her imagination as a place for

---

[1] These two stories were published in *The New York Times* and *Newsday* respectively. Since the first story was written on the set while the film was in production, unlike every other story in the book, had not seen the film before writing the story. The impetus here was to observe Akerman at work in a different setting and on a bigger scale.

immigrants." She was also familiar with Brooklyn, having shot a previous film there in French, the 1988 *Histoires d'Amerique: Food, Family, Philosophy*, a string of Jewish jokes told against a background of Brooklyn exteriors.

Seated on a camera dolly, the 45-year-old Ms. Akerman is the center of a swirl of activity. Having directed more than 25 films, including the 1992 French movie *Night and Day*, which Vincent Canby called "a small, seriously comic extravaganza," she is used to the hurly-burly of production. The demands of shooting this script call for a crew of 60, which is large for her. And the film is being shot in English, a first for the director.

Ms. Akerman established herself as a formidable avant-garde presence with her first two feature films, the sexually uncompromising *Je Tu Il Elle* (1974), in which she starred, and *Jeanne Dielman: 23 Quai du Commerce, 1080, Bruxelles* (1975), a three-and-a-half-hour film, shot in long takes, about a housewife-prostitute (played by Delphine Seyrig) who murders one of her customers after sex.

Ms. Akerman, who has been acclaimed by some critics as the most important European director of her generation after Rainer Werner Fassbinder, has made movies that range from the mordantly satirical to the charmingly playful.

"This film is a challenge for everybody," says Ms. Konckier, "because it's the first time Chantal is doing comedy like this with such actors. It's a lighter subject than usual, so of course the way of shooting is different. She has to cover more."

After 13 days of shooting in New York, the French and American crew members are learning to co-exist on the set. "Brooklyn so far is the most helpful neighborhood I've ever shot in," says Gaby Laferrière, assistant director.

The street scene is lively and colorful with 130 extras, mostly children. The setup for the 300-foot, two-camera tracking shot is complicated. Ms. Akerman confers with her German cinematographer, Dietrich Lohmann. Her camera operator is French, and the focus puller, who is keeping Mr. Hurt in focus as he walks down the street, is American. Grips and electricians are repositioning light fixtures: A young woman in fatigues at a public telephone checks three lighting strips that illuminate Mr. Hurt's face when he makes a call. A Steadicam operator walks backward, trying to keep a tight shot on Mr. Hurt's face while the dolly runs down the track.

Mr. Hurt, walking briskly past men playing dominoes in front of a bodega, looks deep in thought, tries several variations of the walk, hands in pocket, arms swinging, glasses on, glasses off.

Across the street, residents are critiquing the background action "People don't walk like that in Brooklyn, all the same speed, same distance from each other," a girl says. "That's how they walk in Manhattan."

Her friend agrees. "They'd stop and chat to their friends, because here, everybody knows each other."

QUEENS SCREENING SHOWS A FILMMAKER'S VERSATILITY

March 11, 1997—Juliette Binoche, who played a nurse in *The English Patient*, gets to hear people's troubles again in a new comedy *A Couch in New York*, when

she's unexpectedly saddled with a whole slew of patients, as well as a golden retriever, after answering an ad for an apartment swap with an Upper East Side psychiatrist. The latest film by the prolific and versatile Belgian-born writer-director
Chantal Akerman, *A Couch in New York* will premiere March 22 as part of a retrospective of her work now under way at the American Museum of the Moving
Image in Astoria, Queens. *Window Shopping,* a 1985 film, is set in Paris' Golden
Fleece shopping mall. It features the late Delphine Seyrig, who played the title
role in Akerman's 1975 magnum opus about an obsessively immaculate housewife,
Jeanne, Dielman, 23 Quai Du Commerce, 1080 Bruxelles. Window Shopping also
has eight original songs with lyrics by Akerman woven into the screenplay. It's a
story of romantic intrigues set in a hairdressing salon and a clothing store, facing
each other in the mall.

"It's about love and business, but it's not romantic at all," Akerman said during
a recent interview in Manhattan. Seyrig's character "is a bit like my mother. My
mother ran a clothing store, and my father made the leather clothes, which she
sold in the store."

Other films to be screened this weekend at the museum include *The Eighties,* a
1983 experimental film also made in a shopping mall. Sunday's schedule includes

Director Chantal Akerman with actor Sylvie Testud on the Croisette at the Festival de Cannes, 2000.
Photo © Liza Béar.

a 1983 film, *The Man With the Suitcase,* in which Akerman plays a filmmaker who can't get rid of an annoying and unwanted guest in her apartment.

Of *A Couch in New York,* which will close the four-weekend-long festival, Akerman says, "I wanted to do a very classical comedy as a homage to the Thirties. I've always loved Ernst Lubitsch and Billy Wilder."

Akerman, who also counts among her influences Robert Bresson, F.W. Murnau, and Yazujiro Ozu, has been hailed by *Variety* as "the most accessible of avant-garde filmmakers." Critics have also praised Akerman for her flawless composition and witty subversion of genre film.

Sonia Wieder-Atherton, Akerman's partner since 1988, wrote the score for *A Couch in New York.* She has also collaborated with Akerman on the 1989 feature *Histoires d'Amérique: Food, Family, Philosophy,* shot near Brooklyn's Williamsburg Bridge and on musical videos about Schubert and the modern French composer Dutrilleux. She has also worked on the soundtrack for Akerman's film-video installation at the Jewish Museum, *Bordering on Fiction: D'Est,* based on her 1993 documentary of Eastern Europe, *From the East.* The installation runs concurrently with the American Museum of the Moving Image exhibit.

Akerman says many thematic and dramatic elements in *Couch* allude to her previous films, like obsession and the use of monologues.

"The William Hurt character, the psychoanalyst," says Akerman, "is very tight and obsessed, just as Jeanne Dielman is. So is the girl in my first film, *Blow Up My Town,* who's always cleaning everything." She refers to a 13-minute short filmed in 1968 about a girl who blows up her high-rise apartment complex after cleaning the kitchen.

One of Akerman's next projects, she said, will be a purely literary work devoted to the memory of her father.

ABEL FERRARA

The Addiction

What does it matter, man. Why does everybody always talk about the bread? I can make $20 million look like $200. Or I can make $500,000 look like $10 million. And you can make $10 million look like 50 cents. So who cares. I don't even know how much this film costs.

Abel Ferrara, 1995

Deadly serious, dead on target, with a keen nose for the perversity of human nature, Abel Ferrara's films plunge into the icy rivers, into the most extreme forms of human behavior. No feet of clay there: Double rape in Ms.45 *(1981). Drug trafficking in* King of New York *(1990). Gang warfare in* China Girl *(1987). Serial killings in* Fear City *(1984). Yet his often delirious portrayals of murder and mayhem are tempered with irony and a sense of balance—not so much the scales of justice as the law of the jungle: Violent crime breeding the violence of retribution. In the past, Ferrara's films have had a tantalizing ambiguity—they've come on as powerful moral parables while conveying the seductiveness of evil—the devil gets an awful lot of good lines.*

Ferrara's latest film, The Addiction, *opening in New York this October, and written, like almost all the others, by Nick St. John, seems to mark a turning point. Structured as a vampire movie, with Lili Taylor in the lead, it portrays the pure horror, the wasting torments of addiction per se.*

This interview was done late at night over the phone while Ferrara was deep in the throes of pre-production on The Funeral, *a gangster film set in 1935. Casting was still in progress as we talked.*

12 Midnight, July 27, 1995.

Liza Béar: Are you ready? Can we start?

Abel Ferrara: Please.

LB: So you know this is a q and a.

AF: Well, don't make these questions too hard.

LB: I'll try not to!

AF: Had you seen the movies before or had you just rented them all?

LB: I'd seen *Bad Lieutenant.* And *The Addiction.*

AF: 'Cause that's a little much, if you have to sit and watch them all at once.

LB: I did it over a period of time. *The Funeral,* the one you're working on now, that's your 11th feature. Does preparing for the shoot get easier or harder?

AF: This one's a nightmare.

LB: Why?

AF: I'm dealing with a bunch of psychotic actors and their neurotic agents. And lunatic managers.

LB: How do you get yourself to relax?

AF: [laughs] How do I get myself to relax. I try not to relax.

LB: How do you get your actors to relax?

AF: Ah. That's my secret. I'll never give that one up.

LB: So what's your main challenge as a director at this point?

AF: [laughs] What's my main talent as a director?

LB: Challenge. At this stage, not during the shoot.

AF: To come to terms with the script. So I understand it now, not when you're watching it in the movie theater. To try to figure it out before I release it.

LB: A lot of actors have stayed with you film after film.

AF: We're the only ones who offer them work.

LB: Who's in the new film who's been in your previous films?

AF: Annabella Sciorra theoretically, otherwise we're going with a lot of new actors. Isabella Rossellini. Um. Let me see. Valery Golina, Chris Penna, and Benicio del Toro.

LB: Your films range from fairly small ones to really big budget, $20 million?

AF: Yeah, *Body Snatchers.* This is in the middle. It's not too big, it's not too small.

LB: 9–10 million.

AF: What does it matter, man. Why does everybody always talk about the bread? I can make $20 million look like $200. Or I can make $500,000 look like

$10 million. And you can make $10 million look like 50 cents. So who cares. I don't even know how much this film costs. It's a gangster film set in the Thirties, that's the scale of the production.

LB: Black and white?

AF: We've got to get people in hats. No, fuck black and white. We did our black and white.

LB: With *The Addiction.*

AF: Nicky St. John wrote it when he wrote *The Addiction.* He had this one very creative period.

LB: The only film where you collaborated on the script was *The Bad Lieutenant,* with Zoe Lund. You've worked with Nick St. John for a very long time. Do you generate the story idea and Nick . . .

AF: No no no no. We work all kinds of ways. Like *The Addiction,* I didn't even know he was writing it. He gave me the whole script just the way you saw the film.

LB: But do you guys have such a close relationship that you know what's going on in each other's heads, or in each other's lives?

AF: No. I hope not.

LB: How often do you talk? Every day?

AF: There are times we talk all the time, and there are times we don't talk for a long time. He lives upstate. We've been together since we're 15 but the guy's always surprising me. He's always coming up with shit.

LB: Once you get the script from Nick St. John or Zoe Lund, they're the only two writers you've worked with, how much do you rehearse?

AF: We've been rehearsing a lot lately cause we find it's a better way to go. You take the script, and then you work on it. The writer's on the set.

LB: The other film I liked a lot was *Ms.45,* with Zoe Lund. Although on the surface it seems very different from *The Bad Lieutenant,* because it's a revenge film, it's also about the abuse of power, because she takes revenge to an extreme and becomes a feminist vigilante.

AF: Yeah. Falls in love with the power of that gun.

LB: Right. Anyone can. I thought *The Addiction* is the most abstract of your films. Because addiction is the root cause of the evil that the characters in the other films portray.

AF: Say that again?

LB: Well, I tried to look at *The Addiction* in relation to the other films. In a way it felt the cleanest—the simplest story line. Addiction is the root cause of all the evil in many other films.

AF: Say that again? I'm sorry, that was a good point you were making, I just forget. Addiction . . . just repeat what you said.

LB: I know that people look at it as a vampire movie but to me it was more about the horror of addiction. The bad lieutenant is addicted to drugs.

AF: He's addicted to everything, not just drugs. Hold on, hold on . . . He's addicted to alcohol, to gambling, to casual sex. Power. The power of the badge.

LB: Kathleen in *The Addiction* is a philosophy student. All of your films have this moral infrastructure that stems from Catholicism, even if you're critical of it at times . . .

AF: We're not critical of Catholicism in *The Addiction*. That's an expression from a devout Catholic, Nicky St. John. And that's the reason he didn't work on *The Bad Lieutenant*.

LB: What I was getting at was Kathleen is a philosophy student and typically philosophers are at odds with religion . . .

AF: Not all of them.

LB: No, not all. But the philosophic turn of mind makes you question, rather than accept things on authority. What you're taught is to question everything.

AF: There are some great philosophers who were devout Catholics. [talks to someone in the production office] What? Could I call him back in two minutes? Where is he? He's at home? But he's going to stay there? Hold on one second.

LB: She's studying Nietzsche.

AF: As one of many things, again.

LB: But the reference to Nietzsche is *Beyond Good and Evil*. Nietzsche really despised Christian morality.

AF: Exactly. And she was getting to the point where she was asking what is the intellect without the soul? Where are you at? That alone isn't going to get you anywhere. Your mind is not enough. And your body's not enough. You have to find the soul. You dig what I mean? Or you're not going to make it. Intellect alone in this world is just going to leave you . . .

LB: Cold and dead.

AF: Addicted.

LB: Addicted to filmmaking, right? When you started out, you picked up a camera rather than a paintbrush or a pen.

AF: I couldn't really play the guitar as good. I tried it. I didn't grow up in the nineteenth century. Everyone in my generation had the option of making films, the way you had the option of painting or playing the guitar. It was the only way I could express myself the way I wanted to express myself.

LB: Do you still play the guitar?

AF: Yeah, *The Bad Lieutenant* was a song.

LB: I noticed you wrote some of the lyrics for *China Girl* too. So in the beginning, did you use films to control—to take a hold of your life?

AF: Wait. Hold on.

Pause while Ferrara takes care of some business.

LB: What's going on in the production office right now?

AF: We're trying to replace someone in the cast of the film.

LB: Oh, that's really nerve-racking isn't it. At the last minute.

AF: Very nerve-racking.

LB: So do you have some options?

AF: I hope so. Wait, hold on one second.

Another longish pause. When we get back . . .

LB: Some things in your life—your filmmaking life, have been very stable. For instance, you've been in the same place since '76. You've worked with a lot of the same people, Mary Kane, Joe Delia . . .

AF: Well, in this town you can't afford not to. Rent control.

LB: That space on East 18th was what gave rise to your first commercial film.

AF: *Driller Killer.* The guy who lived here before was a painter.

LB: How come that was your only acting role? You didn't like acting?

AF: I couldn't do it as good as . . .

LB: You were a better director.

AF: Yeah. The best actor wins.

LB: When did you first work with Christopher Walken?

AF: *King of New York.* After I saw him in *Deer Hunter.*

LB: It seems like he's made for you.

AF: I wouldn't say he was made for me, but I'm glad he was made.

LB: You spent a year in England, right?

AF: Yeah, I lived in England. London, Oxfordshire. Cotswolds. I shot my first 35mm there. with a BBC crew. Just a short. It was kind of nice 'cause I was a kid, 18, 19.

LB: You haven't ever made films in Europe since?

AF: No. We're trying to. We have a project with Walken and Giancarlo Giannini.

There is another break while Ferrara takes care of business. I read a quote from
The Bad Lieutenant.

LB: "Vampires are lucky. They can feed on others but we can feed on ourselves. We've got to come, so we can go, we've got to suck ourselves off . . . "

AF: [laughs] Where did you get that? You memorized it?

LB: Well, I wrote it down. [goes on reading] "And we've got to eat away at ourselves until there's nothing but appetite." They're Zoe's lines. Was that the premise for *The Addiction*?

AF: No. Zoe and I wrote one script and Nick wrote the other. But what's that saying, "great minds work in the same way . . . "

LB: "Think alike." Since *The Addiction* is coming out we should probably say quite a bit about it, or rather you should, not me.

AF: [laughs] Let's not feel obligated.

LB: Quite. What's the most important thing about that film for you?

AF: I think that no matter where you're at, or how far down you think you are, that your life force, your basic human spirit can overcome any situation you might have gotten yourself into or have been thrown into.

LB: You mean, you have the key within yourself.

AF: Yeah.

LB: To get out of it.

AF: To persevere.

LB: To transcend it?

AF: Yeah, transcend it. That's a good word. A beautiful one.

LB: Well, I like persevere. That's a nice word too.

AF: And not to despair.

LB: So do you find that making films is less of a struggle than life?

AF: There's no difference. It is my life. There's no separation. For as long as I can remember. Or care to.

LB: Every other year you seem to make another film. Is it a struggggle to convince people to get behind you?

AF: Yep.

LB: So that doesn't really change.

AF: No. Even tonight. Whether they do well or not do well. It's an ongoing trip. That's where it's at. And that's the work. You're either into it or you're not. You've got to believe in it. In the process. In the act of filmmaking. The act of reaching out. Communicating. That I'm not just here alone, spinning through . . . you know what I mean? Through this fucking universe. Or Manhattan. That people sitting in a room can feel what I feel, desire what I desire.

Pause.

LB: There's something I really liked about *Bad Lieutenant*. One strand of the plot has him gambling on those seven Mets-Dodgers games throughout the film. What he's doing there is what he's doing with the rest of his life.

AF: Say that again?

LB: Am I being too technical?

AF: No, no. Seven games is the championship, not the World Series.

LB: The TV screen and the game come up in all kinds of odd places, like when he's arresting the two guys who raped the nun, handcuffing them, they're watching the game. You hear the game on the radio when he's driving, in the background . . .

AF: In the foreground.

LB: It makes you super aware—that all of his life is a gamble. He's taking so many risks. And yet the sports gambling is a way for everybody . . . Not everybody who watches your film has done the things the bad lieutenant does. Because when you do drugs, you're gambling with your life, don't you think?

AF: Umm . . .

LB: You're gambling with your health.

AF: Well, certain drugs might save your life.

LB: Yes, but I meant narcotics . . . how do you mean, save your life, antibiotics?

AF: I don't know. You're saying, when you use drugs, you gamble with your life?

LB: Well. When you take alcohol you gamble with your life. Alcohol destroys your brain eventually.

AF: Well . . . I'm not a doctor, so.

LB: Everything I've read says addiction is physiological, it's not weakness of will. It's how your system works. Or maybe you don't accept that?

AF: Well, alcohol isn't the best thing in the world for you.

LB: In *Ms.45,* because the Zoe Lund character is mute, the plot points have to be made visually, so you can watch what she looks at, and guess what she's thinking. There's a point of view shot of her at work looking at a green garbage bag, and then later you see what she uses the green garbage bag for.

AF: Well, it's the movie as mind control.

LB: When she's shopping in the supermarket, she doesn't buy fish or chicken, she buys a chop. So you make the link, when she cuts up the body of her assailant.

AF: Yeah, she's into red meat.

LB: Was that in the script?

AF: I don't know. We went out there with Zoe, and who knows why she bought, why she was in the meat counter.

LB: It happened again with the iron. She used the iron to kill the guy and then she burns the clothes at work with the iron because she's so distracted the day after.

AF: Well, in a way it's a silent movie. That's what's great about it. People think we made her mute because the actress couldn't talk. Meanwhile Zoe—did you ever meet Zoe?—she's eloquent. She has the most beautiful voice. Well, you heard her do that speech you liked so much.

LB: Which of your movies do you like the best?

AF: In which way?

LB: As a director. In which you did all the things you wanted to do.

AF: Well, I like *China Girl,* personally. I like the situation, I like the characters. It's a shot by shot of *Romeo and Juliet.*

A 15-minute break. When he gets back . . .

LB: Do you make a living from your films?

AF: Yep. We keep the show on the road. Wait a minute. Hold on.

LB: Sara Chiang, the lead in *China Girl*, is also in *King of New York*.

AF: How do you like the Chinese actors? Joey Chin, he's in *The King of New York* as well. It's an interesting dynamic down there.

LB: Between the Chinese and the Italians. And you kept the love story really sweet and simple.

AF: I'm telling you, it was a scene-by-scene remake of *Romeo and Juliet*. That's Shakespeare. It shows you how powerful and beautiful and how eloquent he was plotwise.

LB: Aside from that, you tend to focus on evil, on the dark side of life, and to portray characters who are depraved, decadent, or corrupt, or weak.

AF: Like who?

LB: The Frank White character in *The King of New York*, the gang members. Almost everybody has some venal sin, or they're involved in violence or vice. They do drugs. Or they deal drugs. Although Frank White tries to redeem himself by giving money to the hospital . . .

AF: He's a gangster. But there's the police. They don't do drugs. There's the other side of that. There's the Victo Argo character in *King of New York*, right.

LB: Yes, he's the good guy but he seems powerless and he gets killed.

AF: There's three of them.

LB: Yeah, but the emphasis seems to be on corruption.

AF: Well, I'm just seeing the world I live in. Hold on.

LB: It's not a criticism. Do you think that everything has gotten so twisted and society is so cynical that say you did become interested in the other side, it would be impossible to create convincing characters.

AF: There's the Lili Taylor character in *The Addiction*. She's convincing. Look at her at the end of the movie.

LB: But she dies.

AF: Well, not the person in the cemetery.

LB: Just the bad part of her dies. But throughout the film she's under the spell of the addiction.

AF: I don't understand what you're saying. Are we making films about people who invent a cure for polio? We're making films about the conflict. People caught in the grip of good and evil. Two sides to the coin. Where are you at and how do you deal with it. That's what the movies are about and that conflict is the fucking film.

LB: The Harvey Keitel character in *The Bad Lieutenant* goes from bad to worse.

AF: No, not at the end. He plays out what the nun wants him . . . Lets them off, gives them the money. He could have saved himself and he chose to save them.

LB: Is that good considering the crime they committed?

AF: Well, that's the question. The nun has forgiven them. He's not letting them go because he thinks they committed a great crime and therefore they should be rewarded. He's letting them go because that's what the victim asked him to do.

LB: Right. But isn't he also letting them go because the justice system is such that they would get off anyway because they're juveniles.

AF: I doubt if they'd get off.

LB: But that's what he says to the nun in the church, they're going to walk. See, I read it . . .

AF: Wait, hold on. He wanted to kill them right there, but he let them go.

LB: The way I read your take on the justice system, in *King of New York,* is that it favors the scumbag. It's almost impossible for the police to do their job. Same thing in *The Bad Lieutenant,* we get the sense that justice will not be served, so the lieutenant has to pick the lesser of two evils. He's sending the kids on the bus so that they'll be out of town.

AF: No. He's giving them a second chance. He says to them, "Your life ain't worth shit in this town." Those guys'll be killed in prison. They wouldn't be given a fair trial. They'd be killed before they even got to prison.

LB: So then you don't have much faith in the justice system, right.

AF: Well, it's kind of overwhelmed. But it's trying.

LB: Your view of the individual and society is closer to tragedy. The individual tends to give in to his worst impulses. The social system is such that with the best intentions justice can't really be done because the courts are strangled with rules and regulations.

AF: It's tough. But hey, people are trying. Whether they accomplish it or not is another thing. Are you going to be up for a while? Call me back in 20 minutes.

2 A.M.: Ferrara explains what's going on . . .

AF: See, It's a casting situation. I have this brilliant lawyer. His name is Jay Julian. He represents Keitel and Walken and Joe Pesci and a lot of filmmakers too. He started off as a Broadway producer. He used to represent De Niro and Scorsese. Not any more. Anyway, he's amazing. I don't know his age, but he's up there. This is when we do the wheeling and dealing, at this time of night. We're very close to shooting. There's this incredible amount of pressure. You know what I mean? With these actors it's so fucking difficult.

LB: Is he in LA?

AF: No. He's in New York right on Broadway on Times Square. He's like a Damyon Runyan character, he was there in the Actors' Studio at the very beginning. He was a wild character. He helps me finance the films.

LB: Oh, he's very important to you then.

AF: He is. He's not a producer but he helps finance the films because he represents actors. In this day and age, the actors are the key. As it should be.

LB: Without the actors you don't have the deal.

AF: No. Which is the base of the problem.

LB: So is all the financing in place for *The Funeral?*

AF: Um . . . I hope so.

LB: Pretty much, huh?

AF: Well, I tell you, the money is coming from October Films who're going to distribute *The Addiction* and these young dudes who did *Kids.* Have you seen that?

LB: Not yet, no.

AF: Good flick, man. And the guys who put up the money are 25–26 years old. Mike Chambers and Pat Panzerella. It's a good group of people. What's good is the money is coming from the distribution.

LB: So the film is guaranteed distribution?

AF: Well, we'll see.

LB: Nothing's guaranteed until the film's in the can.

AF: You know that, right.

LB: And even then.

AF: You haven't stopped making movies, have you?

LB: Actually I wrote a book of short stories since I made my film.

AF: Really? So now what, you're going to sell them to the movies?

LB: I've optioned one story, "Crocodile Tears."

AF: "Crocodile Tears." That's a great title. It's like *Snake Eyes*. Did you see the Madonna movie?

LB: Yes, of course, *Dangerous Game*.

AF: The original title was *Snake Eyes*.

LB: I like *Snake Eyes* better.

AF: Yes but there's a porno film called *Snake Eyes*. We couldn't use it as a title. MGM was agraid of getting sued so they had a generic list of titles to choose from. It's funny, because whenever we are in between films and people say, what are you going to do next . . .

LB: That's all people ever say, isn't it.

AF: Yeah. So I used to say, *Snake Eyes*.

LB: Oh, I see, like rolling the dice.

AF: Yeah, that's what it means. Snake eyes is a losing hand. If you roll two ones, that's a losing throw. When I wasn't in a mood to get into a conversation, and people'd ask, what movie are you going to do next, I'd say, *Snake Eyes*. And they'd go, wow, sounds good, 'cause there's something about it that sounds official, but meanwhile there never was a movie that went with it. All we had was this title to shut people up.

LB: You're pretty good at doing that, aren't you?

AF: [laughter] Definitely.

LB: Something must have happened.

AF: We admitted defeat.

LB: No you didn't. What happened between then and now? Something good, right?

AF: I wouldn't say good but we resolved something. I got some good legal advice, let's put it that way.

LB: Do you have all the locations for the film?

AF: Yeah. Jersey City and Brooklyn. The story takes place in Mount Vernon. It's the first town north of the Bronx. You know where the Bronx is?

LB: Yeah. When you lived in Peekskill you came into New York to look at Warhol movies?

AF: Yeah yeah yeah. Joe Dallessandro, Pasolini . . .

LB: Italian new realist cinema.

AF: Godard.

LB: God.

AF: Do you like Godard?

LB: I like *Breathless* and *Pierrot Le Fou* and *Masculin Feminin* and *Vivre Sa Vie* and *Week-End*.

AF: The last one was good, *Nouvelle Vague*.

LB: So how did you get that break with Ed Pressman?

AF: What do you mean, "break"? *Bad Lieutenant* was less than $2 million. We did big films before him. *Fear City*, ever see that one? With Tom Berenger and Melanie Griffith.

LB: Not yet.

AF: *China Girl* was way bigger than *Bad Lieutenant*.

LB: Oh, because of all the action sequences with the gangs.

AF: No, no, he's a great producer.

LB: How do you feel about making so-called Hollywood movies?

AF: Which one?

LB: *Invasion of the Body Snatchers*.

AF: I liked that film. But it was the typical process. It's not a film I feel like doing every day.

LB: You have less control? Or more people to hassle with?

AF: Yeah. When the budget's $20 million . . .

LB: The pressure's 20 million pounds on you.

AF: Exactly. Ten times the pressure of a $2 million film.

LB: I was wondering. Could we talk a bit in person?

AF: No, we can meet. Have you ever seen me? Have we ever met?

LB: I've seen you on screen.

AF: That was a long time ago.

LB: '79.

AF: I'm 44 now. It was just my birthday.

LB: When?

AF: July 19.

LB: Weren't you too busy to notice?

AF: Actually I had a very interesting birthday.

LB: What did you do?

Silence.

AF: Hello?

LB: I'm listening.

Originally published in *Bomb*.

JAFAR PANAHI

The White Balloon

I agree that the less the director intimidates the actors, the better it is for the film. It will enrich the process of filmmaking as a collective experience. As far as I'm concerned, if the actors don't see other movies I would like that even better: complete purity as far as exposure to cinema.

Jafar Panahi, 1995

An exquisitely crafted debut feature, Jafar Panahi's The White Balloon *is a compelling tribute to the aesthetic merits of simplicity. A little girl wants to buy a special fish for the New Year's celebrations; to get to it, she must forge her way through a sly, treacherous world of adults in the back streets and alleyways of Tehran. The film so imaginatively inhabits the macro mindset of a seven-year-old, for whom the tiniest setback is a momentous hurdle, as to bring high drama and a delicious humor to every step of her single-minded journey. Under Panahi's impeccable direction, Aida Mohammadkhani plays her role with grave charm and unflinching determination.*

A Cannes 1995 Camera D'Or winner, The White Balloon *is also a salute to the strong collaborative tradition of Iranian filmmaking that has emerged in the wake of that country's devastating social upheavals. By the time I first saw* The White Balloon *at the Montreal Film Festival, the story of the making of the film was already legendary. As it goes, Panahi told Abbas Kiarostami his idea for the scenario while working as Kiarostami's assistant director on* Through the Olive Trees. *Kiarostami not only encouraged him to make the film but offered to "write" the script by narrating the story into a tape recorder as they drove from one location to another.*

This interview was conducted with the invaluable help of a Farsi interpreter while Mr. Panahi was in town for the screening of his film at the New York Film Festival.

Liza Béar: Do little girls always get their way in Iran?

Jafar Panahi: [laughing] Probably as much as anywhere else in the world!

Aida Mohammadkhani stars as Razieh in *The White Balloon* aka *Badonake Sefid* (1995, Iran). Directed by Jafar Panahi. Courtesy of Photofest.

LB: Especially if they're so determined. The red bill that Razieh loses says 5,000 on it. How much is that worth?

JP: It's a 5,000 reals bill, equivalent to 500 toumans. It's worth $1.50. But that's like one third of a day's pay for that family. If you're making $200 a day here, that's like $70.

LB: As well as having the initial story idea for *The White Balloon,* you directed and edited the film, you were responsible for the art direction and you built the set. How did you manage it all?

JP: For two reasons we couldn't have a very large crew for this film. One was the [small] scale of the production and the size of the budget: we just couldn't afford to. The other, just as important, was the presence of a kid. The more people you have on the set, the more the kid may be bothered by their presence. For instance, I never use a continuity supervisor, I take care of that myself. Also, I don't use a person to operate the slate because that's disturbing for the child. I want the child very naturally to flow into the part without somebody shouting, Now we're ready!

LB: You got the locations to match perfectly, which was very important for a film that takes place in real time.

JP: It's very hard to get that kind of a match. I spent an incredible amount of time doing it. For example: the little girl's house is in Tehran, but when she opens the door onto an alley, that's another town. Because I knew the kind of passageway that that kind of a house should be a part of. So, in a sense, I created my own architecture by putting different locations together.

LB: Which part was the set?

JP: It's in the very first scene, when you have that circular movement of the camera. The place was there, but it just had the bare minimum for us, and we had to completely set-dress it and build our own set within that space. The tailor's shop was a real shop but not in Tehran, somewhere else. The snake charmers were in Tehran but at quite a distance from the house. No two locations that you see as adjacent in the film are in close proximity to one another in real life.

LB: How did the story elements come together?

JP: A film school friend of mine, Parvis Shabahzi and I had an idea for a short film. As it happens, he was also my assistant in this film and now he just got an opportunity to make his own feature film.

LB: That's great. Do you both have children?

JP: Parvis does not but I have two children, a thirteen-year-old son and a seven-year-old-girl, the same age as Razieh in the film.

The story for the short film was very simple: a little girl wants a special fish for the New Year. All the other characters and situations in the feature-length version were added by Abbas Kiarostami, except for the old lady who helps Razieh find the money, which was part of the original script for the short film. The Afghan boy's character was originally supposed to be an old man, but we changed it to an Afghan boy. As a result we had to change the last ten minutes of the film.

LB: What other ethnic groups were represented in the film?

JP: The old lady is of Polish origin, part of the Polish emigration that took place during the Second World War. The tailor is from the Turkish minority. The fish vendor is from a city in northern Iran, which is on the Caspian Sea and has its own dialect. And the soldier is from another part of the country altogether.

LB: Did you have to travel a lot during the casting to find exactly the right actors?

JP: To some extent I did travel but in some instances I got extremely lucky. The very first day of casting we found the lead character, Razieh. We had scheduled to go to two different classes with a video camera and do a test of several girls we thought might be suitable for the part, but when we went into our very first classroom, there she was.

LB: She'd never acted before, right.

JP: If she'd had the slightest bit of experience I wouldn't have cast her. Sometimes in five frames you can tell whether the person is right for the part and at others times you spend hours and days looking around. You know you're not going to find the person in a particular place but you still do the test. But sometimes there's a particular moment when, basically, your eyes cross and you think, this is it. That's what happened to me with Aida.

LB: Did anyone in the film have acting experience?

JP: The only character who had a very little film experience, although she's not really considered a professional actress, was Razieh's mother. In fact, she's married to a friend of mine who's also an Iranian filmmaker who made a very good movie called *The Fish,* which went to a lot of film festivals. She was the subject of a documentary on her life by another Iranian filmmaker. But to give you an idea of how much she knew about filmmaking, the very last day of my work with her, she asked me whether I was also a cameraman like the other director.

LB: In a way, you could take it as a compliment that she didn't feel intimidated by you as a director.

JP: I agree that the less the director intimidates the actors, the better it is for the film. It will enrich the process of filmmaking as a collective experience, and as far as I'm concerned if the actors don't see other movies I would like that even better, complete purity as far as exposure to cinema.

LB: What was your own childhood like growing up in Tehran?

JP: I grew up in the same environment, the same streets and alleys that you see in *The White Balloon*, with the same kind of family. I had the same kinds of problems myself. My father was a house painter.

LB: Did he have a secret second job, like the unseen father in the script?

JP: No, but he was really a film buff, crazy about going to the movies. I used to go to work with my father when I wasn't going to school, in the summer or during the holidays. My father loved to go to the movies himself but he didn't like me to go see the movies that he was seeing. But I was just as interested in going to the movies as he was and since he wouldn't take me, I would go on my own. Sometimes he would put me in charge of the workers on a contract job. And he would say, I have to do something, I'll be right back. I was about 12 years old and more at the time. So he would go, and when he didn't come back after half an hour I would realize that he must have gone to see a movie. Once I'd figured that out, I would also abandon the workers and go to see a movie, sometimes a different one, but sometimes it might happen that I ended up going to the same movie as my father. If my father found out, there would be punishment later at home and he would promise never to go the movies again.

LB: Sounds like the beginning of a good scenario.

JP: I used to complain, how come you go to see them, but you tell me that they are not good for me?

LB: Just like the little girl in the film!

JP: Yes, when she's told not to stop at the snake charmers and she does. But now as it turns out my own son, 13, is totally in love with American action-adventure movies. They're only available on lousy quality videocassettes on the black market. And I keep telling him, don't watch them. I try to keep him from seeing those kinds of movies, just like my father tried to stop me. And my son's response is exactly like mine, I just want to find out why you think this is no good for me.

LB: Did you go to film school immediately after high school?

JP: When I graduated from high school the Iranian Revolution broke out and the colleges closed for a long time, two or three years. I had to look for other things to do, including going to the war front, and taking still photographs. And after a while when I had made some contacts there, I asked them to give me a 16mm film camera so I could shoot a documentary. This was the Iran-Iraq war. The front was in the southern part of Iran.

LB: Did you see action? Were you involved in combat?

JP: Yes, I was enlisted.

LB: It must have been great training for the eye.

JP: The war documentaries were very encouraging to me because I realized I was doing film work, so after the war was over I came back and—there's an entrance examination in Iran which is very important—so that was an incentive for me to work really hard to prepare for it. It's like the French baccalaureat. The first year in film school we weren't required to specialize in any particular field but I realized that my first love as a filmmaker was editing. That's why I would get my hands on any surplus footage or reels that I could just to put something together. Sometimes I would beg my friends to let me edit their projects for them. And once I had done some work as an editor, I started to feel that I should be making my own films. So I became one of the seven directors out of 60 students that had gotten into the film school, to be trained and graduate as a director.

LB: That's a pretty selective system compared to the U.S. film schools. How many films have you made altogether?

JP: Three short documentaries and two short dramatic films, which won awards in a number of domestic film festivals.

LB: Did you travel anywhere other than to the war front?

JP: My very first foreign trip in my entire life was to France to participate in the Cannes Film Festival this year.

LB: Maybe because you were all working on home turf, the dialogue in *The White Balloon*, for instance the snake charmers, the bickering between tailor and client, sounds particularly lively and authentic.

JP: I wanted to capture day-to-day life in Tehran through the dialogue, but also the script was strong enough to create situations that would allow the characters to engage in that sort of disputatious dialogue. And what was also important to me was the representative nature of the characters—they each represent a different segment of the population, a particular frame of mind and through the dialogue they can make their points.

LB: Was any of the dialogue improvised?

JP: I'm not quite sure to what extent we used improvisation because of the style of working with the actors. We never gave them the script. We would just explain a situation to them and talk about it. We would say, in this situation you have to express such and such a feeling and this is your goal. Now you put it into your own words. We might also say a few words to get them going, but that's really how we worked with them. And this is also the beauty of working with non-professionals. But there's no way you can work like that with a professional actor. He would say, I want my lines, I can't work any other way.

LB: So your background in documentary must have contributed to this way of working.

JP: Not only is the documentary approach very helpful in terms of creating dialogue and improvisation, but it's also very helpful when it comes to découpage, which means the visual dynamic of the shooting script basically and of the editing. It almost forces you to be spontaneous about it, because that's what working with a non-professional actor will do to you. No matter how carefully you create a certain découpage in your mind, you still have to make some changes due to the abilities or lack of abilities of your actors. And also that's why I think it's an advantage if you edit your own films in a situation like this. It's amazing: not only was our cast non-professional but so was the crew. It was my first film, my cameraman's first film, my soundman's first film. It was a debut for everybody. Even so the craftsmanship is amazing.

LB: You shot in 35mm too.

JP: An Arriflex. We used three kinds of tripods and one of them was the high hat. Mostly we shot the film in natural light and even in the use of reflectors we had to be very careful because I wanted to be non-intrusive. I didn't want anything imposing like a huge reflector. There were only a couple of instances where we really had to light the scene, like inside the tailor's shop. I was very careful to pick locations which most of the day were in shadow so we wouldn't have to deal with variations in sunlight.

LB: I understand the use of the goldfish in the New Year's ceremony is not part of the Islamic tradition per se, it goes back to an older Persian tradition that predates Islam and that some Iranians have fought to preserve.

JP: I'm not sure exactly at what point in time the fish became part of the New Year's Eve ritual but in terms of what it means, it's a dynamic symbol of life.

LB: What are the seven "Sins" associated with the ceremony?

JP: We have a letter "Sin," which is like S in our language. If I want to write the name Sally in our alphabet I start with the letter "Sin." The seven elements start with a "Sin" but the fish isn't one of them. The fish was added, as was the mirror. "Fish" in Iranian starts with the letter M. *Maohi* is the Iranian word for fish. The other elements are a coin, garlic, flour, a dried fruit not found in the U.S., and a rice dish. Some people believe that if they have the first 5 or 6 elements together, for the last one or two they can improvise. I forgot one—*sabze,* which means grass. *Sabze* represents green things, spring, the sense of new life.

LB: *The White Balloon*'s been shown at Cannes, Montreal, Telluride, Toronto, and the New York Film Festivals. What was the special award you won in Tokyo?

JP: It won the best first film award, shared with a U.S. film, we think *The Usual Suspects.* It also won an award called "The Flying Dragon," which is given by the Mayor of Tokyo for the best film of the festival. Obviously I'm very happy about it, not only because I'd just lost all my money in Tokyo, just like Razieh in the film, but mostly because the amount of the award, $160,000, will enable me to produce my next two films. They'll also both be stories about children, one almost entirely in Tehran and the other in Iran but outside of Tehran.

LB: Well, I hope you haven't lost any money in New York.

JP: No, not yet!

First published in *Bomb.*

MARLEEN GORRIS

Antonia's Line

[My] first three films were all pretty bleak. They say things that make you despair about the human condition, because all's not well with the world. But with the passage of time, I wanted to express something more . . . benign.

Marleen Gorris, 1995

Dutch filmmaker Marleen Gorris is sitting at what may be the only vacant table on this October night in East Hampton, New York, the home of the Hamptons International Film Festival. Gorris's latest film, *Antonia's Line,* has just been shown, and her fans have trailed us to the crowded patio of the Blue Parrot Bar and Grill. Swarms of correspondents for foreign news organizations covering the festival are perched on adjoining chairs.

"You're being besieged!" a fan named Antonia announces cheerily, handing the director some Antonia's perfume.

"It's lovely, very thoughtful," Gorris smiles, graciously accepting the gift. With her steadfast gaze and mischievous grin, the 46-year-old director looks tiredly happy. She has just flown in from Amsterdam for the festival, where her utopian film met with wild applause. It had already generated similar excitement at the 1995 Toronto International Film Festival and at the Cannes Film Festival (where the buzz started when the film was first screened for women buyers and press only). It went on to win the People's Choice audience award at Toronto over 295 other films, and has been chosen as the Netherlands' entry for Foreign Film at the Academy Awards.[1]

After her fans leave, Gorris leans in away from the noise and backtracks to 1982, the start of her career. Her directorial debut was the controversial murder mystery *A Question of Silence.*

---

[1] *Antonia's Line* won the Oscar for Best Foreign Film in 1996.

Marleen Gorris, director, *Antonia's Line* (1996, Netherlands). The film won the Oscar for Best Foreign Language Film, 1996. Courtesy of Photofest.

"*Silence* was willfully misunderstood," Gorris says. "It isn't about condoning a murder. It is about why that murder was committed."

The murder in question is of a male boutique owner, killed by three shoppers: a housewife, a secretary, and a waitress, none of whom know each other, or the victim, before the crime. A court-appointed psychiatrist must assess the trio's competence to stand trial, and against all expectations, this soignée, exemplary professional woman vouches for their sanity. Acclaimed as a tragicomic allegory, *Silence* vented the suppressed, mounting rage of the ordinary woman at the routine indignities and insults of day-to-day male condescension.

Yet, only a few years before Gorris wrote the screenplay, she didn't consider herself actively feminist. "In Holland there was a very strong feminist movement in the seventies," Gorris recalls. "But I wasn't a part of it at all, because you know what people are like: they don't see what they aren't ready to see."

A writing course in the late seventies produced the script of *A Question of Silence*. She approached avant-garde Belgian director Chantal Akerman to direct the film, but Akerman encouraged Gorris to direct it herself. The film won several European awards, after which Gorris made two more features in the same unsettling vein, *Broken Mirrors* (1984) and *The Last Island* (1990).

"I suppose those first three films were all pretty bleak," she says. "They say things that make you despair about the human condition, because all's not well with the world. But with the passage of time, I wanted to express something more . . . benign."

Antonia's Line is a striking change of pace. Beginning with the period after World War II, Antonia, 40 and a widow, returns to her rural childhood home in southern Holland. Her mother is dying, and Antonia seeks to make a life for herself and her teenage daughter, Danielle. Tracing a matriarchal lineage, the film portrays Antonia and four generations of female progeny as caustic, take-charge survivors who live and love to the fullest. With its dazzling blend of cinematic craft and sexual politics, *Antonia's Line* brings a new feminist maturity to the screen. Birth, death, love, and hatred are set in a context of an extended family, and shot through with Gorris's brand of humor. For example, Crooked Finger, the village recluse, becomes the surrogate father to Antonia's granddaughter, Thérèse. Meanwhile, Danielle, Antonia's daughter, sets up house with Lara, Thérèse's music teacher, and the lesbian couple coexist naturally with the other pairings. I ask Gorris if this acceptance of social diversity is central to the film.

"Absolutely," Gorris says. "Tolerance without indifference. Because very often tolerance is used to mask indifference to others." She pauses, then rephrases carefully. "It's more: allowing people the liberty to be how they are."

Not that the film doesn't have its dark moments—rape, incest, murder, suicide, hypocrisy. "The world is full of torment and devils," says the bespectacled Crooked Finger in the film, quoting Schopenhauer, when Therese announces that she's pregnant, "Why would you want to bring a child into such a world?"

"Crooked Finger is very dear to my heart," Gorris says. "I take his despair very seriously. But through Antonia, which of course is me as well, I put him in his place. 'If you have to choose between philosophy and life,' Antonia says to him, 'this is the time to choose life.'"

Originally published in *Ms.*

BENJAMIN ROSS
The Young Poisoner's Handbook

If you want to feel good about yourself, take prozac, smoke a joint, but you're not going to get it from my movie. I wanted to make a feel bad movie.

Benjamin Ross, 1995

The proximity of one's next-of-kin makes poisoning the perfect crime of opportunity, and the perfect subject for a film, according to 31-year-old English filmmaker Benjamin Ross. He based his debut feature, *The Young Poisoner's Handbook,* on schoolboy mass murderer Graham Young, whose deadly exploits had fascinated and horrified him as a child. After attempting to poison his stepmother in the early '60s, Young was sent to Broadmoor, one of England's top security mental institutions. The case acquired considerable notoriety in Britain when Young was released nine years later and became a repeat offender, killing eight of his workmates by putting thallium, a tasteless odorless poison, in their afternoon tea.

Patrick McGrath, a British novelist now living in New York whose fiction taps a similar vein of New Gothic humor as Mr. Ross, has vivid recollections of the Graham Young scandal from a different family perspective—his own.

"When Graham Young was caught, the British press were baying for blood, and it was my father's blood they were baying for because he was the psychiatrist who discharged the real Graham Young from Broadmoor. Graham Young had been a model patient. After nine years of treatment he wasn't considered dangerous."

Hailed as a black comedy of manners and an astute insight into a psychopath's mind by the British press, the $2 million film premiered at the Sundance Film Festival in 1995.

"At first," Mr. Ross said during an interview in New York, "my dream was to come to America, embrace commerce, go Hollywood, become anything but English."

His early Super 8 films, including *Rent Boy,* a mock documentary about a Picadilly Circus male prostitute, won him a Harkness Fellowship to Columbia

Tea and no sympathy. Hugh O'Conor in Benjamin Ross's *The Young Poisoner's Handbook* (1995, UK). Courtesy of Photofest.

Film School in 1988. He studied with Emir Kusturica. But after a couple of years of cultural displacement, Mr. Ross decided that, as a filmmaker, he would have to ground his stories in familiar places and characters.

"I wanted to make films about the England I knew and recognized," said Mr. Ross.

The son of a conveyancing solicitor, or real estate attorney, from a modest Polish-Jewish background, Mr. Ross's home turf is the London suburb of East Finchley, a stone's throw from the stuccoed uniformity of Graham Young's Neasden, another London suburb.

"I had the idea for the script in the bath of my Columbia apartment one day and wrote the first draft during the Gulf War," Mr. Ross recalls.

Back in London, Mr. Ross found a writing partner, the actor Jeff Rawle, with whom he collaborated over a 2-year period to write 20 more drafts. In the final script, the story is told from the young poisoner's point of view using first-person narration. The historical events serve as a starting point for the film, all of whose characters, other than Young and his immediate family, are fictitious.

Like the real Young who had an above average IQ, the fictional Young is drawn as a precocious misunderstood child who clings to his scientific mission to escape the hatefulness of his milieu and his family's taunts.

According to Dr. Jonathan C. Howard, Fellow of the Royal Society, Young's particular scientific achievement is to have calculated the precise doses of antimony necessary to assure slow death and to avoid detection. "Poisoning is the ultimate crime of cold blood," Dr. Howard said. "In poisoning, the act of killing is separated from the act of dying."

In the film, a musical performance by a lounge crooner in Golders Green, a North London neighborhood known for its cemetery, is the occasion for Young's first experiments in poisoning when he seeks to eliminate a romantic rival by spiking his lunch. He uses mustard to mask the tart taste of antimony sulphide, one of his two poisons of choice. The other is thallium.

"I wanted to encourage you, through whatever dramatic means, humor or satire, to identify with the killer in youself," said Mr. Ross. "If you want to feel good about yourself, take prozac, smoke a joint, but you're not going to get it from my movie. I wanted to make a feel bad movie."

A slightly different version of this story was published in the *New York Times*.

NICOLE HOLOFCENER

Walking and Talking

If we can get in those places in life where we are coming of age with some grace, we're lucky. If not, we can turn it into a movie.

Nicole Holofcener, 1996

July 25, 1996—Two days before the Manhattan opening of *Walking and Talking,* a movie about a crisis between two thirty-something women friends, its 36-year-old director, Nicole Holofcener, paced up and down the corridor outside Catherine Keener's 11th floor room at the Regency Hotel clutching a cellular phone, taking care of last-minute details.

Inside the room, Catherine Keener—who plays independent woman Amelia in the movie—is wrapping up her fourth interview of the day, curled up on a chair, the contours of her face lit by daylight from the window.

Holofcener, in slacks and T-shirt, squeezed past the bed and sat next to Keener at a small, round table in the crowded hotel room. The two women have an easy camaraderie and finish each other's sentences.

"People have been obsessing about my hair for days," said Keener, as she poured the coffee. She's now disconcertingly blond, having changed her natural rich dark hair color for Tom DiCillo's *Box of Moonlight,* recently shot in Tennessee. And she's keeping it blonde for DiCillo's *The Real Blonde,* which starts production in September.

Holofcener first spotted Keener in DiCillo's *Johnny Suede* when it was screened at the 1992 Sundance Film Festival, where Holofcener's own short film, *Angry,* was playing. She later saw her in person on the StairMaster at a West Hollywood gym reading Newsweek in a plastic sleeve. A casting director they both knew passed the *Walking and Talking* script to Keener. Actor and director immediately took to each other at their first meeting at an L.A. coffee shop.

"When I first saw Catherine in *Johnny Suede*," Holofcener said, "I thought she'd have the ability to feel the sadness and loneliness for Amelia's character very easily without self-pity or lack of self-respect."

As it happens, the first scene of *Walking and Talking*, in which the dark-haired Amelia meets her blond best friend Laura (Anne Heche), also takes place at a coffee shop, not in Los Angeles but in New York, at Chelsea's fashionable Le Gamin. In the scene, the obnoxious waiter ignores Amelia's order but immediately takes Laura's order when she arrives. Amelia is not fazed.

"She gets overlooked, but she's still fighting," Keener said.

Holofcener was raised in New York and Los Angeles, got her first taste of filmmaking at San Francisco State and graduated from Columbia film school, eight years ago. Her thesis film, *It's Richard I Like*, a subtle analysis of uncertainty in a boy-girl relationship, was picked up by PBS's American Playhouse. Keener grew up in Miami and got into acting while an English major at Wheaton College in Massachusetts. "Amelia was based on me," Holofcener said. "I wrote about what I experienced when my best friend was getting married. And *Walking and Talking* is really Amelia's story, even though the problem in the friendship is what carries the plot!"

For Keener, it was how Amelia's sadness was handled in the script—its humor—that drew her to the character. "What was really interesting for me about this movie was that it's told from Amelia's point of view," Keener said. "As an actress I often read scripts where there's a female lead, and then there's a best friend. And this movie was about the best friend. It reversed the normal setup. The best friend became the lead. Usually the best friend is relegated to a couple of scenes."

"Usually they're caricatures," Holofcener said.

"And they can't be as pretty as the lead," Keener said.

"When I was casting the movie, Amelia was always recommended as being a plain Jane," Holofcener said.

"Quirky," Keener said.

"The quirky one with the zany vintage clothes," Holofcener said. "I'd say, 'Whoever said struggles in relationships are about who's prettier?'"

In the movie, the two women are portrayed as former roommates who also shared a large, furry cat, now dying of cancer. Like a stone thrown into a pond, the news of Laura's impending marriage changes the social dynamic of their small New York milieu, setting off ripples of anxiety in Amelia, who feels her friend will have less time for her. The big event also puts a strain on Laura's relationship with her future husband, whom she forces to have a mole removed, presumably afraid he might get cancer, like the cat. Or maybe it's a sign that she can't accept him, warts and all.

Analyzing the contrast between the two women in her story, Holofcener said that she saw Laura as the one with the power in the relationship.

"Laura looks like she's in control more than Amelia does," Holofcener said. "Amelia doesn't look like she's in control and she doesn't fake it. Laura, even when she's not in control, acts like she is. Laura is less needy."

While growing up, Holofcener, now married to a writer, said that she hadn't necessarily wanted to get married.

"I don't feel there's anything trapping or demoralizing or unfeminist about getting married," Holofcener said. "I met somebody and it was the most romantic gesture."

Among the film's many nice ironies: Laura, a therapist who fantasizes about one of her patients, points out to Amelia, who goes to therapy, that marriage isn't the be-all and end-all of life.

"When you're longing for something so much," Holofcener said, "when you're not in the club, it looks so much more glamorous than it really is. Amelia doesn't have anything near it. But in my movie I wanted people to feel moved by the longevity of friendship. If you can withstand the growing pains, you'll benefit from a lifelong relationship."

"If we can get in those places in life where we are coming of age with some grace, we're lucky. If not," Holofcener added, smiling, "we can turn it into a movie."

Published in *Newsday.*

KARIM DRIDI

Bye-Bye

I made this film to prove to Chirac that "these people" can also smell good.

Karim Dridi, 1996

July 16, 1996—"There may be more knowledge of Arab culture in France than in the U.S. because France is closer to North Africa," says Tunisian-born Karim Dridi, whose second feature, *Bye-Bye,* opens next week. "But in fact, throughout Western society, *Muslim* is practically synonymous with *terrorist.*"

Bye-Bye is a richly textured drama about North African immigrants in Marseilles. Says Dridi: "About a year before he was elected, Chirac made a scandalous remark about immigrant Arab families. He said, 'These people have a bad smell.' I made this film to prove to Chirac that 'these people' can also smell good. That's why in my film here's a lot of food, you see the kitchen and people eating meals, cooking and eating like anyone else."

Initially, Dridi, 35, wrote a first-person novel rather than a script, and he tried to give the film a novelistic feel. Taking place in a seething tenement neighborhood, *Bye-Bye*'s clashes are as much between genders and generations as they are racial flare-ups. The story unfolds when 25-year-old Ismael and his 14-year-old brother Mouloud arrive from Paris to stay with their cousins. Ismael is haunted by the death of his handicapped brother in a fire for which he feels partly responsible. A fabulous soundtrack ably underscores the film's many moods and Ismael's brooding sense of guilt.

Dridi's father, an officer in the Tunisian navy, met his mother, a nurse, on the battlefield during the Algerian-Tunisian war. "Being half-French and half-Tunisian," says Dridi, "both an insider and an outsider, enabled me to see each culture from the other's point of view."

"At 13, I went to live with my aunt in Tunisia for a year so that I could learn Arabic," says Dridi, who has lived in France since he was two. "That visit had an enormous impact on me because I was there alone without my parents. The aunt's

Sami Bouajila (back) and Frederic Andrau in *Bye-Bye* (1995, France Algeria), directed by Karim Dridi. Courtesy of Photofest.

character in the film is drawn from my real aunt. She's a woman who really holds her home together. She doesn't reject tradition but at the same time she's thoroughly modern."

As a filmmaker, Dridi is self-taught, but his quicksilver camera captures the hustle and bustle of immigrant life and the tension between traditional and contemporary values. When Mouloud reads the lyrics for his new rap song to Ismael, Ismael comments dryly, "You don't know it by heart yet. Also, dic is spelled with a k."

Although Dridi says 80 percent of new French directors now go to film school, he got his start at 18 making industrial films. "At 20, I sold my first short to TV and then made six more." After his short *Zoe, the Boxer* won several awards, he was approached by producers to make his first feature, *Pigalle*, a portrait of the notorious Paris neighborhood.

Dridi relies heavily on rehearsal and improvisation: "A month before the shoot, I rehearse full-time with all the actors and rewrite the dialogue. Once we're in production there's no more improv. My mise-en-scène originates from the performance and not a storyboard. I don't start out with a visual plan."

Claiming he has more affinity for British directors such as Stephen Frears, Ken Loach, and Michael Winterbottom than for current French cinema, Dridi has been commissioned to make a documentary about Ken Loach for BTF (French Television). Contrasting his ideological approach to that of U.S. filmmakers such as Spike Lee, Dridi says, "In *Do the Right Thing* and *Jungle Fever*, Spike Lee opposes whites and blacks. He pours oil on the fire. Whereas in my film even if I do show differences between two cultures, my objective is to provide an intimate portrait of a family and to show how similar families are whatever the race."

Dridi's next film, *Hors de Jeu,* will have nothing to do with immigrant life (or with football) because he doesn't want to be pigeonholed. It will be about two people who want to be players but are metaphorically offside.

"Instead of mixing French and Arab culture," says Dridi, "I'll be mixing the in-crowd with the people who are totally unknown."

Published in *The Village Voice.*

PATRICE LECONTE

Ridicule

I adored the script. I found it smart and original. I agreed to direct on condition that not one comma be changed. It was perfect as it was.

Patrice Leconte, 1996

Patrice Leconte's next project will be an action film. That may sound like a major departure for someone who just directed a satirical, highly verbal costume epic set in eighteenth-century France. But those who have seen *Ridicule* in the two weeks since it opened in Manhattan will no doubt tell you that it's not much of a stretch.

"The notion of French wit was at its apogee in the late eighteenth century," Leconte said during a recent visit to Manhattan to promote the film. "At that point it was no longer a game or even a sport but a power trip. Wit had the power to make and break reputations. I had always thought of eighteenth-century wit as delightful and effervescent as a glass of champagne, but in *Ridicule* it works like a Colt in a western."

Set in 1783, six years before the aristocracy was deposed, the critically acclaimed *Ridicule* tracks the vicissitudes of a young country nobleman and engineer, Grégoire Ponceludon de Malavoy (Charles Berling), at the court of Louis XVI in Versailles. Ponceludon's peasant workers are dying of malaria. He wants the king to finance a drainage project for the mosquito-infested swamps in his region.

"Be witty, sharp and malicious," the Marquis de Bellegarde (played by Jean Rochefort), who is also a doctor, instructs his protégé, "and your province will be cured of its problems."

At Versailles, a nobleman with an agenda seeking an audience with the king would face intense competition. Access to the royal purse strings means learning the ways of the court; in the anterooms, being quick on the draw with *bons mots,* quips, wisecracks and repartee is what it takes to create a buzz in the royal ear. Well, almost. There's a slight detour via the Countess de Blayac's boudoir.

Fanny Ardant (as Madame de Blayac) and Bernard Giraudeau (as l'Abbé de Vilecourt) in Patrice Leconte's *Ridicule* (1996, France). Photo by Catherine Cabrol. Courtesy of Miramax Film Corp. All Rights Reserved.

Although Leconte has written or co-written the screenplays for all his 13 previous films, the 49-year-old director had no problem at all working with Remi Waterhouse's script, which, according to Leconte, "came in out of the blue."

"I don't know why [the producers] picked me," Leconte says. "Maybe because I had never made a period film. In any case, I adored the script. I found it smart and original. I agreed to direct on condition that not one comma be changed. It was perfect as it was."

The film was shot in eight or nine chateaux akin to the ones in the historic Loire Valley around Leconte's hometown of Tours. "We couldn't shoot in Versailles itself," Leconte says, "Too much red tape."

For the visual style of *Ridicule*, Leconte said that he "tried to forget all the period films and also eighteenth-century paintings, opting instead for impressionism, elliptical narrative and use of evocative detail to advance the action. "The court of Louis XVI was as strange and self-enclosed as a Martian planet," Leconte says. "Totally cut off from the peasants' reality. [There were] deplorable working conditions in the rest of the country. The revolution was lying in wait, and the courtiers were oblivious of it. They'd established a code of sorts and a pecking order based on wit and ridicule that more or less worked for them. The court was a hotbed of conniving, intrigue and manipulation."

An example: "I would be flattered by your advances," the Countess of Blayac (Fanny Ardant) tells the film's protagonist as she rejects some tactical flirting, "if my chamber didn't lead to the king's." Then she gives him some advice. "Learn to hide your insincerity," she says, "so that I may yield without dishonor."

After attending film school in Paris, Leconte, the son of a doctor, wrote and drew strip cartoons for a satirical publication for five years while making short films. *Monsieur Hire* (1989), a thriller also recognized by critics as a subtle evocation of romantic obsession, brought him international acclaim. He won renown for his tart comedies such as *The Hairdresser's Husband* (1990) and *Tango* (1993). But most of that renown was confined to Europe.

"Most humor doesn't travel well," says Leconte, who lives in the Montparnasse section of Paris with his wife of 25 years and their two daughters.

Asked about scaling the rungs of the movie industry, Leconte says it helps to know exactly what you want but not to take yourself too seriously.

"Taking yourself too seriously," says *Ridicule*'s director, "is a sure way to come a cropper."

Published in *Newsday*.

MILOS FORMAN
The People vs. Larry Flynt

If you love the beauty and freedom of the jungle, you have to live with the leeches and mosquitoes and snakes, the tigers and the sharks.

Milos Forman, 1997

A savagely funny burlesque/courtroom drama based on real trial transcripts, The People vs. Larry Flynt, *Milos Forman's latest film, wrings a hard bargain from the contradictions of American culture—and to maximum effect. With Rabelaisian flair and an unerring nose for irony, the film cleverly manages to satirize the grotesqueries of capitalism represented by* Hustler, *the hypocrisy of the religious right and to pay homage to the First Amendment in one breath, somehow without ever falling prey to the scuzz that Flynt exemplifies. The film may well reap another slew of Oscars for its formerly Czech director.*

Partly a wrenching love story between shock/schlockmeister Flynt (wickedly played by Woody Harrelson) and his fourth wife Althea Leasure (Courtney Love in a dazzling turn) who died of AIDS, and part ode to the Supreme Court, the first-rate, incisive script tracks the rise and fall of the Kentucky-born rebel's fortunes across three decades, from bottomfeeding smut peddler to First Amendment hero by default. Flynt's outrageous challenges to authority (he famously wore the U.S. flag as diapers in court) and his constant need to outdo himself in print, eventually taxed everyone's patience, including his wife's and his lawyer's, and sparked intense opposition, not only from the moral majority. But the arc of his life, with his rags-to-riches ascent as porn king, obscenity trials, attempted assassination, religious "conversion," and tenacity in the face of growing opposition, has all the ingredients for raunchy comedy and high drama. Having been permanently paralyzed by a sniper's bullet, Flynt takes his fights to a more exalted plane when the Reverend Jerry Falwell sues him for libel in a Virginia court for a satirical lampoon (Falwell having sex with his mother in an outhouse) and is awarded damages for "emotional distress." Flynt and his indefatigable lawyer, Alan Isaacman, appeal the case in Washington, D.C., make the Supreme Court laugh, and win a unanimous ruling in his favor.

In its heyday, Hustler *easily outstripped its peers* Playboy *and* Penthouse *by being the first glossy, in porn lingo, to "show pink." It quickly escalated in sensationalism and sheer grossness, with graphic sections like "Assholes of the Month" and "Beaver Hunt," blending crude humor with debasing imagery and broadening the scope of its targets to cultural icons like Santa Claus and the Wizard of Oz (shown in the film), then focusing on prepubescent nudity and coprophilia (not shown in the film).*

In a very different way, Forman's life has been as dramatic as Flynt's: he lost both his parents at the hands of the Gestapo at an early age, made his first three internationally-shown films in Czechoslovakia, and, after moving to New York, won Academy Awards for One Flew Over the Cuckoo's Nest *(1975) and* Amadeus *(1984). The People vs. Larry Flynt, with Woody Harrelson, Courtney Love, and Edward Norton as Alan Isaacman, premiered at the 1996 New York Film Festival and opens nationwide in December. With the fate of the Communications Decency Act—declared unconstitutional by a 3-judge court—pending, and censorship, actual and implied, threatening the untrammelled exchange of protected speech on the Internet, the film's release couldn't be more timely.*

Milos Forman is at his house in Connecticut. There's no train station in the vicinity and I don't drive, so I'm on the phone in New York.

Liza Béar: Sorry I couldn't make it to Connecticut.

Milos Forman: That's all right.

LB: Have you become a recluse?

MF: No, but I haven't been here for such a long time, only on Sundays or weekends. And I'm enjoying being here a little longer, because I have to build a fence for my dog, so it doesn't wander onto the road . . .

LB: What is your house like?

MF: It's an old farm, from 1748.

LB: Oh, does it remind you of Caslav, the place where you grew up?

MF: The nature, the countryside, is very similar, yes. I guess that's why I'm here.

LB: Well, my first question is very, very serious. Which do you prefer, Hugh Hefner's *Playboy,* Bob Guccione's *Penthouse,* or *Hustler?*

MF: Let me tell you, I never bought *Hustler* in my life!

LB: Uh huh.

MF: And I never bought *Penthouse* in my life. I bought *Playboy* only once because there was an interview with Jimmy Carter. When I was buying it at the newsstand at the corner of 57th Street and 6th Avenue, I was blushing and had the feeling that everybody was looking at me and hissing.

LB: I'm sure no one noticed!

MF: Not that I didn't see these magazines at somebody else's house.

LB: Of course, of course. You made your last film, *Valmont,* seven years ago. What triggered your interest in Larry Flynt? [long pause]

MF: [emphatically] Ev-e-ry-thing. Everything. The story. The characters. The humor of it. And I felt that it's not meaningless to do the film.

LB : Not meaningless?

MF: It makes sense to make the film at this point.

LB: Oh, to put it mildly. Understatement.

MF: Right.

LB: Before you read the script by Scott Alexander and Larry Karazewski, what image did you have of Larry Flynt?

MF: It was kind of funny because when I get a script I always read at least 25 pages of it, and if it doesn't grab me, then I put it aside. This one, I read the title and I put it aside right away, because the only association with the name Flynt in my imagination was sleaze and exploitation.

LB: So you weren't bowled over.

MF: No. I wasn't bowled over to do another *Showgirls.* But then I was repri-manded by my agent Mr. Lantz who said that I should read it as a courtesy to Oliver Stone, but I hadn't known that Oliver Stone was involved because the cover page said Ixtlan Productions. I was puzzled. I didn't know that was his company. Of course, if it comes from Oliver I will read it because I respect him and like his work very much.

LB: It came with the right pedigree.

MF: So I read the script and that was it. I realized that the sleaze and exploita-tion is one part of Larry Flynt, but he has other parts, the pros, which balance the cons and even outweigh them.

LB: There's a line in *Amadeus* which came to mind seeing Larry Flynt. Mozart tells the king, "Your Majesty, I am a vulgar man, but my music is not vulgar." I thought, you must really enjoy the paradox. Demystifying Mozart.

MF: It's funny, I was in London for two days casting *Ragtime* and my agent called me to see if I wanted to go to the theater. There were people in the room so I didn't even ask what the play was, but British theater is usually very interesting, so I said yes. And in the taxi I learned it was a play about Mozart. I wanted to jump out immediately! Films or plays about composers are usually the most boring ever. I want to hear Mozart's music, not see a revered figure on a marble pedestal. But from Shaffer's play I found out there were other sides to Mozart's character.

LB: There's a rumor that your friend Vaclav Havel recommended Courtney Love for the role of Althea, Larry Flynt's wife and partner.

MF: He didn't recommend her, but I was really torn between three girls, and I had a screentest tape with me in Prague. They were all wonderful, each very, very different. That made choosing between them difficult, because if they'd all been similar, after a while you figure out which one of them is the best. Havel and his wife enthusiastically picked Courtney.

LB: Who were the other two?

MF: Rachel Griffith and Georgina Cates.

LB: That was a controversial choice, casting Courtney.

MF: We had to fight hard for her. We even had to pay the insurance from our own pockets because the studio just didn't want her. To them she was not a name.

LB: Well, she's a name in the music biz.

MF: What do they know about rock and roll? They have soundproof windows. I had a wonderful casting director, Francine Maisler, and she suggested a lot of people. Of course I had to meet them all. But what's important that studios often don't realize is that I have to have fun to make a movie, and if they impose on me their idea of casting which I am not happy about, I wouldn't be able to work. "Fun" doesn't mean only having a great actor or actress. Sometimes I turn down a better actor for somebody who is not as good but somebody with whom I'll have more fun. If you have to get up everyday at six in the morning, Jesus Christ, and be with these people from 8 to 6 in the evening every day for several weeks, you'd better surround yourself with people with whom you have a good time.

LB: And then presumably it's fun for the audience to watch it, especially if it's a serious subject.

MF: That's right. Because the theaters are not comfortable enough for them to stay in their seats otherwise.

LB: Talking about unusual casting choices, you had the real Larry Flynt play the judge at his first obscenity trial.

MF: Oh, that gave me a big kick. And Mrs. Giuliani, when she accepted to play Ruth Carter, that gave me a big kick too. I love that kind of thing.

LB: Also the surgeon.

MF: Yes. He'd really operated on Larry Flynt's spine, this man. And D'Army Bailey, the black judge. He's a real judge. He's a legend in Memphis, Martin Luther King veteran. He started the Hotel Lorraine and turned it into a civil rights museum.

LB: How do you get the non-actors to integrate with the professional actors?

MF: I do screentests with these people and you immediately feel if it clicks or not.

LB: Well, one-on-one is one thing, but what happens when, say, Woody Harrelson is on the set?

MF: That's why it's important to have fun on the set, because otherwise there are all these uptight, serious considerations of me-being-a-performer-in-this-impor-tant-movie—that's what makes you stiff. And Woody and Courtney and Edward [Norton] were wonderful in helping create a good atmosphere on the set.

LB: You wrote the scripts for all your early Czech films, *Black Peter, Firemen's Ball, Loves of a Blonde.*

MF: Co-wrote.

LB: Then after *Taking Off*, your first New York film . . .

MF: *Taking Off* was a disaster financially, for two reasons. I started out in Czechoslovakia as a screenwriter, but you really cannot function—you can function, but not one hundred percent, in a language and a culture which you didn't digest as a child. You just don't hear all the nuances. The second reason is—although I consider working on the script half of directing—because I want good writers to work with me again, why should I ask them to give me credit?

LB: Well, but you obviously take a huge delight in pointing out the extravagances in American culture. Do you miss the writing, or do you now enjoy putting all your observations into the mise-en-scène?

MF: Oh no, I don't. When you work with writers like Peter Shaffer or Larry [Karazewski] and Scott [Alexander] and Michael Weller, it's pleasure, it's wonderful.

LB: Are you a perfectionist?

MF: Well, it depends. There can't be more than one perfectionist on a set. If I find another perfectionist on the set, then I have to step back and stop being one . . .

LB: You mean, like the DP [director of photography].

MF: Otherwise the film would never be finished.

LB: Give me an example.

MF: If I wanted to be absolutely perfectionist in getting the best from the actors, then I would kick the cameraman out. And the cameraman, if he's a perfectionist, he hates the director. Because I let the actors improvise. I let them move freely, and that disturbs his lighting. You can't have a cameraman-perfectionist and a director-perfectionist.

LB: A lot of people don't realize that.

MF: It's similar with actors. If the actor is a perfectionist and I'm a perfectionist and we differ . . .

LB: You've worked with the same DP, Mirek Ondricek, for a long time, but for this film you had someone new.

MF: Yes, because that Czech friend of mine was working on a Penny Marshall film. But I'm very, very happy and excited about Philippe Rousselot.

LB: And it must have been a demanding production, with all those big courtroom scenes.

MF: Yes. Usually I never have less than 100 shooting days. This one was 74, most of it in Memphis, two weeks in Los Angeles, and one day in Washington, D.C. We also shot in the prison in some small town, I forgot the name, around Memphis.

LB: Did you read the novel by Jaroslav Harek, *The Good Soldier Svejk,* when you were growing up? Its humor makes me think of your films. It has great cartoons.

MF: Oh yeah. I would love soldier Svejk to meet Yossarian from *Catch 22.* Neither wants to fight.

LB: That wasn't censored in Czechoslovakia?

MF: No. *Good Soldier Svejk* was not censored because the Communists explained that it was anti-war and anti-monarchy.

LB: One of your very first jobs was as the host of a talk show on Czech TV.

MF: I got the job when I was still at the university because I needed money. I had one decent suit, so I could go in front of the camera. The censorship was totally ridiculous. You had a conversation with some filmmaker, let's say, or musician, and it's supposed to be on the spot . . .

LB: Spontaneous.

MF: Spontaneous. But in Communist countries you had to submit every single word and line to the censors beforehand. And if you deviated from that, you were in trouble.

LB: But if you're going on live, how could they control it? They take you off the air?

MF: No, they wouldn't stop it but the next day they would fire me. And not only that, I'd probably have to go and work in the coal mine.

LB: That's pretty drastic.

MF: So I and whoever I was interviewing, we had to learn by heart our "spontaneous" conversation.

LB: Here in the land of free speech, there are other kinds of controls at work.

MF: You know, Bob Dole and Newt Gingrich and even Al Gore are sort of proclaiming, No no no no no, we don't want to ignore the First Amendment, we don't want the government to impose censorship: We just want you to be more responsible.

LB: Ah hah.

MF: That's the first step towards repression, because that's imposing self-censorship.

LB: Sort of like the Hays Code in the movie industry in the Thirties.

MF: "If I don't want to be attacked tomorrow by Gingrich, I'd better tone this down"—that kind of thinking is probably even worse than outright censorship.

LB: U.S. law is pretty convoluted. Did you have to learn a lot about the workings of the libel laws doing this movie?

MF: Yeah. Boring.

LB: In the script, the main opposition to *Hustler* comes from the Reverend Jerry Falwell and the Moral Majority. I was wondering why the radical feminist protests that took place against the more obnoxious *Hustler* covers, like the image of a woman going through a meat grinder with the caption "Grade A Pink," weren't also included.

MF: It's there, it's there. Althea, Flynt's wife, is furious. She tells Larry people are vomiting, puking. That's exactly what she's pointing at when she says it, the meat grinder.

LB: Oh, I see, so you felt that Althea represented the feminist objections. You did it through her character, is that it?

MF: Yes. But I'll tell you something—at the time, Jerry Falwell was not at all discredited as the ridiculous character he is now. He was as powerful as this guy, what's his name, Ralph Reed.

LB: Oh yes, from the Christian Coalition. Dreadful.

MF: Jerry Falwell was as powerful and as eloquent and as charming as Ralph Reed is now.

LB: I understand what you're saying. In a way, I think Ralph Reed is more dangerous because he has this terrible clean image. At least Jerry Falwell, you look at him and you can tell he's devious. But Ralph Reed is the clean-cut all-American boy.

MF: Well, Falwell was a little thinner in the Seventies, so he looked a lot more respectable back then.

LB: Yes, but look at his mouth, he's a hypocrite.

MF: You are right. The beatific smile always on his face. Really suspicious from the word go.

LB: The mass media are so afraid of not being fair to Ralph Reed that people like Charlie Rose bend over backwards to give him time on TV. So have you made your peace with Czechoslovakia? You went back to Prague to shoot *Amadeus.*

MF: Well, no, in the early eighties Czechoslovakia was still under the Communists. But if *Amadeus* had not been shot in Czechoslovakia, the film would never have been done.

LB: Really. Why not?

MF: We could only shoot in three cities: Vienna, Budapest or Prague. Nowhere else would have the right architecture. Vienna was too expensive. We would never have found the money to shoot there. Budapest is so damaged by different wars in the last two centuries that you will not find a street where you don't suddenly have two or three modern buildings. And to build sets somewhere, nobody would pay for that. So the only solution was to do it in Prague. And you know, to make *Amadeus,* I would have gone into cahoots with the devil.

LB: It was that important to you, huh?

MF: Yes.

LB: But there was trouble about you getting back in to Czechoslovakia?

MF: I didn't know if they would let me in. Since I became a U.S. citizen in 1977, I applied twice for a visa and they always declined. So I was a little nervous. But this time when I asked for a visa to do business, to bring in dollars, they gave me the visa!

LB: I see.

MF: Dollar has the same smell for everybody. For the capitalists, communists, fascists: The power of the dollar. Which, by the way, is a Czech word. In the fifteenth century it was minted in Joachimstown in Bohemia. That's where they started to mint coins. They called them Joachimstallor. Later, it was just tallor and it became dollar.

LB: You've been back to Prague fairly recently.

MF: I was there about ten days ago, yes.

LB: So have they absorbed more of the good or the bad from Western society?

MF: Both. They're lapping it all up. They're going crazy about it. It's very difficult for these countries to get used to the fact that yes, if you love the beauty and freedom of the jungle, you have to live with the leeches and mosquitoes and snakes, the tigers and the sharks. It's difficult for former Communist countries. They would love to have all the freedom and beauty of the free world, but first they have to kill off half of the animals.

LB: The moral of the Larry Flynt film is tolerance, at least in print, even for things that are hateful. From the response to the film so far, do you feel you got that point across?

MF: I hope so. I really believe that freedom of expression is absolute.

LB: Oh you do? Regardless of the consequences?

MF: Regardless of the consequences. That's the price we have to pay.

LB: Right. I suppose we tend to take it for granted. But what if someone's freedom of self-expression intrudes on someone else's, you know, well-being . . .

MF: Look, how should I explain it? The fanatical conservatives, they will always demand law and order, censorship, control. The fanatical liberals will always demand that freedom of expression is absolute. The problem is that the liberals will never win over the fanatical conservatives.

LB: Why is that?

MF: Because it's ridiculous. You really can't give a hundred percent absolute freedom of speech. You can't do that.

LB: You can't shout "fire" in a crowded theater, you mean.

MF: Right.

LB: So there have to be limits. And that's the difficult part, knowing exactly where to place the controls. And who does the placing.

MF: Right. But if you stop fighting for absolute freedom, then the conservatives will win. Look at what happened when the people in Russia and Czechoslovakia relaxed. The fanatics, the conservatives, won.

LB: And at this point in U.S. history it's important because the right has made such huge inroads.

MF: You never find a country or have a society in which you can really go and scream "fire" in every theater. But—you had a Hitler. You had a Stalin. You have Ayatollahs.

LB: Do you think that's our biggest threat right now?

MF: No, because in this country, people will never stop fighting for the freedom of expression. And that's why I am absolutely positive that nothing so extreme will happen here. But you had the McCarthy era. That was probably as far as this country can go. You have to fight to maintain the freedom you have every day. Relax, and you will go to the right. So far, so good. People are not different here or there. There are a lot of potential fascists and communists and fanatics in this country too, and the only way these people are kept in check is by a free press. A free press is the only way to stop things from going to extremes.

Originally published in *Bomb*.

JAN SVERAK

Kolya

When my father told me this story, I had a strange feeling in my throat. I was speechless. For me that's a signal the story works. Then I was really curious to see whether the emotion would sustain itself over a full-length script.

Jan Sverak, 1997

When Czech director Jan Sverak embarked on his debut feature five years ago, he had no qualms about turning to his father for help. No, not for a handout to feed the crew nor to spring the dailies from the lab, but for, well, a script.

Luckily, his father, Zdenek Sverak, a well-known screenwriter, obliged, and the father-son team won an Oscar nomination for the 1991 comedy *Elementary School.*

Sverak's fourth feature, *Kolya,* opening Friday in Manhattan, is another father-son effort, and its Oscar[1] potential got a significant boost when it won a Golden Globe Sunday as best foreign film. Sverak père not only wrote the bittersweet script, but played the lead as a disgruntled 55-year-old Czech bachelor whose life is irrevocably changed by Kolya, a five-year-old Russian boy (Andrej Jhalimon) left in his charge.

"When I was born, my father already had his own theater," said the 31-year-old Sverak fils during an interview in Manhattan shortly before *Kolya* opened at the Sundance Film Festival last week.

"He also worked for the radio and wrote and acted in TV and features," Sverak said. "So he had no time for me. We became friends once I was an adult and learning to make films. Now we have much more time for each other. We spend our days together doing something."

After *Elementary School* came *Accumulator* (1994), a science fiction film and a parody of Hollywood action films like *Terminator II.* (*Accumulator,* too, was

---

[1] *Kolya* won the Oscar for Best Foreign Film in 1997.

Zdenek Sverak (as Louka) and Andrei Chalimon (as Kolya) in Jan Sverak's *Kolya* (1997, Czechoslovakia) which won the Oscar for Best Foreign Language Film in 1997. Photo by Zdenek Vavra. Courtesy of Miramax Film Corp. All Rights Reserved.

written by Sverak's father.) That same year, while waiting for the script of *Kolya,* Sverak made *Ride,* a Czech version of *Easy Rider.* Zdenek Sverak also has written the script for two films by Jiri Menzel, *The Life and Extraordinary Adventures of Private Ivan Chonkin* (1984) and *My Sweet Little Village* (1985).

"First I wanted to be a painter, then a cinematographer," said Jan Sverak, who eventually studied documentary filmmaking at the same élite Prague film school that Milos Forman attended. "My father knows this about me, that my power is in visual creativity, and that I like to play with small details. So he puts them into the script. Or maybe it happens naturally. As he's writing, he's already preparing the scenes."

The idea for *Kolya,* said Sverak, was suggested by Pavel Taussig, a friend of his father's, who recommended that he write a script with himself in the lead, and that, at Sverak Sr.'s age it would suit him to interact with a small boy. In a few sentences, Sverak said, Taussig then outlined a story about a Russian girl who's offering money for Czech citizenship papers via marriage.

"When my father told me this story," Sverak said, "I had a strange feeling in my throat. I was speechless. For me that's a signal the story works. Then I was really curious to see whether the emotion would sustain itself over a full-length script."

Clearly, from audience acclaim so far, there was no cause for concern. Since its release in the Czech Republic seven months ago, the film has gained an audience of more than a million, which is 10 percent of the Czech population.

"I think the script draws on our experiences with our own kids," said Sverak, whose younger son is five, like Kolya. "Including my sister's two, my father has four grandkids. So his experience with small kids is very fresh. We used this as a source of information and images."

The Sveraks drew on these experiences in *Kolya*'s exquisite country sequences, which form a crucial part of the developing emotional ties between the child and his adoptive father.

The historical context of the story is the former Prague of 1988–89 during the last days of the Russian occupation and the fall of the Communist regime.

"Everything in Prague is radically different since the revolution," said Sverak. "The houses now have private owners and have been rebuilt or repainted. Capitalism started then, and there are advertisements and billboards everywhere. Before the revolution there were only Czech, Russian and East German cars. That means only five models. Now we have all sorts of cars which we had to pull out of the streets when we were shooting and replace with old wrecks. We had to recreate the old reality, the time when 115,000 Russian soldiers, fully armed, were stationed in our country."

As a child, Sverak said, he grew up not only in Prague, but also in the country, where the Communists provided every family with a low-cost cottage which they had to repair themselves.

"History has taught us to be very practical," said Sverak. "My father's idea of relaxing, for example, is to build a wall. Well, mine is to sleep and watch movies."

Published in *Newsday*.

JUDY DAVIS

Children of the Revolution

I'm not by nature a revolutionary kind of personality. I really like a peaceful life. But I don't like abuse of power. That's come up as a problem occasionally.

Judy Davis, 1997

Mention Judy Davis, and immediately many women (and men) will respond "My favorite actress." I'm one of them.

Born in Perth, Western Australia, her explosive debut at 23, straight from Sydney drama school, was the lead role in Gillian Armstrong's My Brilliant Career *(1979), the story of a 16-year-old aspiring writer determined to get out of the bush. The movie launched both their careers, and instantly etched Davis as a unique screen presence. She represents the quintessential woman of her generation—firebrand existentialist defining herself on her own terms, striving not to mold herself to another's image. Which is, of course, a paradox for an actress, but one from which, through her masterly acting skills, Davis is able to draw an electrifying tension. As the lead again in Armstrong's* High Tide *(1988) about a back-up singer who's reunited with her abandoned daughter in a coastal trailer park, Davis thrills with her portrayal of powerful complex emotions.*

Not surprisingly, in spite of international acclaim, Davis's aptly selected support-ing roles show a preference for auteur films—Woody Allen's Husbands and Wives, *Burroughs's slain wife and a Jane Bowles pastiche in David Cronenberg's* Naked Lunch, *a ghostwriter-lover in the Coen Brothers'* Barton Fink. *They also show a decided literary bent—the repressed Adele Quested in* A Passage to India *(for which she got an Oscar nomination), Harriet Herriton in* Where Angels Fear to Tread, *the intransigeant George Sand in* Impromptu. *On the screen (I didn't get to meet her in person) Judy Davis's face rivets with its lunar pallor and full-lipped sensuality. Yet a Judy Davis character—strong-willed, high-strung, contrary—radiates an emotional intelligence that's always on the qui vive, edgy, subtle and intense, with an inner truthfulness that compounds her erotic appeal.*

Judy Davis in *Children of the Revolution* (1997, Australia), directed by Peter Duncan. Photo by Philip LaMasurier, courtesy of Photofest.

After a number of American films, Davis's lead role as Joan Fraser, an ardent Austra-lian communist/parent in the current Children of the Revolution *seems ideally suited for her and won her the Best Australian Actress Award for 1996. In this epic satire, set over four decades, Joan Fraser's visit to Moscow and tryst with Stalin engenders a mon-strous offspring who becomes head of the biggest law-enforcement agency in Australia, driving the country to the brink of civil war. Earlier this spring, seemingly eons after its global capitulation, I spoke long-distance to Davis in Los Angeles about Communism's swansong and other matters pertinent to our resignedly full-blown capitalist times.*

Liza Béar: Did you fly in straight from Australia?

Judy Davis: Yes, I did, yes.

LB: From shooting a movie?

JD: No, from my home in Sydney.

LB: I haven't seen your latest films, *Blood and Wine* or *Absolute Power*, but I saw *Children of the Revolution* at Sundance.

JD: Did you like it?

LB: Oh, I loved it. I thought it was a hoot . . . Uh, do you like it?

JD: Yeah, I do. I love it too.

LB: But you don't like all the films you're in.

JD: No. Not all of them necessarily work in the end. That's to be expected, really.

LB: Do you think *Children* worked all the way through?

JD: Well, it's very ambitious. This was Peter Duncan's first script and first directing job. Logistically it was very challenging.

LB: How so?

JD: He had nine weeks to film it in. And yet he had to somehow give a sense of two countries, Russia and Australia. And he had to stretch from the 1950s through to the present. He had to go through anti-war demonstrations, have all his key characters aging. It was almost epic in its scope. And on a really tiny budget, maybe $5 million. Given what for me would be utterly daunting obstacles, I think he managed sensationally.

LB: What was your reaction to the role of Joan Fraser when you first read the script?

Long pause.

JD: I was surprised that a young man—he's 34—had written such a role for a woman. A woman who is as vibrant, if not more vibrant when she was older as when she was younger. Woody Allen writes really wonderful roles for women, and doesn't seem to have a prejudice about age, but mostly writers lose interest in women as they get into their 50s and 60s. They don't find them as potent. And in Peter's case, I think he actually found Joan increasingly potent. In the script she was meant to represent the revolution. When the [Berlin] wall comes down, it's only a matter of time before Joan herself will die. There's really nothing left for her. She crumbles as well. Perhaps the director was free in his approach to Joan because her character is based on his grandfather, who was a Stalinist.

LB: The time transitions were beautifully done. Did you find Joan a challenging role?

JD: Oh yeah, really challenging. I wasn't nervous about the aging. I was as nervous about being young Joan as being old Joan. I don't know how old I looked, but I was trying to play somebody in her late 20s when Joan went to Moscow. I was trying to get that sense of naiveté, which can be quite a difficult thing to catch when you're 40 and getting a little bit cynical. I found that quite as difficult as being older. But the opportunity to be able to play an old woman who wasn't a cliché, who was this gnarly potent ferocious creature, was just the kind of older woman I'd longed to see on the screen.

LB: You get to be a parent and a fighter—the role brings out two extremes. Did you try to keep a tension between the two aspects of Joan's character?

JD: Ummmh . . .

LB: Well, I suppose it's not terribly developed in the film since the film's a comedy rather than a character-driven film. Do you relate to that sense of fighting for the revolution?

JD: Me personally? No. Not at all. No no no, I'm not a political animal in that way. Although I admire people who are. I feel rather envious of people who can believe so utterly in something. I can't, myself.

LB: You mean, you can't believe in something outside yourself.

JD: Yes, like a religion or a political belief.

LB: I thought the script was rather subtle. There was a constant ambiguity about certain of Joan's lines that could apply to one's own personal revolution. Like, "Do we want a discreet revolution?"

JD: Yeah, yeah . . . so you're asking whether . . .

LB: I mean, do you feel you're constantly fighting on your own terms in your life, in your work?

JD: I think probably when I was younger. There are so many preconceptions about what a young woman should be like, should speak like—what her attitude should or shouldn't be. When I was in my early twenties in Sydney, working in the film industry. . . . It's different now, but then it was very male-driven, and I found it very difficult.

LB: Were people condescending?

JD: No, it was more that some men that I came across found me rather shocking, and I puzzled over that. There really is nothing shocking about me. And I came to the conclusion that in some instances they were shocked because I expressed opinions about things.

LB: About your role, for instance?

JD: Yes, I suppose. The way I thought about . . . the way I questioned things, or perhaps suggested improvements during the making of the film. The [film] industry then wasn't used to that. And sometimes it became difficult. Not always. But I'm thinking of one director in particular whom I would rather not mention. He actually accused me once of being self-opinionated, which I suppose is very condescending. It assumes that because you're a young woman you shouldn't have opinions. Or if you have them, you should keep quiet about them. And I found that truly shocking, that kind of attitude.

LB: So this was in the late '70s?

JD: More 1980.

LB: Well, some people don't get it, do they.

JD: [laughs] It was a very backward view, yeah.

LB: I checked Peter Duncan's biography on the Internet and I noticed he had acted in three films.

JD: Oh yeah? I didn't know that. He was great. He was remarkably open for being a first-time director with his own script. He's a tremendous admirer of Woody Allen. I think Woody's been a bit of an inspiration for him.

LB: Did you have any input into your role?

JD: A little bit. The speech where she rants at the television when she sees Gorbachev and Reagan—that scene came about because I'd suggested to Peter that we hadn't seen Joan for a while and maybe the audience would like to know how she was getting on and responding to events. And I'd met Howard Barker, an English playwright years ago who'd told me his father was a Marxist and they'd spent years sitting in their lounge room screaming at the television set. That's a wonderful image. So I suggested something like that to Peter, whose own grandfather was also a Marxist. And had done a similar thing. Peter went away and came back with this fantastic speech. I made input in that way.

LB: Is it difficult as an actress to sustain a role in a film that stays on the level of satire? Towards the end of the film I found myself wishing that it would shift gears and become more like a drama, and less like a satire.

JD: Ah, that's interesting. I think that's what Peter was trying to do, actually. And if some of the scenes that ended up on the cutting room floor were still in the film, it would be even clearer that the film was going in that direction. But it would have been longer.

LB: Do you feel you're the child of any kind of revolution?

JD: Well, I missed the '60s revolution. I was in primary school then.

LB: You did run away to Thailand at 17 though, didn't you?

JD: Yeah . . . My family and educational background were rather cloistered, so I felt the need to break free. I say that, and yet there was one particular woman at the school I went to who was a wonderful creature.

LB: Was it a girls' school?

JD: Yes. There were boarders there, but not me. She was an amazing woman. But in fact that system punished her too. She was forced to leave Perth and shifted over to Sydney. This was the late '60s and the Catholic church was going through its own turmoil then. We were caught in the middle. I'm not by nature a revolutionary kind of personality. I really like a peaceful life. But I don't like abuse of power. That's come up as a problem occasionally. You don't have to look too far to see abuses of power. And I've always found it very hard to come to terms with that.

LB: Male power and power of position, right?

JD: Not necessarily male power. What power does to people. And how people respond to power. There are a lot of people who don't respond to power very well at all. Some people do and they're great.

LB: When you had a child, did that make a big change in how you viewed the world, or your work? Did everything change?

JD: Yes, it transformed almost everything. I really grew up very quickly. I was just a big indulgent baby before I had a child. And certainly money was not a concern of mine at all. I was rather arrogant about it, in fact.

LB: Why? 'Cause you made plenty or . . .

JD: No, no. I thought I was above it all. I was above that kind of coarse need. But the minute Jack was born, I started to think seriously about how I was going to . . . how we were going to support him. It did make me grow up. It changed my attitude to acting too. I got more businesslike about it. I was wasting a lot of time before then. I never have been a consistent worker—job after job after job. Temperamentally I always need space in between roles to collect myself again and to develop a need to produce something else. But I started to take it much more seriously once Jack was born. All sorts of social things too. Before I had a child I wasn't really aware of living in a community. I felt quite separate from it, being an actress. That's not unusual, especially if you're doing a lot of theatre, which I was. You work at night, part of the day gets lost. You drift about a bit in this subculture of actors . . . That all changed. Now the community that I live in is my child's community, and it's become mine as well. And it's become very important for me to feel we're all a legitimate part of that. It really helped me as an actress too.

LB: That gives you a whole other strand to work from, right?

JD: Obviously, it should always have been there anyway. It's such a concentrated experience, those early years of trying to learn how to act, trying to learn the craft, find your way through the maze of an industry. You can suddenly find yourself quite isolated.

LB: Are you committed to living in Australia?

JD: I didn't want to force my child to be a migrant. It hasn't proved to be necessary to move.

LB: What do you think's special about Australian film?

JD: What's made it easier for Australian filmmakers than young American filmmakers is this government subsidy system. Certainly up to this point anyway the films have cost a lot less money to make. There're only 17 million people in the whole country.

LB: So you think individuality is still valued there?

JD: [long pause] Anywhere you go on the globe I don't know whether things can vary much. We are a social animal, and we exert tremendous social pressure on each other. Most people are conformists, and then you try to figure which society is the more tolerant of aberrations that occur within it. I don't know whether Australia is any more tolerant than America. In some ways, Australia is the great conformist country, where anybody who had the audacity to appear wildly different could be attacked. I think that's true historically. Maybe it's getting better. But certainly the Australia that I grew up in in the '60s was quite a conformist country.

LB: How do you see things changing in the world your son's going into?

JD: I'm still trying to figure that out. He goes to a state primary school, and I find that very conformist, in fact.

LB: Do you think he'll have the freedom and the space to be who he wants to be?

JD: He's going to demand it, that's his nature. It's the way we've brought him up. I've always been interested in what he thinks about everything. Before he could speak I was asking him for his opinion on things. It was ridiculous. I don't know how often that happens with kids, that adults show a genuine interest in their opinions. Anyway, that's certainly what we've done with Jack, and it may create problems for him within systems, but in the long run it's best for him . . . You know, I don't mean to suggest that Australia is more conformist than any other country. Conformity isn't necessarily a bad thing, either, as long as it doesn't lead to a narrow-minded view. Sadly, it often does. I've never been very good at conforming myself. I could have tried to, but I wouldn't really have been able to pull it off.

LB: Other than Joan Fraser, what do you rate as your most rewarding film roles?

JD: Well, *High Tide* for one. That film was very emotionally draining. I'm not entirely sure what it taught me. I got pregnant straight after that film. Maybe that's why it's a bit of a blur. It's curious that after playing that role I actually became a mother. So I was given a very clear indication of the distance between what I imagined and the reality.

LB: Maybe because you were so successful in the role it gave you the freedom to be a mother afterwards.

JD: Oh, that's a nice way of looking at it. It produced a fantastic baby.

LB: Do you prefer to use "actress" or "actor"?

JD: Actress, actually. We can all call ourselves actors, but it doesn't mean the parts get any better.

LB: How do you make sure you get the psychic space that you need on the set, especially when you're dealing with first-time directors?

JD: I found over the years it's been useful not to collect a series of essential rituals. It would be too difficult to force that issue. And my preparation time for, say, a difficult sequence, has decreased too. I needed more time [to get into character] when I was younger. Or I thought I did. So I'd kind of overkill it a bit. But if an actor or an actress needs time, you've just got to have the courage to say so. I haven't often felt the need to do that. Certainly on *Children of the Revolution* that didn't arise. There would have been no problem at all if it had. Peter was very open to anything. On a film set I don't use up too much energy sitting around and chatting and gossiping. I find that kind of social interaction extremely draining. I probably keep myself a little isolated when I'm not actually on the floor working. Every actor's different. Some actors need to chatter a lot before they go into a take, for whatever reason.

LB: Do you work out, or do anything physical?

JD: I occasionally work out.

LB: You're not a big exercise freak.

JD: That's the tricky thing, because you can overdo exercise. I did a film here in Los Angeles once, *New Age*, and I thought, well, I'm going to have to go to the gym everyday, because that's what they do here. It's going to make me feel like a local. So I got incredibly fit—too fit. When I left and went off to France and I couldn't get to a gym everyday, my body very quickly started falling apart because it had been so tuned to that constant pumping. And it's a very unnatural thing too.

LB: I haven't seen your latest film, *Absolute Power*.

JD: I haven't either. It hasn't opened in Australia.

LB: What role did you play in *Absolute Power*?

JD: I play the president's Chief of Staff. A very, very different character from Joan Fraser. I can say what I thought I was playing but, not having seen the film, I'm not quite sure how it's ended up. The character I was aware of playing was really hardnosed, tough, amoral, committed to the President—you know those Washington people. It was very interesting going to Washington. Really a shock. It didn't look anything like I'd expected. It was rather like a museum. It's full of very imperial buildings from a time when people really believed in institutions like government. We're all a bit cynical about them now.

LB: Is there anything about Communism that you miss now it's all gone? About its ideals, I should say.

JD: The film may be poking fun [at Communism], but the way I played Joan, I wasn't poking fun at her at all. When Joan believed in something, I was believing it too. And because of that I felt I was giving her, and people like her, respect. The film ultimately doesn't mock Joan. I think the director was saying, with the best intentions in the world people like Joan can be very dangerous. Which is a very legitimate thing to say about any zealot. But having said that, when in the film Joan talks about what she thinks is wonderful about the Soviet Union, who could disagree? It's just that there is an enormous chasm between the theory and the reality. And that was always the dilemma with Marxism. But, in a sense, Joan is a theorist. She's excited by, devoted to the theory.

LB: Don't you think the film satirizes capitalism equally? The ending's so cynical. When Joe finally finds out he's Stalin's son he sells his life story to a publisher and options the movie rights.

JD: Yeah. Money.

LB: What's your next project?

JD: I did a Woody Allen film which should be coming out at the end of this year. It's called *Deconstructing Harry*. A lot of people like Demi Moore are in it. But, you know . . . Woody doesn't like you to talk about his films in advance.

Published in *Bomb*.

MOHSEN MAKHMALBAF

Gabbeh

I realized that what is needed for us to achieve social justice and freedom is cultural change—to change people's perceptions of one another, and their perception of power.

Mohsen Makhmalbaf, 1997

On June 15, *Gabbeh* was screened at the Midnight Sun Rim Festival in Lapland, 130 kilometers north of the Arctic Circle, where reindeer herding is still the primary means of subsistence. I had hoped to speak to Mohsen Makhmalbaf there: the perpetual daylight seemed an appropriate setting in which to discuss his tale of Iranian nomads, which basks in its own golden glow of wry humor and childlike innocence. But the director never made it to Lapland. Later, on the telephone from Tehran, Makhmalbaf explains that he receives so many invitations to festivals (170 in his career) that he was not even able to come to New York for his recent MoMA retrospective or for the opening of *Gabbeh*, the first of his 14 films to be distributed in the United States.

Currently scouting locations for his next project, a film about music called *Silence*, Makhmalbaf talks about the radical transformation that has recently brought Iranian filmmakers international acclaim.

"The kind of Hollywoodish cinema that existed in Iran in my grandmother's time was close to hell," says the 40-year-old rebel-turned-auteur. "After the revolution, I went to my grandmother's grave and said, 'I wish you were still alive, because there's now another kind of cinema in Iran. It's a humanist cinema, and people are not making movies solely to make money.'"

Originally banned in Iran—as were four of his previous films—*Gabbeh* explores the magic carpet of Persian legend. Structured like a fable, the film concerns a young woman who magically emerges from a rug and tells the story of how she was prevented by her father from rejoining her lover. Asked what prompted him to make *Gabbeh*, Makhmalbaf answers without hesitation: "Love of life—at a time when this love is being threatened by commerce and politics. What you see in

Gabbeh is a love of nature and the willingness to live life to its fullest. That's something lacking in urban life.

"When I was traveling in the Fars province in southwestern Iran," he continues, "I was really affected by the nomadic life of the people there, especially how they were making these beautiful carpets called gabbeh. The inspiration for all these carpets came from events in their lives, what was happening around them. My approach to *Gabbeh* is exactly the same: nature inspiring art."

To thwart the Iranian censors, the movie was originally pitched as a documentary about rug-making. A recurring scene in which a schoolteacher demonstrates the natural origins of color takes political subtext to the heights of lyricism: Iran is, after all, a country where color—in women's dress, for instance—is highly politicized.

In marked contrast to the film's sublime images of scarlet poppies and wind rippling through wheat fields, shot in the Iranian countryside, Makhmalbaf spent the first ten years of his life in a poor neighborhood in Tehran, working from the age of eight to support his family. He joined a revolutionary group at 15 and engaged in guerrilla activity against the Shah's government.

"My dream was to help bring social justice and freedom to my country," Makhmalbaf says. "I was 17 when I was shot and then arrested in the course of guerrilla activities."

Specifically, Makhmalbaf stabbed a policeman who was trying to disarm him.

"That part of my life is partially documented in the film *A Moment of Innocence,* says the director, who spent four years in prison and was freed when the revolution broke out.

"After the revolution, I concluded that it's not enough to go from one totalitarian regime to another," recalls Makhmalbaf, who still lives in downtown Tehran, is married and has three children. "I realized that what is needed for us to achieve social justice and freedom is cultural change—to change people's perceptions of one another, and their perception of power."

Still, *Gabbeh*'s politics are far from explicit, and since it eventually opened in Iran to wide acclaim, it's hard to say exactly what the authorities found so objectionable.

"If you want an exact answer," said Makhmalbaf, "you have to ask them. I think it was the happy, upbeat nature of the film and the fact that it was so full of color and life, which is not an accepted norm in this country.

"I'm at a point in my life right now where I think peace is even more important than justice," Makhmalbaf adds. "I couldn't be more fed up with wars and conflicts, because the first thing that becomes a casualty of a conflict is humanity. The wars and the conflicts haven't given us anything. They have always taken away from us."

Originally published in *Time Out NY.* Makhmalbaf was interviewed via teleconference in Tehran; the interpreter was in New Jersey.

CÉDRIC KLAPISCH
Chacun Cherche Son Chat

When I shot the demolition I didn't know how I would use the footage. Finally I discovered that it was part of the subject matter of the film, it wasn't a digression. And during the editing I found a place for it.

Cédric Klapisch, 1997

July 4, 1997—"The form of a city changes faster than the human heart," wrote the nineteenth-century French poet Charles Baudelaire. More than a century later, French filmmaker Cédric Klapisch chronicles the eye-blink rate of urban upheaval in his new film *Chacun Cherche Son Chat [When the Cat's Away]*.

Asked by his producers to turn a short film about contemporary Paris into a feature, Klapisch spun a tale about a shy 22-year-old girl, Chloe (Garance Clavel) who recruits—and unveils—a whole neighborhood in the search for her lost cat, aptly named Gris-Gris (*gris* means gray in French).

Ordering lunch in the Museum of Modern Art restaurant in our own battle-scarred city before the opening of his film last month, Klapisch, 35, said he had picked the rapidly gentrifying La Bastille neighborhood because it represents what's happening in Paris today.

"I really wanted a strong contrast between trendiness and the typical Parisian way of life," he said. "In La Bastille you have a very trendy Jean-Paul Gautier show-room next to an old Parisian-style furniture factory."

"The other reason for picking La Bastille," Klapisch said, "is that Chloe's story is based on an anecdote told by a friend of mine who really did leave her cat with Renée Le Calm, the 76-year-old lady in the film. And because La Bastille is Renée's neighborhood, it was easier to stay close to home.

"I shot everything on three adjacent streets, one block almost. I thought it was good to be accurate and not lie about that one spot in Paris."

Two of the neighborhood's real cafés, the newly chic Pause Café and the older corner Café des Taillandiers (where a café au lait or a *petit noir* is half the price), are used as locations. Born and raised near Place de la Contrescarpe in the Latin

Quarter, Klapisch considers himself pure Parisian. *When the Cat's Away,* his third feature, is the first to receive international distribution.

He says he has wanted to make films since he was 4 years old, and eventually studied film at New York University in the '80s. Starting out as a cameraman (for Todd Solondz) and in documentaries (shooting the Kenyan Maasais tribe, for example) Klapisch's observational bent might derive in part from his gene pool: His father is a nuclear physicist and his mother a psychologist.

Moviegoers who have spent any time in Paris will find that the film's mise-en-scène creates such an authentic neighborhood feel that it makes the skin tingle with recognition—and premonition. "Every French person I've seen in New York has told me the same thing," Klapisch said. "It's great, because that's exactly the feeling I wanted to communicate."

Aside from a woman who loses her cat, the impetus for the story was the network of sprightly old ladies who help her find it. "I thought that was really funny," Klapisch said. "And also a great excuse to show Paris today. My friend would take me to different locations where I met all these local characters.

"At one point I realized that Renée, the old lady she was talking about, had been an extra in my previous film. I knew she was a really great old lady and could act. So I auditioned her to make sure she would be able to act a whole page of script. Very often the script was based on people that I met during casting who gave me ideas for scenes.

"In many scenes I used people on the spot. Like when the Algerian character Djamal [Zinédine Soualem] tries to wake up a homeless man sleeping in the street, the people who come up to him are real homeless people who happened to be there the day of the shooting. We just rehearsed with them for ten minutes. I didn't want to kick them out and then put fake homeless people in their place."

Of all the characters in the film, the character of Chloe is probably the least improvised, he said.

"It's based on what single friends of mine have told me about going to gay bars to avoid being hassled by guys. That's a very modern attitude. And Chloe shares an apartment with a gay guy. She feels comfortable with him but at the same time there's something lacking in her life.

"After a while the cat is forgotten and the film focuses on the people Chloe meets during the search," he said. "It's really a search for her self. It's not so much that the cat is lost, it's Chloe who is lost. The film's French title *Chacun Cherche Son Chat* has more of a double meaning than the English translation, because it can mean that you're looking for affection, happiness, a love object."

While his crew was shooting a scene, a historic church was being demolished in the same street, Klapisch said. He turned the cameras on the collapsing structure.

"When I shot the demolition I didn't know how I would use the footage," Klapisch said. "Finally I discovered that it was part of the subject matter of the film, it wasn't a digression. And during the editing I found a place for it."

Asked whether he thought it was possible for real-estate development to be sensitive to the neighborhoods of Paris, "It's possible," Klapisch said. "And I was really glad to see that this film had an effect on the Mayor's Office in Paris. I just heard that the mayor really loved the film and that now he would be more concerned about neighborhood associations, people who are trying to save the spirit of the neighborhood. The problem is that politicians work so much outside reality."

So unintentionally the film has a political thrust? "It was intentional," Klapisch said. "The actor who plays Djamal is a second-generation Algerian. In the story, being an Arab, his character is not as well viewed as other people. And yet he plays a very important role in this neighborhood. Because he's unemployed, he has time to help people. So he's always the one that people call when they need to carry something or to find things in the neighborhood. Djamal makes the point that even if you don't have an official role in society, you can still find one.

"My next film, called *Perhaps,* will be about the future, after they've done the damage," he said. "I will try to show it in a good light. It'll be a new Paris, but I would like to be there."

Originally published in *Newsday.*

MIGUEL ARTETA

Star Maps

The metaphor of prostitution fits so perfectly with the desperate and sick nature of Hollywood. People will do anything to get a movie made. The whole town seems absurd.

Miguel Arteta, 1997

In Miguel Arteta's satire/melodrama *Star Maps,* a startling Latino takes on the dark side of Hollywood, the fabled casting couch gets a nasty new twist as Carlos (Douglas Spain), a young aspiring actor from Mexico, is turned into a street hustler by his father, peddling maps to the stars' homes as a front.

Here in New York, in the sun-filled garden of Rialto, Little Italy's metal shop-turned-bistro, the film's L.A.-based writer-director Miguel Arteta recalls that entrée into the business was a bit less traumatic than Carlos's.

"I was very lucky," acknowledges Arteta, who initially studied film at Wesleyan. "My car mechanic introduced me to Jonathan Demme, and I showed him one of my student films, a musical satire about a world where everybody can sing and dance at any moment, very Busby Berkeleyesque. One character is too inhibited to sing and dance, so he joins a self-improvement group."

After seeing the short, Demme gave Arteta a job as second camera assistant on the documentary *Cousin Bobby.* "He asked me whether I knew how to load an Aaton," Arteta recalls. "I lied and said yes." The director later recommended him to the American Film Institute.

Growing up, Arteta traveled throughout Latin America (his father is Peruvian; his mother is Spanish). "I think that's why I'm a filmmaker," says Arteta, 32. "I've been a foreigner all my life, looking at cultures from the outside. I lived in San Juan till I was 13. Then we moved to Costa Rica when my father sold his auto-parts shop. Previously, he worked for Chrysler during the revolution in Cuba, and Che Guevara put him in jail for working for a U.S. company."

Douglas Spain in *Star Maps* (1997, US), directed by Miguel Arteta. Fox Searchlight, courtesy of Photofest.

Arteta says he decided to make Carlos Mexican "because most of the Latinos in LA are Mexican."

But, as he's quick to point out, "My film is not specifically a Mexican story. This could have been any immigrant family."

One of a handful of Latinos at AFI, Arteta remembers it as "a very intimidating environment, very Hollywood—very, very political. All the students were making $200,000 short films with Mel Gibson. And here I was—a Latino trying to get into Hollywood. I had to do things that I wasn't really proud of; I got caught up in the desperation of this film school. Bette Midler's husband and Jennifer Jason Leigh's boyfriend were my classmates. After a very nurturing environment at Wesleyan and working for Jonathan Demme, who's one of the nicest people in the industry, here I was dropped into the pit of Hollywood." Without batting an eyelid, he adds, "I fell flat on my face."

As a result of that experience, Arteta started thinking about the lengths to which people will go in order to make their dreams come true, the theme of *Star Maps*.

But there would, of course, be more to the story. "I also wanted to satirize how I was seen as a Latino," says Arteta. "People had such weird expectations of me. They thought I would be doing gang films with crack addicts. And the liberals in the school felt I should be making *Stand and Deliver: Part II.*

But Arteta was determined to make a movie on his own terms. "I feel like there hasn't been a Latino independent filmmaking voice out there," he says. "Robert Rodriguez is really a Hollywood director."

By having Carlos peddle star maps as a front for prostitution, Arteta highlights the shallowness of the movie industry. "The metaphor of prostitution fits so perfectly with the desperate and sick nature of Hollywood," explains the director. "People will do anything to get a movie made. The whole town seems absurd. It's a place where 40 percent of the population is Latino, yet they're invisible. Most of the Latino population lives in East LA, where the Hollywood culture doesn't even go. They're terrified of crossing the LA river. Living in Hollywood you see Latinos as busboys, gardeners, maids and map vendors on street corners."

Carlos is no more willing to accept such Latino stereotypes than Arteta. "I wanted the audience to be left with the idea that Carlos would continue to pursue his dream," says Arteta, "but that now he knows how to do it the right way."

Originally published in *Time Out New York.*

Masayuki Suo

Shall We Dance?

What I found in the course of my research is that I personally became more and more involved and interested in dance, and the film, as a result, is more like a story of people who've fallen in love with dance.

Masayuki Suo, 1997

July 30, 1997—Meticulous as an anthropologist, or maybe even a number-crunching salary-man, Masayuki Suo, Japanese director of *Shall We Dance?*, logs the hour and minute we start the interview in a notebook and turns on his own tape recorder.

Is this media surveillance? Research for his next film, a musical, perhaps? No. Via the interpreter, Suo explains he is simply keeping a detailed record of his first trip to New York, to be published when he gets back to Tokyo. After all, he is recognized in Japan for his documentaries as well as comedies.

Set in the world of Japanese ballroom dancing, *Shall We Dance?*, Suo's fourth feature, is a warm, humorous, liberating story about a timid accountant who yearns to escape from the tyranny of the bottom line. He secretly takes dance lessons—and finds his freedom by learning to keep his balance on the dance floor.

The title may hark back to *The King and I* rather than to Janis Joplin's famous line, "If I can't dance, you can have your revolution," which *Shall We Dance?* turns on its head. But in spirit, having touched a nerve and set off a small box office revolution in Japan, it would have made the rock singer happy. At the Japanese Academy Awards this year, the film won in 13 of 14 possible categories.

"For a long time I'd been thinking in vague terms about shooting a love story featuring a middle-aged, salaried worker," says Suo, who at 40 is two years younger than his lead character Sugiyama (Koji Yakusyo) and not at all timid. "These are the people who go to the movies the least in Japan. Then one day, just like in the film, from the window of a commuter train leaving Tokyo, I saw the window of a dance school. And I thought, what would it be like if a middle-aged, salaried

Reiko Kusamura, Yu Tokui, Hiromasa Taguchi, and Koji Yakusyp in *Shall We Dance?* (1996, Japan), directed by Masayuki Suo. The film is about a timid Japanese accountant who attempts to escape from the tyranny of the bottom line through ballroom dancing. Courtesy of Photofest.

worker were to glimpse a beautiful woman standing at the window. I imagined he'd want to dance with her once. So this could be the start of a love story."

That's what the film became, in more ways than the filmmaker had intended.

"I started off making a film about the love story of a middle-aged salaried worker," says Suo, "and what I found in the course of my research is that I personally became more and more involved and interested in dance, and the film, as a result of that, is more like a story of people who've fallen in love with dance."

Though now widely practiced in Japan, ballroom dancing is still considered a subversive activity. According to Suo, who was born in Tokyo but raised in nearby Karasaki, ballroom dancing was imported from England during the Meiji era 130 years ago for the upper classes. The Meyi emperor, with an attitude of "if you can't beat 'em, join 'em," completely embraced Western culture, says Suo. For example, if there were guests from abroad, Japanese in Western clothing would mix with the Westerners and dance together as a kind of formal social interaction. Under the next emperor, he says, dance halls provided an opportunity for men and women to meet and dance.

"The men were ordinary people," explains Suo, "but the women made a living by being professional dance partners. There was never a situation where a married couple would go out together to a dance hall." In this setting, ballroom dancing developed a seedy reputation, which lasted until very recently.

Like most Japanese men, Suo says he would feel very embarrassed to go out with his own wife and dance—even though his wife, Tamiyo Kusakari, is a ballerina and the female lead character in the film. "Historically, ballroom danc- ing became a means for men to get together with women other than their wives if they were married," he says. "Not necessarily with sexual liaisons as an objective. Even people who are dancing for the sheer fun of it won't admit it because of the seediness associated with the activity."

In developing the relationship between dance instructors Tamako Tamura (Reiko Kusamura) and the younger Mai Kishikawa (Kusakari) and their charis- matic students, the focus of *Shall We Dance?* is very much on the dance steps: the social waltz and tango; the modern dances, slow fox trot, the quickstep, Viennese waltz; the Latin rumba, cha cha, paso doble, samba and jive. The learning process that Sugiyama goes through with the eccentric Aoki (Naoto Takenaka), the short Hattori (Yu Tokui) and "fat guy" Tanaka (Hiromasa Taguchi) is occasion for some slapstick routines, in which, Three Stooges-like, they triumph over gawkiness and ineptitude.

Kusakari met Suo during the casting process for *Shall We Dance?* The film marks her acting debut.

"I was looking for somebody who stood well, who had a certain kind of poise," says Suo, smiling discreetly as his wife sits down next to him, "somebody who with one look would set a salaried man's heart racing. Somebody who would be very different from the typical Japanese ideal of a wife. And the character had to be able to dance better than anyone else in the movie . . . When I met Tamiyo, it wasn't so much that I knew she would be able to dance very well—I had no idea how to approach her. She was very difficult to approach, someone who's living in a completely different world from mine."

Asked whether she also found the director difficult to approach, Kusakari says she knew Suo only in name as the director of the 1992 wrestling comedy, *Sumo Do, Sumo Don't,* a major hit throughout Asia.

"My first impression when I met Suo was of a very sensitive man," says Kusakari, "although I couldn't quite grasp where he was coming from. I wasn't quite sure how to react to him."

Quiet on the set. Roll it!

Was it love at first clap of the slate?

"During the filming," says Suo, "all I could think about was my film and how Tamiyo would make my film interesting. I never thought about how she could make my life interesting. And so our relationship started after the film was com- pleted, edited and we were going to screen it together. That's when we first began to relate on a personal level."

"Suo is very good at explaining very precisely what it is he wants to do," says Kusakari, "and so for me, as a first-timer in a film, it was a great help."

"If there's a role that's right for my wife," says Suo, referring to his next film, "I'll begin negotiations with her, but I'm not planning to create a role especially for her."

Published in *Newsday.*

SHIRLEY BARRETT

Love Serenade

I always feel like Dimity is me on my bad days. She's gauche and ineffectual . . . but she acts heroically in the end. Dimity is always trying to make sense of the world. She's puzzled by questions like do fish have souls, do fish feel pain, do worms have babies, all those kinds of things.

Shirley Barrett, 1997

In her surreal comedy, *Love Serenade,* Australian director Shirley Barrett brings a slightly nutty flavor all her own to the spunky quirkiness of films from down under.

The film won her a Caméra d'Or—director's prize awarded for a first feature—at the Cannes Film Festival.

In the South Australian backwater town of Sun Ray, the routine of 20-something sisters Vicki Ann (Rebecca Frith) and Dimity (Miranda Otto) is rocked by the arrival of next-door neighbor, 44-year-old big-city deejay Kenny Sherry (George Shevtsov), who spins soul music on the tiny radio station and steals their hearts, one by one.

"My husband grew up in Robinvale, Victoria, the town where the film was shot," said Barrett. "We'd go there every Christmas to visit the in-laws. At first I found it almost hostile, but then its strange, melancholy atmosphere grew on me. It had the kind of bleak charm, which hadn't been captured yet on Australian film. There was nothing to do all day except swim and then climb the silos at sunset.

"I liked the way the silos loomed over the town like giant sentinels," Barrett said. "It felt like a powerful place to set a climactic scene."

Barrett, 35, was born in Melbourne and lives in Sydney. After dropping out of college, it took her three years to be accepted at the Australian Film and Television School (also the alma mater of directors Gillian Armstrong and Jane Campion).

The effort paid off. Her final student short, *Cherith,* starring Shevtsov, won several awards and got her work directing "slightly better class soaps and series television."

From left to right, Rebecca Frith (as Vicki-Ann Hurley), Miranda Otto (as Dimity Hurley), and George Shevtsov (as Kenneth "Ken" Sherry), in *Love Serenade* (1997, Australia), directed by Shirley Barrett. Photo by Elise Lockwood. Courtesy of Miramax Film Corp. All Rights Reserved.

"In *Cherith* he plays a fundamentalist preacher," Barrett said of Shevtsov. "I just love that low-key malevolent quality he exudes. In fact, I wrote the part of Ken Sherry with George in mind."

Barrett's own father was a Presbyterian minister before converting—to communism—when she was 10. Barrett said she and her three older siblings learned Russian as children because her father wanted them to immigrate to the Soviet Union. They didn't.

Cherith also caught the eye of producer Jan Chapman (*The Last Days of Chez Nous*), who worked with Barrett on the *Love Serenade* script and helped get the rights to the '70s soul classics.

> "The silos loomed over the town like giant sentinels. It felt like a powerful place to set a climactic scene."

"Originally I set out to make a comedy," Barrett said, "but I also wanted to write about inappropriate girlish infatuation. I like that topic. Because I'd always been very susceptible to girlish crushes. I also wanted the music to be an integral part of the storytelling. I was particularly keen on using Barry White and all that very orchestrated, smoldering and highly atmospheric music. I especially wanted to evoke that sense of yearning, of missing out on something out there that becomes this idealized love."

Barrett, who is "just shy of 6 feet," said she always felt outlandishly tall and gawky as a teenager, "with all the boys too short in a big way." There had been a Ken Sherry in her life, very briefly, when she was about 18.

"I wrote a lot of diaries at the time so I documented this saga very well," said Barrett. "And when I look back on it, it's quite hilarious really because I'm so pathetically deluded. I wasn't thinking about scripts then, but I did record some of his dialogue, and that came in very handy later.

"I had a sister who was five years older than me and I suppose she's quite bossy," Barrett said. "But at the same time we don't have a Vicky Ann/Dimity relationship," she said, referring to the film's characters. "We're not as intimately bound as those two are."

Barrett said that, of the two sisters, she felt closer to Dimity, the Miranda Otto character, who works in a Chinese restaurant and is the first to fall prey to Ken Sherry's wiles.

"I always feel like Dimity is me on my bad days," said Barrett. "She's gauche and ineffectual . . . but she acts heroically in the end. Whereas Vicki Ann struggles to hold onto her dignity and Rebecca Frith really brought a kind of nervous energy to the part. Dimity is always trying to make sense of the world. She's puzzled by questions like do fish have souls, do fish feel pain, do worms have babies, all those kinds of things. When Ken betrays her for Vicki Ann, she starts to see him as fishlike. I had an image in my mind of the fish as cold, legless and unloving.

"At one point when I was stuck with the script, I found myself writing a scene where Dimity is walking down the corridor and she hears this gargling sound. Ken is gargling mouthwash but the bubbles are coming out of . . . gills. It had a kind of logic to it, so I kept that motif.

"The beauty of winning the Caméra D'Or," she said, "is that you get a lump sum of money toward developing your next script. Fantastic!"

And what might that be?

"I'm honestly a complete void," she said. "Because after we made the film I had another baby. Now we have two under two. But it'll be another comedy."

Published in *Newsday*.

RUPERT GRAVES

Profile

There's a huge amount of snobbery in the film business in England. The second sons who don't do too well in the business world go into film.

Rupert Graves, 1997

Tall, narrow-shouldered and reed-thin, British actor Rupert Graves springs across the lobby of a Manhattan hotel toward the round tables in the lounge, then folds his limber frame into a chair.

Graves, 34, is in New York to promote three films opening this fall: Richard Spence's *Different for Girls,* a 1990s transsexual romance; Philip Goodhew's *Intimate Relations,* a '50s black comedy, and Marleen Gorris's *Mrs Dalloway,* adapted from the 1920s classic by Virginia Woolf.

After seven days on tour and more than 70 back-to-back interviews, the actor who is best known, perhaps, for his role in the English exports *A Room with a View* and *Maurice* is as loose and feral offscreen as he is on. With his smoldering dark eyes and spiky hair, he radiates physical energy.

He is also disarmingly self-effacing.

"As a kid I wasn't very good-looking. I was very spotty and terribly thin," he says. "I often missed school and played truant a lot."

Born and raised in Weston-super-Mare, a seaside resort on the Bristol Channel in southwest England, Graves was the son of a father who taught piano to children and a mother who performed in amateur opera and "went around knocking on doors, trying to find places for French students to stay."

The actor's mercurial fluidity—he has played characters ranging from a straight-laced Victorian to a suicidal World War I veteran to a young man in love with a transsexual—is almost certainly a result of his early training. He dropped out of high school to join a traveling circus at 15, then went on to perform in children's theater at Butlins Holiday Camp (budget family vacation spots found throughout England), where he acted in 14 different one-hour plays a week. Eventually, he joined the prestigious Old Vic theater company and came to the United States in a production of George Bernard Shaw's *Candida*.

He got his first screen break at 24, when a casting director spotted him in a West End play and cast him as Helena Bonham Carter's brother in *A Room With a View,* the 1986 Merchant-Ivory adaptation of E. M. Forster's novel. A year later, he played the gay gamekeeper in *Maurice,* starring a then unknown Hugh Grant.

In *Intimate Relations,* Graves plays Harold Guppy, a neurotic sailor who is blackmailed into sex by his landlady and her 14-year-old daughter.

"My starting-off point for Guppy's character was what institutionalization does to somebody," Graves says. "Guppy was kicked out of home by his mother when he was 10 and grew up in a reform school, as tough as a prison . . . It made him entirely unprepared for life on the outside. When Guppy's blood sugar went down, he would turn violent, which is why he eats sweets all the time in the film. I like the fact that he was a potential murderer."

Motorcyclist-messenger Paul Prentice, Graves's character in *Different for Girls,* is another type altogether.

"Guppy is apathetic, passive, being acted upon," Graves says, while Paul is "guided by will and defiance. 1977 was a defining moment when punk broke. Paul had such a good time that he never moved out of it. He's looking at society, and he wants to rebel.

"[But] what really drew me to the film was Paul's dilemma: the difficulty of acknowledging that you're falling in love with a transsexual who used to be your male friend. I thought it was pretty saucy."

There were other differences between the two films. "I get a little embarrassed about love scenes," Graves says. "In *Different for Girls,* the love scene is a lot more intimate, more voyeuristic . . . as Harold Guppy, with the landlady, it wasn't about love, and we weren't naked, so you didn't get the same kind of heaviness."

Finally, there is *Mrs Dalloway,* starring Vanessa Redgrave in the title role and Graves as Septimus Warren-Smith, a shell-shocked World War I soldier who would rather kill himself than be sent to a mental institution.

"It's a fascinating story," Graves says. "I totally fell in love with Virginia Woolf. I read all the letters, biographies, but then looking into [her] background—she used this male character as a kind of confessional. When she had her breakdown, she heard birds talking in Greek to her outside her window. As a child, she was abused during Greek lessons. [Warren-Smith] becomes an embodiment of Virginia Woolf's actual breakdown. It's harrowing stuff."

From Forster to Woolf—is there some reason why Graves so often lands parts in literary adaptations?

"It's kind of strange because I'm uneducated, and I'm not posh," says the actor, who now lives in London's East End. "There's a huge amount of snobbery in the film business in England. The second sons who don't do too well in the business world go into film. After all, there are plenty of Oxford-educated actors, like Hugh Grant, who have read the books . . . "

Is he an anomaly then?

After *A Room With a View* came out, "I felt like an impostor," Graves says. "People would invite me to their parties. As soon as they found out I wasn't of their class, they were really surprised, a little offended. I suppose it's ironic because I've got a look and my name is Rupert.

"I was named not after Rupert Brooke the poet but after Rupert the bear," he adds, referring to a Winnie the Pooh-like storybook character popular in England.

"Of their class" or not, Graves finds the situation "fine . . . hilarious, really." He even concedes that he sometimes fakes an Oxford accent when he's in certain social circles.

To faze people?

"To fit in," Graves says. And laughs.

Originally published in *Newsday*.

JIM JARMUSCH

Year of the Horse

We had been threatening them the whole time, we're going to interrogate you, we're going to interrogate you. The guys in the Horse would go, "Whooo, real scary, man, I don't see any interrogation
room set up."

Jim Jarmusch, 1997

Little Italy, October 17—There's nothing like a Jewish high holiday to curb New York's hyperactive pulse. A few days before the opening of Jim Jarmusch's frenetic new film, *Year of the Horse,* in the Rialto's becalmed outdoor garden, we have an ambling conversation over a cup of tea about music, film, crows and other life forms.

With a major retrospective at the American Museum of the Moving Image, and now the release of *Horse,* Jarmusch is hard-pressed finding time to write the script for his next film.

"I've never been pulled out of writing like this before. It's frustrating," Jarmusch said. "Doing press for *Horse* is ridiculous because I made it for them so my soul really isn't in it. There is a soul in it, but it's their soul."

In the late '70s, before *Stranger than Paradise* transformed the landscape for independent film, Jarmusch worked on Howard Bruckner's documentary about William Burroughs.

"My favorite rock and roll movies are *Don't Look Back* and *Cocksucker Blues,*" said Jarmusch. "*Horse* is closer to *Monterey Pop.* It's just a good blast of their brand of rock and roll. Making a film like *Horse* is very different from making a feature film with a story that you've written. Though when making any film, I try to let the material tell me what to do with it. Here it was liberating for [the editor] Jay Rabinowitz and I because there was no choice. There was no road map, no blue print, no structure at all while shooting."

For live interviews of Neil Young, Neil's father Scott Young and the other members of Crazy Horse Jarmusch had an unusual set-up consisting of a single

Jim Jarmusch, director. Photo by Sukita. 1991. Locus Solus, Inc.

chair in the center of the room facing the camera, with a washing machine in the upper right-hand corner of the frame—an apt metaphor for the interview process.

"That was in Dublin backstage," Jarmusch said. "We were on tour with them for their last European show. And we had been threatening them the whole time, we're going to interrogate you, we're going to interrogate you. The guys in the Horse would go, 'Whooo, real scary, man, I don't see any interrogation room set up.' In Dublin we had the choice of a few rooms back stage and this one had a stainless steel sink and washing machine. I kept expecting some Irish women to come in and say, 'We've got to use the machine, could you please move out of here. Our washing's got to be done.'"

In another sequence on a bus, Jarmusch reads to Young from Ezekiel in the Old Testament.

"Rock and roll friends of mine have said, 'Well you really nailed that,'" said Jarmusch. "On the road you start reading from the Bible 'cause that's all there is in the hotel room. And I had this book, *Ken's Guide to the Bible,* which catalogued a lot of the more lurid passages. Violence is part of our greatest stories. In San Francisco, where we edited and shot and where Neil had done the score for *Dead Man,* a lot of the hotels have the Bible and the Buddha. What a cool town."

Half-Moon Bay, a wild, rocky, dangerous surfing beach 30 miles south of San Francisco, was the main location for the music video of Neil Young's *Big Time,* which Jarmusch shot in super 8. That video was the genesis for *Year of the Horse.*

"The image quality is so raw and yet luminous," Jarmusch said, "and the sound of the music is recorded in digital Dolby 40 track—I like the contradiction of the huge high tech sound and the very raw imagery. It fits the band . . . Unlike lot of newer and younger musicians, [Crazy Horse's] energy is totally lacking in irony. But these guys [the Horse] dress like garbage men. They're not interested in the pose of being rock stars. They're really obsessed with their music and how to make it pure, which is very refreshing. And when they're on stage they're like 50-year-old teenagers."

A huge music fan, Jarmusch refers to music as his favorite form inspirationally.

"I love all kinds of music. I listen to everything," said Jarmusch. "There's a lot in every genre that I hate. There's 10 percent of any genre that I love. To me hip-hop in the last 10 or 15 years is the most interesting innovative form. The only genre I have trouble with is swing. I love jazz from the '20s and '30s and I'm a heavy bebop fanatic. And I don't like show tunes. Lately I've been listening to a lot of hip-hop, Ornette Coleman and very pure blues like Son House and Mississippi Fred MacDowell."

Explaining the origin of the film's title, Jarmusch referred to David Briggs as "sort of the fifth member of Crazy Horse and their producer from the very beginning." Briggs died in late 1995.

"While he was dying," said Jarmusch, "Neil went to see him and asked him, 'What should I do now, David?' And David said, this has got to be the Year of the Horse, meaning, go back on the road with Crazy Horse . . . We thought of calling the film *Horse Shit, Smell the Horse.* They're pretty open about drugs in their past, though. I didn't put that much of it into the film [except for] the Danny Whitten overdose. And of course 'Tonight's the Night' is about Bruce Berry, their roadie, who o'ded. They accept their past and their history. They're not afraid of it. They're not a politically correct type of people. They're interested in what the truth is. Neil has said to me often or to others when we've done interviews together, the worse thing that can happen to a musician or to anyone whose work goes out to other people is to start believing your own press. Once you do that, you've lost touch with yourself. What happens in your life is what happens and there's no shame. Neil's just not the kind of person who wants to create a Neil Young mythology."

A temptation which many think Jarmusch has also resisted. In 1983, with the release of *Stranger than Paradise,* Jarmusch was canonized, or maybe "canbyized" by Vincent Canby as "an American original."

"Uncle Vince," Jarmsuch says, "I never met him but I really miss him."

"You could have been caramelized and turned into candy," I point out.

"Or cannibalized," Jarmusch says.

Unlike many filmmakers, studio or independent, Jarmusch has been able to retain control of his movies.

"I was helped out in the very beginning by Jim Stark who helped me design this process," said Jarmusch. "Basically we finance my films by split rights presales. So I get money from say, France, Germany, Japan, and in exchange they get the distribution of the film in their territory when it's finished. And the people who finance the film do not have any artistic control over it. So I'm able to produce the films through my own company the way I want to because I own the negative. I have control over the script and who's in the film and what music is used and how they're edited. It's shocking to realize how many people don't have final cuts over their films—sometimes not even Scorsese."

Jarmsuch says this labor-intensive system hasn't prevented him from producing more scripts since *Stranger*—*Down by Law, Night on Earth, Dead Man, Ghost Dog*, as well as his thesis film *Permanent Vacation* were all made over a 15-year period.

"Aki Kaurismaki calls me the world's slowest film director," Jarmusch says. "He called me a month ago saying, 'I have to finish my script.' It was a Thursday. And I said, 'When are you shooting?' He said, 'I'm shooting on Monday.' Then he left me a message three days ago: 'I wrote the script, I filmed the script, I'm done with the editing.' And I haven't even finished starting to write my script. He's just really annoying."

In the distance, crows caw emphatically above the hum of nearby venting systems.

"I've always been a big fan of crime fiction and real film noir, which ended in 1951," says Jarmusch, whose films are not test-marketed. "Violence in and of itself isn't a negative thing in storytelling. It's really important. But now [in Hollywood films] they've taken the guts out of violence as a powerful narrative element . . . It's gratuitous after the test market, someone's got to get shot in slow motion . . . Sad. The only innovative things happen when people take chances and play with the form, or use an existing form in a classical way that's respectful of it, of its power."

"Crows are smart birds. I was in the very last town in California before Oregon," Jarmusch recalls, "when there was a big wind coming in off the sea. The gulls like to hang in the air, static, right on the beach. And among maybe 15 gulls was one crow, 8 feet up, doing it too. He was checking out the game they play."

ALAIN BERLINER

Ma Vie en Rose

I've always been attracted to stories about someone who's different, who can't really find a place in the mainstream.

Alain Berliner, 1998

February 12, 1998—French director Alain Berliner said he took pains to set his satire of childhood innocence and homophobia, *Ma Vie en Rose,* in a suburb of his hometown, Bruxelles, the kind of neighborhood where families have four children, and wives do not work.

A slightly surreal black comedy about a 7-year-old boy who thinks he's a girl, *Ma Vie en Rose* won a Golden Globe and has been acclaimed as a send-up of bourgeois pretensions and gender conventions.

The boy's family has "sunk all their savings in the purchase of a suburban home, which represents their social ideal," Berliner said. So when homophobic graffiti appear on the garage door, the family's ideal has been sullied and they feel obliged to find a more tolerant environment.

"I've always been attracted to stories about someone who's different, who can't really find a place in the mainstream," he said. As for Berliner's personal life, he's a doctor's son, married with two small children.

In the film, Ludovic (Georges Du Fresne) dresses in girls' clothes and plays with dolls. To the dismay of his family and neighbors, he also wants to marry his best friend, Jerome, and in the film's early sequences the two boys are seen staging elaborate wedding ceremonies in full regalia. That is, until Jerome's father, who is Ludovic's father's boss, puts a stop to his son's participation.

"Ludovic's logic," Berliner explained, "is that he will grow up to be a girl because he knows that boys don't marry boys"—at least not in this well-heeled neighborhood of identical mansions and garden parties.

The film is based on a script by Chris van der Stappen, 38, who works in a public relations firm and was introduced to Berliner by a mutual friend.

Georges Du Fresne in *Ma Vie en Rose* (1997, France) aka *My Life in Pink*. Directed by Alain Berliner. Photo Sony Pictures Classics, courtesy of Photofest.

"It's her story, not mine," said Berliner. "She wrote it from her awakening consciousness of growing up as a lesbian." Berliner and van der Stappen rewrote the screenplay together, changing the age and the gender of the protagonist, and bringing the reactions of family and neighbors into the story.

Asked why the hero of the film was so young, Berliner said that van der Stappen had told him that for her, consciousness of sexual identity began at the age of seven and that this experience was corroborated in talking to other gay friends.

The screenwriters thought that seven was also a critical age, said Berliner, because in traditional French culture, seven is considered the age of reason, when children have to choose between boyhood or girlhood—at least outwardly by the way they dress. And while being a tomboy is semi-tolerated (the French expression, *garçon manqué,* means literally a failed boy), there is no parallel expression for boys.

For Berliner, the film opens up questions about personal identity which might make some people feel uncomfortable. "It took me some time to understand," Berliner said, "that [Ludovic's] problem was of being a man or a boy in the wrong body."

Many aspects of van der Stappen's experience, for instance her relationship with her mother, were quite different from Ludovic's in the film. "The first time she spoke to her mother about 'it' [her sense of being a man]," Berliner said, "was when they saw the movie together." Berliner said that as a teenager he wanted to make music, not movies. He played in a lot of bands and made some records. But at the age of 18, he became dissatisfied with the rock-and-roll lifestyle and working menial jobs. He applied to film school, and was thrown out at the end of the first year.

"That's when I realized I wanted to make movies," said Berliner. He reapplied, and persistence paid off. A visit from Frank Daniels, then co-chairman of Columbia University's film school, convinced Berliner that writing scripts needed experience and technique as much as inspiration. He wrote a couple of scripts for a Belgian producer, then moved to writing for French television.

Six months into the rewrite of *Ma Vie en Rose* (adapted from the title of an Edith Piaf song), said Berliner, he and van der Stappen decided that the tone and style of the film was so unusual that Berliner should direct it.

"What I really like to do," said Berliner, "is to mix the two genres—drama and comedy. For instance, in the film, Jerome's sister is dead. That's usually something considered too dramatic for comedy."

Berliner found the perfect suburban location for the film's shooting, outside Paris, a neighborhood where the shutters on the houses and the garage doors were painted white. "The only thing I had to add was color," he said. "I made sure the garage doors and shutters matched."

Berliner said he stole the set design of *Edward Scissorhands,* in which all the houses are painted different colors. He said, "I have no problem admitting it."

Published in *Newsday.*

Takeshi Kitano
Sonatine and Hana-Bi [Fireworks]

If I were to use a baseball metaphor, in *Hana-Bi* I'm learning to bunt as opposed to always hitting the grand slam or a home run.

Takeshi Kitano, 1998

April 5, 1998—Surrounded by his entourage, Takeshi Kitano—comedian, actor (as Beat Takeshi), director, talk-show host, author and Japan's premier entertainer for 20 years—walks into the conference room of Manhattan's Kitano Hotel and makes slight bows in formal greeting.

A low-keyed demeanor, scarred, impassive face and deadpan expression hide the swift comedic reflexes and the latent ferocity of the killer roles that he plays onscreen—and the energy he brings to his career. In his many roles, he has two films to promote: His latest, *Hana-Bi* [*Fireworks*] is playing in Manhattan; the earlier *Sonatine* opens in Manhattan Friday. Politely, he clamps an empty cigarette holder between his lips. His is a packed-to-the-gills schedule.

Aside from film production, he has written 53 novels and several albums of pop music, and does six weekly magazine columns and six weekly TV shows. The only sign of wear and tear from long hours in airplanes and dry hotel rooms is tired eyes, which he moistens frequently with eye drops.

Kitano's deadpan, explosive cinematic style features stylized violence in the occasional service of social satire. In the gangster drama *Sonatine*, which was made in 1995, Kitano plays Murakawa, a middle-aged underboss approaching retirement. In *Hana-Bi*, a kind of metaphysical crime thriller that won the Golden Lion at the 1997 Venice Film Festival, Kitano stars as Nishi, a retired cop who has a violent streak, a paralyzed colleague and a terminally ill wife. Between the two films there's a marked shift in his approach to violence.

Portrait of Takeshi Kitano. © Robin Holland.

"My earlier films had often been labeled as intense depictions of violence, and I started to feel a little bit fed up with such criticisms," Kitano said through a translator. "I decided to make an adjustment to the conventional way of shooting these violent scenes. So although the main characters in both films end up dead, in *Sonatine,* Murakawa chooses death as a means of escape. In *Hana-Bi* Nishi also chooses death, but he is willing to confront it face to face in order to take responsibility for his family and friends. If I were to use a baseball metaphor, in *Hana-Bi* I'm learning to bunt as opposed to always hitting the grand slam or a home run."

Kitano, who turned 50 in January, was raised in a rough section of Tokyo he calls "the Japanese version of Brooklyn." "Until I went to junior high school," said Kitano, "I really wanted to become either a baseball player or a boxer, but my mother was very strict and I ended up entering the engineering department of Meiji University in Tokyo. This was during the '60s student revolution, so I dropped out of college and drifted into Asakusa, the striptease area of Tokyo, and became an elevator boy."

One night he filled in for a missing stage actor at the France-Za strip club, then appeared regularly in stage acts. By the age of 25, he had become popular as a stand-up comedian. "The first film in which I felt a sense of accomplishment as an actor,"

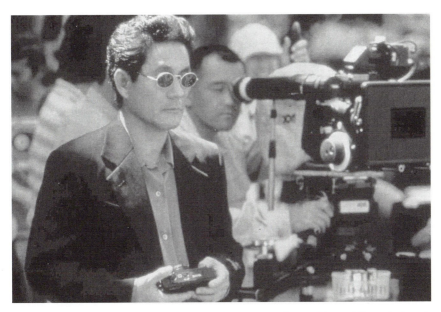

Director Takeshi Kitano on the set of *Fireworks* (1998, Japan). The multifaceted Kitano is Japan's premier entertainer. Courtesy of Milestone Films.

Kitano said, "was Nagisa Oshima's *Merry Christmas, Mr. Lawrence* [1983]. I sneaked into the theater to see how the audience would react, and I expected that they would be appalled at my tremendously serious acting, but the moment I appeared on screen, everybody in the theater, including the employees, burst into laughter, which was humiliating for me. It took me 15 years to be recognized as a serious actor."

Writer-director-actor-editor Kitano added another medium to his resume in *Hana-Bi*—when his detective partner, Horibe, turns to painting after being paralyzed in a shootout, those are original Kitanos on display. In typical fashion, he taught himself to paint after a bike accident in which he was hit on his skull.

"I anticipated that I would become a genius like Van Gogh or Renoir," he said, "but when I tried to imitate [their styles] it was a disaster." The final result: highly stylized, allegorical paintings—a sunflower, for instance, becomes the head of a lion.

"It struck me that it would not be inappropriate to characterize Horibe as a beginner in painting like myself after the accident. So then it would make sense to include my beginning paintings in the film, so it turned out quite okay."

Originally published in *Newsday*.

WAYNE WANG

Chinese Box

I'm not a Hong Kong person anymore. I'm much more American now, and I don't pretend that I could completely understand Hong Kong. So I chose to do it from the Jeremy Irons [character's] perspective.

Wayne Wang, 1998

Wayne Wang has never shied away from the places to which he has emotional ties. In his earliest films, Chan Is Missing *(1982) and the delectable comedy of manners* Dim Sum *(1989), the Hong Kong-born director took an unflinching look at the cultural dynamics of his adopted home, San Francisco's Chinatown. A versatile and fluent visual stylist, Wang's first big box office draw was the more mainstream* Joy Luck Club *(1993), an adaptation of Amy Tan's novel, followed by the precisely crafted* Smoke *(1995) and* Blue in the Face *(1995), Paul Auster-derived character studies set in Brooklyn and Manhattan neighborhoods.*

The new Chinese Box—*written by Jean-Claude Carrière—takes the pulse of Wang's former homeland at a historical turning point, the return of the former British colony to mainland China. Set during the six-month period prior to June 30, 1997, Wang's fictional salute to the big changeover evokes the complex, mysterious hybrid of Chinese and British cultures that defines Hong Kong, and reveals his own ambivalence toward it in the process.*

The film charts the turmoil of three Hong Kong denizens trying to tie up loose ends in an anxious climate. The legendary Gong Li (Ju Dou, Raise the Red Lantern, Temptress Moon) *makes her English-language debut as Vivian, a Chinese immigrant nightclub owner and former hostess. (It's also her first role as a modern dame in blue jeans and shades.) Jeremy Irons* (Reversal of Fortune, M. Butterfly) *plays John, a dying English journalist with a family back home who makes a last-ditch attempt to declare his passion for Vivian. He's also shooting a Hi-8 documentary of Hong Kong street life during the last months of British rule, in the course of which he meets hustler Jean (Hong Kong superstar Maggie Cheung), who has her own troubled story. Ruben Blades plays photojournalist Jim, John's guitar-playing backup man.*

Liza Béar: Tell me why you made *Chinese Box*.

Wayne Wang: Well, I was born and raised in Hong Kong until I was 18, and even after I emigrated to go to school in the U.S., I kept going back there to work. My immediate family stayed until 1984. My wife and her family are from there, too. So Hong Kong was still my home, at least the Hong Kong before the Chinese took over last June. And I had done a little film called *Life Is Cheap But Toilet Paper Is Expensive,* a kind of angry, instinctive film about Hong Kong, very small, a gesture. I felt like there was unfinished business there. But I kept running away from doing this film. Instead I tried to do a studio film. Finally by October 1996, I knew that if I didn't do it, I would never do it, and I would hate myself. So I jumped in there, got the financing together, got a script together and just did it.

LB: In this film you're registering the passing of an epoch . . .

WW: Registering the passing of an epoch, and also how four people—who are somewhat representative of people in Hong Kong, and very different—the choices they have to make about their lives. That's really what the movie is about. It's very much like a [Milan] Kundera novel. It's about people and their relationships, set against a political backdrop.

LB: How close were you to the changeover when you started production?

WW: We started writing the script in October. We had something by mid-January, and we just started shooting. So it was very quick. Everything was very rough and a little bit off the cuff. I wanted to have something down [on paper], but also to be free and instinctive with it. We went back during the real change-over and shot for maybe a week to 10 days there.

So that's basically the process and why I did this film—to understand what it means to me to have Hong Kong be handed back to China. I found that the best way to do that was through an English journalist who really knows quite a bit about Hong Kong, and yet is still, in a way, an outsider.

LB: How much of the story did you have in broad strokes before you started?

WW: Mmmm. Very little. Truthfully, all I knew was that I wanted a man dying during this period. I was very interested in the idea of loss, and dealing with loss, which is my feeling about Hong Kong. And I was interested in death and how somebody would deal with love when he knows he's dying. I've always been fascinated by that.

LB: What are some of the things the British did in Hong Kong that you didn't like?

WW: Well, first let me say what I liked. If there's anything the English left Hong Kong with, it's this incredible dignity with which they do things. The ritualistic ceremony of retreat was so wonderfully done, it's quite moving. As a child growing up, their ceremonies and rituals were some things that, combined with the Chinese rituals, were very important to me.

The other thing that the British provided for Hong Kong was a structure, an organization. They really stopped corruption in Hong Kong. They did a very good job of that. I remember as a child growing up, you had to bribe the postman, 'cause otherwise he wouldn't get your mail right. So that was a 180-degree change because of the British.

Then the bad part about the English is they're colonialists and they're really racist. They won't say it out loud, but they're really bad with the Chinese. The court system is a good example. It's old-fashioned, it's all done in English. A Chinese who might be completely innocent but doesn't speak a word of English is assigned an English lawyer and has no idea of what's going on, and they don't care. As a child growing up, there were so many incidents where I felt the British were just treating the Chinese like shit. For me, that's reflected in the film through the Jean character and her traumatic past with the parents of the boyfriend, who basically destroyed their very innocent love for each other.

> "I went to a British public school—a Jesuit school, very strict, very religious, very Catholic. When I grew up I wanted to be—for a while, I wanted to be English. Some of my friends were English, and it was also hip to be English."

LB: The story is mainly told from the perspective of a British person, rather than from a Hong Kong person, so that you're focusing on the passage of the old—because we don't know what's coming next, is that it?

WW: Right. And because I really wanted to make the main character a bit of my own alter ego. The English journalist [emigrating from Hong Kong] is probably closer to who I am.

LB: Than an incoming Hong Kong entrepreneur?

WW: Yes. I have no interest or relationship with that kind of person, except as an outsider. I'm not a Hong Kong person anymore. I'm much more American now, and I don't pretend that I could completely understand Hong Kong. So I chose to do it from the Jeremy Irons [character's] perspective. Although I did put in a Hong Kong character, Vivian's boyfriend, as a main character, I felt more comfortable talking about the film from the Jeremy Irons perspective.

If I were living and breathing in Hong Kong and a Hong Kong filmmaker, I would have chosen another route. But I am an ex-Hong Kong person, brought up by the English. I went to a British public school—a Jesuit school, very strict, very religious, very Catholic. When I grew up I wanted to be—for a while, I wanted to be English. Some of my friends were English, and it was also hip to be English. The culture was very pervasive, and we were very influenced by it. I listened mostly to English rock 'n' roll. And even after I left Hong Kong and went back, I was still hanging out with the hip colonial crowd, and in a way I know that world very well.

LB: Cricket?

WW: Oh yeah. Bowling, horse riding, racing, cucumber sandwiches, sandwiches with a lot of butter and the crusts cut off, little triangles, Ovaltine, Ribena. I still love Ribena. You can get it in Chinatown. So I know that world, and I love it and hate it.

LB: Both at once?

WW: Of course. I'm supposed to be Chinese and in a way I don't know my Chinese side as well. And these [British] people are also racist. And I was racist along with them. I would say, "Look at those stupid Chinese, they spit on the street, no culture at all."

LB: How did you come to terms with your heritage? Was America the big window opener for you?

WW: Yes. I came to Oakland to study art. My mother encouraged me. I was living with a very liberal American family. They were involved with every movement possible, anti-draft, Black Panthers, and all of a sudden my world and my window to it opened up. This was '68 through the early '70s. The revolution. The whole world opened up to me. I saw how narrow the colonial world was, how narrow the Hong Kong Chinese world was, and that's when I changed—a lot.

LB: What do you feel will happen to Hong Kong now that capitalism can't have unlimited sway?

WW: What's happening is very deep-rooted and may not be visible immediately. Things like, for example, education. There's a definite shift from teaching English to teaching more Mandarin. That was already made a law, right after the changeover. Teaching more Chinese, more Mandarin and more emphasis on singing the Chinese national anthem.

LB: China is becoming much more consumer-oriented. Is it the new China that's going to affect Hong Kong rather than the old Communist regime?

WW: Yes. The new China. Now you walk down the street or go into the subway, half the people you see are non-Hong Kong born residents, they're new immigrants from China. That's changing the texture of the population. The education is changing because they're teaching more about China. But there's a lot of self-censorship. Hong Kong is so reliant on China and also needs to kiss China's ass about everything, whether it's business or government issues or whatever, that the newspapers, the movie exhibitors, are basically censoring themselves.

LB: Why?

WW: Why? Because, for example, the *South China Morning Post* used to be an English paper, English-owned. Now it's owned by some Southeast Asian businessmen who have strong businesses in China. So if you're a journalist and you write a story about Tibet, it'll get put on page 10 rather than on page 1. That's what happens. Three movies—*Kundun, Seven Days in Tibet, Red Corner*—will probably not get shown in Hong Kong. And not because of censorship, but because of self-censorship.

LB: The invisible enemy.

WW: Which is more dangerous and very pervasive. Everything is connected to China and Hong Kong is worried about alienating China. In the end, it's a very dog-eat-dog capitalistic society. Because unless you can make it, nobody's going to care. That's what Hong Kong is.

Originally published on *Salon.com*.

John Hurt
Love and Death on Long Island

What the script succeeded in doing was talking about somebody who was homosexual without it appearing to be so.

John Hurt, 1998

What happens when an older, very English, discerning man of letters on one side of the big pond falls for an all-American teen movie heartthrob on the other?

As the lovestruck writer in *Love and Death on Long Island,* John Hurt's Giles De'Ath eventually leaves his London study, hops on a plane and heads for the fictional Chesterton, Long Island, N.Y., home of Jason Priestley's Ronnie Bostock.

Esteemed by directors for his deep understanding of character during 35 years on screen, Hurt has portrayed Caligula in the PBS series *I, Claudius* (1976), and received an Academy Award nomination for his portrayal of the drugged-out hippie Max in *Midnight Express* (1978). He has always been willing to work with independents and first-time directors, and that's the case again in British filmmaker Richard Kwietniowski's debut feature.

With razor-sharp precision, Hurt gives an astute study of obsession as the fastidious Giles De'Ath, whose Old World lifestyle has resisted vulgar modern-day contrivances from the VCR to the answering machine. De'Ath becomes infatuated with golden boy Ronnie Bostock on a rare visit to his local duplex when—locked out of his house—he stumbles by mistake into *Hotpants College II,* culturally the antipode of the film he'd intended to see, E. M. Forster's *Eternal Moment.*

Hurt responded with enthusiasm during an interview in Manhattan when asked for his first reaction to the script. "My agent called and said, 'See what you think. I'm not sure about it.' I read the script and said, 'Well, I'm very sure. If there's a green light on this, please tell whoever's connected with it I'm definitely interested.'"

"What the script succeeded in doing," he said, "was talking about somebody who was homosexual without it appearing to be so—without tedious and boring details. And by the time you've finished watching the film you suddenly realize you've been watching a relationship about a homosexual obsession.

"But I have a feeling that for the heterosexuals, being heterosexual myself, it transcends the homosexuality. The fact that it was well-written was the first thing that got to me . . ."

Smitten with the all-consuming impact of a schoolgirl crush, De'Ath seeks out every image of Bostock he can lay his hands on, either on video or in print, and assiduously compiles a scrapbook of clippings, which he calls "a file of smiles."

"You constantly had to be aware on two levels," Hurt said. "One, it [Giles's infatuation with Ronnie] was not funny to the characters; two, as an actor you had to play things humorously, because it's intended to be funny to an audience."

One hazard of the role: Hurt had to take up smoking again. "When I started smoking, it was romantic and grown-up and everyone said you should look nervous without a cigarette," Hurt said. "I have given up smoking on several occasions, but Giles in *Love and Death* smokes, so that makes you take it up again, particularly if you like it."

Hurt's career took off with a memorable turn in 1975 as Quentin Crisp, the flamboyant drag queen in *The Naked Civil Servant*. "Quentin was the first character I played that really did cause a storm," Hurt said. "There was a scene in *Civil Servant* where I tried to get into a taxi to get away from some roughs. I had flaming red hair. [After the film], taxi after taxi would refuse to take money from me. I'd never known anything like it."

Born in Chesterfield, Derbyshire, to a Church of England clergyman, Hurt described his father as "a professional Christian, straight and puritanical, and someone who's in another form of entertainment, spiritual entertainment." Hurt's own adolescence, he said, was "very rebellious."

He now lives on a stud farm in Ireland. "I have a cottage surrounded by horses," said Hurt. "I don't leave often. I do have one racehorse. She's a 2-year-old called Heed My Warning."

Hurt makes no bones about his love for independent films, despite his studio box-office successes (*Aliens, A Man for All Seasons, The Elephant Man*). "The reason I like independents is a very simple one," said Hurt. "The smaller the project, the more adventurous the content.

"Acting is my joy, my life, and I'm very thrilled that I chose to do it. You don't do it for the applause. Applause is wonderful, very nice, pat on the back, terrific. The late Ralph Richardson, who's one of my all-time favorites, was receiving an award once and started talking about pride as a dangerous thing, then said, 'but I intend to paddle in a puddle of pride for the rest of the night.' Alliteration and prizes go together.

"Of course, it's wonderful to receive praise—not because it means you're such a clever boy, but because it means a lot of people have enjoyed [the performance]."

Originally published in *Newsday*.

SHERMAN ALEXIE

Smoke Signals

Every moment that can be found in Shakespeare's tragedies and comedies can be found on my little reservation. Hamlet lives there. King Lear lives there. And so do Romeo and Juliet.

Sherman Alexie, 1998

July 12, 1998—Sherman Alexie had no problem tearing apart *The Lone Ranger and Tonto Fistfight in Heaven,* his prizewinning book of short stories, to fashion a script for *Smoke Signals,* the first U.S. feature film written, directed and acted by American Indians.

"I treated the book like I didn't write it," says Alexie, who wrote the screenplay for director Chris Eyre's darkly comic road-buddy movie.

"Most of the narrative drive comes from one particular story called 'This Is What it Means to Say, Phoenix, Arizona,' and the rest of the movie [is taken] in pieces from the other stories. But I didn't treat the book like it was precious."

Smoke Signals, currently playing in New York, follows two Coeur d'Alène Indians, Victor and Thomas, as they travel from Idaho to an Arizona reservation to retrieve Victor's father's ashes. The pair, estranged childhood friends, gradually rediscover their friendship en route.

The film has generated considerable buzz since winning the Audience Award at Sundance, in part due to Alexie's prior literary kudos as a poet and novelist. At 31, he has already published seven books of poetry, two novels (*Reservation Blues,* for which he won an American Book Award, and *Indian Killer*), as well as numerous political essays and cultural commentary. He recently won the 1998 Taos Heavyweight Poetry Contest, a 10-round competition between two poets set up like a boxing match.

(An adaptation of Alexie's second novel, *Indian Killer*—about the serial killings of white men in Seattle, for which an Indian is the prime suspect—is slated for production in October, with Alexie directing from his own screenplay.)

From left to right, Evan Adams (as Thomas-the-Fire) and Adam Beach (as Victor Joseph) in Chris Eyre's *Smoke Signals* (1998, United States). Photo by Courtnay Duchin and Jill Sabella. Courtesy of Miramax Film Corp. All Rights Reserved.

In person Alexie, who is of Spokane-Coeur d'Alène descent, is bracingly direct, tossing out amusing remarks when you least expect them.

"I was pre-med, but I kept fainting in human anatomy class. That's "not good bedside manner," he says, discussing his early plans to be a doctor.

Born in Willipinit on the Spokane Indian Reservation, where he lived until he was 18, Alexie had a hydrocephalic condition at birth that required a prolonged convalescence during which he became a precocious reader—conquering *The Grapes of Wrath* at the age of six.

Still, he had no dreams of becoming a writer. Then, "in 1989, when I took a poetry writing workshop at Washington State University, it was the first time I saw any contemporary poetry by anybody, let alone by American Indians," he says. "I read a poem by Adrian Louis, this Payute Indian poet. There's a line in it—'I'm in the reservation of my mind'—and for me, that line was like 'I sing the body electric' or 'In the beginning, God created Heaven and Earth.' It had that kind of cultural resonance and power. It was literally the lightning-striking, thunder-thundering revelatory kind of moment when I knew that what I wanted to do was write poems."

Acclaim was immediate. After the publication of his first book of poems, *The Business of Fancy Dancing* (1992), "agents and editors would call asking if I wrote fiction," Alexie says. "I said yes, and then I started to write it." But, he adds, "poetry is my first love, and fiction's an arranged marriage."

Arranged or not, *The Lone Ranger and Tonto Fistfight in Heaven,* dedicated to an earlier wave of American Indian writers such as Adrian Louis, Joy Harjo, Leslie Marmon Silko and Simon Ortiz, injected a wry, sometimes brash humor into its portrayal of the harsh life on the reservation—something *Smoke Signals* does as well.

The trip undertaken by Victor (Adam Beach) and Thomas (Evan Adams) is similar to one Alexie had taken with his best friend from the reservation. But the film's father-son reconciliation theme is his own.

"Most of it is [drawn from] my relationship with my father," Alexie says, "My father's still home. He never left. We had a certain estrangement based on his alcoholism and other issues—things that have resolved themselves now. I can tell him I love him and I'm pissed off in the same sentence, so that's a sign of health."

During their trip, the traditionally mismatched road companions—Thomas talks nonstop, Victor doesn't—rekindle their friendship while reconciling themselves to hurtful early memories. In playing the two characters off one another, the film subverts not only cultural stereotypes—Indians as stole warriors, for example—but their views of themselves, too.

"The physical journey is the direct reflection of their emotional journey," says Alexie. "We knew we were going to have unfamiliar characters and situations, so I wanted to hang that on a very familiar frame. The road-buddy movie is the oldest literary or cinematic form in the world. *The Odyssey, The Iliad, Exodus* are road movies.

"The only thing that changes over the years," he adds, "is the snacks."

Developed at the Sundance Filmmakers Laboratory and shot in 27 days, *Smoke Signals* cost about as much as "one chandelier on the Titanic," says Alexie, who also served as co-producer.

With the vast body of contemporary literature by American Indians of different tribal origins available, why has it taken so long for a film by American Indians to be made?

"Nobody had faith enough in any stories we were telling to give us the money," Alexie says. "It took somebody like me, a writer with a successful literary career, to [get] enough respect and attention. And someone who'd come out of NYU Film School like Chris Eyre."

There are other reasons, he says. "It took a while because we're the first generation of Indians who are completely familiar with film and completely obsessed with film the way all other races of people have become obsessed with it. It took until there was a *Brady Bunch* generation of American Indian kids for this film to happen."

Alexie is cautious about predicting any future wave of American Indian filmmaking. There are, he points out, 27 Indian tribes in the state of Washington alone.

"I am one person, one writer, writing about his particular experience," he says. "I don't articulate any group thing at all. Nobody ever asks a white writer to do that. I'm a Spokane-Coeur d'Alène Indian. I'm a member of a tribe and proud of that. Every moment that can be found in Shakespeare's tragedies and comedies can be found on my little reservation. Hamlet lives there. King Lear lives there. And so do Romeo and Juliet."

Published in *The Star Ledger* and the *Denver Post.*

MICHAEL WINTERBOTTOM
Welcome to Sarajevo

Someone's shot, a shell goes off. The next second, there are 25 photographers taking pictures of someone as they die . . . For people watching that, the first reaction is horrific: How can those people just come and take a photograph of that person instead of doing something about it? But equally they have to get the picture. There's no way of resolving that contradiction.

Michael Winterbottom, 1998

Lancashire-born Michael Winterbottom's directorial bravura was first noted in his debut feature Butterfly Kiss, *and subsequently in* Go Now, *featuring Robert Carlyle as a man coming to terms with multiple sclerosis. His latest achievement,* Welcome to Sarajevo, *unlike Srdjan Dragojevic's* Pretty Village Pretty Flame *or Emir Kusturica's* Underground, *views the horrendous Bosnian conflict from the diverse perspectives of a cadre of international journalists covering the Sarajevo siege. It provides a rare dramatic insight into the dynamics—and ethical dilemmas—of war reporting. The American freelance "loose cannon" approach, personified by Flynn (Woody Harrelson) is juxtaposed with the more closely coordinated tactics of a British news team. Amidst rival disasters relentlessly competing for coverage, each reporter or producer must make daily judgment calls about what constitutes "a good story," and strike a balance between observation and personal involvement, between the demands of the job and basic human decency. When the Ljubica Ivezic orphanage, a growing number of whose members are war casualties, is bombarded by artillery fire, the film narrows its focus to the plight of those children and reaches critical mass over a British journalist's promise to a young girl to evacuate her. The means by which he does so, and the ultimate consequences of his action, limn poignancy with suspense.*

Shot on location in the immediate aftermath of the Bosnian hostilities, Welcome to Sarajevo *is based on* Natasha's Story, *a veteran war correspondent's firsthand chronicle of his own experiences. After covering wars for 25 years, Michael Nicholson felt obliged to abandon a pure observer stance and to intercede on a human plane in the life of a Bosnian child, whom he took home and adopted. Earlier this year the film, which stars Emira Nusevic as the child and Emily Lloyd, Kerry Fox, Woody Harrelson, Stephen Dillane and Marisa Tomei as reporters, premiered at Cannes and Toronto. Michael Winterbottom called me in New York from the bustling cafeteria of Soho House, London, while taking a break from auditions.*

Liza Béar: What stage are you at on the next film?

Michael Winterbottom: Actually, I'm editing it. It's called *I Want You.*

LB: Sounds like a change of pace. Is it a romantic comedy?

MW: No, it's quite romantic, but it's dark. It's about various people who're obsessed with other people. There are four [main] characters. It's set in an English seaside town, Hastings, which is a resort but also a fishing town. That's why we chose it. It's completely different from *Welcome to Sarajevo.*

LB: At what point were you when the script for *Sarajevo* arrived on your desk?

MW: It was December '94 and the war was still on. Everyone in England was very aware of what was happening, feeling confused, really, that there was a war going on in Europe in the first place. I was born in the Sixties, and I'd grown up at a time when war in Europe was seen as history, and everything was very stable. So it seemed strange that the war was happening at all, and then doubly strange that it didn't seem to affect things in England that much. Of course you saw it on the news, you thought it was terrible, but it actually didn't make much difference. Because you'd thought of wars in Europe, the First or Second World Wars, as the most important thing in your life. Even the Spanish Civil War. Everything you read was about people going off to Spain and writing about it.

LB: Like Hemingway.

MW: Exactly. Whereas you were reading about [Yugoslavia] every day but it didn't connect. So when I saw the script it seemed like a chance to find out what was really happening there and make a film about it.

LB: So it had been bothering you for a while.

MW: But only in the way it bothered everyone.

LB: Well, I'm not interviewing everyone. I'm interviewing you!

MW: [laughter] What I'm saying is, I don't feel I had a special connection. I was aware of it, but also feeling disconnected as well.

LB: Where did you grow up?

MW: In Blackburn, Lancashire, a small industrial town in the north of England.

LB: You studied English at Oxford, but didn't become a writer.

MW: No, I can't write. I like reading. It's much easier than writing. Then I took a post-graduate film course at the University of Bristol, and another film course in London. At the same time I was a trainee editor at Thames Television. And then I got a chance to work with Lindsay Anderson on a documentary about British cinema that he was making, and after that I made a documentary about Ingmar Bergman. I wasn't really ever a journalist. Then for three of four years I directed a detective thing called *Cracker* for TV, which I think is being shown in the U.S. I also did a Roddy Doyle series called *Family.*

LB: So the plight of the journalist in *Welcome to Sarajevo* wasn't something you'd been agonizing over because you yourself had been in a similar predicament.

MW: No. Not at all. And I hope how the film works is that what the journalists feel and experience is a more acute form of what everyone can feel and experience. It's not specific to them. They're in that quandary of being right there, and not being able to do anything about it, but that's what everyone feels when they watch on TV what the journalists have witnessed firsthand. The original screenplay was more particularly about one journalist and his adopting a girl.

LB: The screenplay was based on the book, *Natasha's Story.*

MW: Yes, written by Jeffrey Case. I read the book as well, but I wanted the film to be about lots of characters, not just one. So that's when Frank Cottrell Boyce came on and we started working on another draft of the screenplay together.

LB: He's a long time collaborator of yours?

MW: Yes. I met him briefly at [Oxford] University and then he wrote things I did for television.

LB: Had you been to Sarajevo before?

MW: No. It wasn't clear whether it would be possible to shoot in Sarajevo, because the war was still on at the time. We worked on the screenplay at the beginning of '95.

LB: When did the war end?

MW: The peace agreement was in December '95. When we finished the script it was about May '95. I had already agreed to make *Jude,* based on the Thomas Hardy novel, so I went away and shot that and finished filming it in January '96, and by that time the peace agreement had just been signed. That's when we first went to Sarajevo, January '96.

LB: What was it like making the film in immediate postwar conditions?

MW: Well, obviously there are practical problems. When we first went there it was very hard to telephone from Sarajevo. Roads weren't great. It used to take about two days to get there because you had to drive in from the airport in another part of Croatia. The water supply . . . We had to clear land mines.

That was the only real danger. We had to be careful. But there was no war going on once we were filming. The situation was relatively stable. In fact, the main problem was persuading the financiers that it was safe enough to film there.

LB: Did they make you get extra high insurance?

MW: Yes, and we also had to do some interiors in Macedonia because they wanted to know whether we had somewhere else to go if we couldn't go on filming in Sarajevo. It was like an extra insurance policy. Channel 4 developed the screenplay. They had agreed to finance half of it, and then Miramax came in before we started filming. The budget was $6 or $7 million, because we had to go to so many places. It was quite expensive from the travel point of view,

LB: Did you rely a lot on actual news footage of the war?

MW: Actually, there's only about ten minutes of news footage in total but it feels like a lot more because it's interspersed throughout the film in very brief moments.

LB: How did the cast come together?

MW: What was interesting about the situation [in Sarajevo], was that the journalists come in from outside and they're constantly meeting the local people. The script called for lots of children who had to be Bosnian and therefore had no experience acting and no English in most cases, and a lot of them were refugees. So they were essentially being themselves. Then we had to have Bosnian, British and American actors. Inevitably it was going to be a strange mix of cast. Quite an unusual range of experience and approaches and cultural backgrounds.

LB: I wondered how you picked the actors . . .

MW: I'd seen Kerry Fox in Jane Campion's films and also she'd done some British TV I was trying to find a mix of people who'd be interesting together.

LB: How did Woody Harrelson get involved in the project?

MW: We had the character called Flynn already [the American freelance journalist], and when we took the screenplay to Miramax he was already supposed to be "the star." We already had the line, "No one knows about Sarajevo in America, but everyone knows me." The script required, in a perfect world, someone who could deliver that line and be believable, and it was lucky that Woody had seen *Jude*—Miramax had arranged for him to see it—and liked it. We met up in Berlin very briefly. At the time, he had just done a few films back to back and wasn't really looking for a film, but the subject matter, the fact that we were going to film in Sarajevo, must have persuaded him it would be an interesting film to work on. Having someone as known as Woody was great because his image and reputation mirrored the image and reputation that journalists were supposed to have in the film.

LB: Other than British and U.S., wouldn't there have been French and German and Italian journalists in Sarajevo?

MW: We wondered about it, but in fact, especially from Frank's point of view writing it, it was difficult enough to imagine the Bosnians' experience as well as the British and the Americans' and we felt the script had enough range. Every nationality had journalists there. But the film already felt as if it was lots of people's stories.

LB: You didn't want it to be too fragmented.

MW: Yeah. And adding another culture to the mix would have been difficult.

LB: *Natasha's Story* was written by a journalist who'd been covering wars for 25 years, so he was quite a bit older than your Henderson character, who seems more like 35,36—your age.

MW: Probably it was subconscious, I felt more comfortable with that age. We thought Stephen [Dillane], who'd done mainly theater in England, would be great for the lead and therefore went in that direction. But [in the casting] we looked at actors older than Stephen as well. Also, we weren't trying to imitate the book. We decided quite early on it was just a question of what worked best dramatically. And it felt like the character should be someone at the peak of his career, still ambitious, old enough to be a senior journalist, which he is. Henderson is close to forty and perfectly capable of being the main foreign correspondent of a TV station, yet he's someone who still has a lot to lose. He wasn't like someone who was about to retire anyway and was disillusioned simply because he'd been through it all and had enough. If anything, there was more at stake than if the character had been a lot older. But the basic thing was that we'd met Stephen and thought he'd be great for the part.

LB: How did you meet him?

MW: We'd seen him in a Beckett play at Donmar Warehouse in Covent Garden.

LB: Do you yourself have any ambivalence about the role journalists play in society?

MW: When they do surveys of the least trusted profession, journalists always get the worst ratings from the public. What was interesting about Sarajevo was that obviously it was a very dangerous situation and journalists were risking their lives, and a lot of journalists were killed. But also a lot of journalists became very committed to the story, leaving aside their individual morality. There was a lot of reporting in England which said, we're showing what's happening, and also, something's got to be done to stop it. Newspapers like *The Guardian* and *The Independent* were running real campaigning [advocacy] stories saying, the government must do something, everyone's sitting by and watching this happen and it's terrible. So journalists were fulfilling the true role of the journalist which is to show you what's happening in the world, show you are connected to those events and that some action should be taken. I like the fact that the film is about a very moral bunch of journalists. The Flynn character that Woody Harrelson plays seems much more frivolous and lighthearted than

Henderson, the English character, but in the end they're all doing the same job which is getting the stories out of Sarajevo. I like that.

LB: It seems that we go through cycles. During Vietnam, journalists were seen as heroes, as in *The Killing Fields,* which Chris Menges shot.

MW: Watching all the documentary material of Sarajevo, there were numerous occasions when you see something terrible happening. Someone's hit in the street. Someone's shot, a shell goes off. The next second, there are 25 photographers taking pictures of someone as they die. It's a complicated thing. But equally, if you don't have people taking those pictures, you never know about it. For people watching that, the first reaction is horrific: How can those people just come and take a photograph of that person instead of doing something about it? But equally they have to get the picture. There's no way of resolving that contradiction. As a film crew going in after the war, we felt a little uneasy being a Western film crew, bringing in all those resources we needed to make the film into a city which had just been through a terrible war.

LB: And suffering from economic disaster.

MW: Exactly. But in doing that we worked with a lot of Sarajevans. Any money that gets spent there is a good thing. Nevertheless, you still feel uncomfortable about it. I'm sure from a journalist's point of view, being in a city where this was happening, that unease is even more extreme because people are getting shot all around and they're relatively secure. They fly back out, they have their flight jackets, they have their armored land rover.

LB: They're still privileged.

MW: Yeah, relatively.

LB: In the film, Henderson actually has two moral crises to go through: fulfilling his promise to Emira to get her out, and once he does, whether to return Emira to her mother or not. Was that in the original story?

MW: What happened with Nicholson the journalist in the original story is exactly what happened to Henderson in the film: When he got back to London with Emira, he realized there was a mother and he therefore had to get adoption papers. When we were working on the script there were suggestions that we should drop that second half of the story. The traditional climax of the film would be: the journey out of Sarajevo, and having got Emira out, that's the end of the film. She's safe; he's got her; he's done the heroic thing. It always felt like that would be too pat, a distortion. If it worked, that sense of him returning to Sarajevo and having to face up to the mother, and having her give her blessing for what he'd done would be more interesting and truer to the situation. We tried to avoid reducing it to one act of heroism, like "save the girl." We wanted to make it more psychologically true, so that he gradually falls into doing what he does. It's not a big dramatic moment where he suddenly sees the light and is converted and then takes action. It's more that he's drawn and sucked into it. And it's only once he's committed to Emira that he realizes the implications, and one of them is going back and getting Emira's mother to agree he's done the right thing.

LB: How did you achieve the incredibly disorienting effect of being at war in the first 10–15 minutes of the film?

MW: A lot of things I do are for half thought about reasons because it feels right. War in Europe is something I'd been taught as history, it wasn't going to happen in my lifetime. Seeing these images from Vukovar that could have been the total destruction of the town—it was hardly possible for me to believe it was happening. So at the beginning of the film, to take the image from black and white to color . . .

LB: Took it from the past to the present.

MW: Yeah.

LB: The jolting hand held camera movements were really unsettling too. You literally don't know where you are, things are coming at you from left and right.

MW: One of the experiences of going there was to see the incredible jumble of contradictions—when you go through a town trying to imagine, where was one side, where was the other side. It was an integrated place originally. One side of a block of flats would be completely destroyed, the other side would be completely lived in. I wanted to get that across, that war isn't a big great homogeneous whole, it's more like lots of weird events. One minute everything's quiet and you can be having a drink in the bar and the next minute, someone's shooting at you in the street. The more jumbled up and contradictory I wanted things to appear, the sharper the cuts between shots.

LB: I suppose your sense of place and direction, of being able to get from A to B, is totally shattered when shells explode and great chunks of physical matter disappear.

MW: For instance the flats that Risto, the translator, lives in in the film—a guy who took us there showed us how at different times during the war he would sleep in a different room. At one point he'd think, this room is safe, there can't be any sniper fire here, and then suddenly there'd be sniper fire there one evening, or in the next room or the next room. It was impossible to tell where the danger was coming from because they were completely surrounded by sniper fire, you'd never know which was the safe direction. We wanted to capture what it was like to live there through that.

Originally published in *Bomb*.

Samira Makhmalbaf

The Apple

I wanted for *this* father and for *these* daughters to have to change their lives.

Samira Makhmalbaf, 1999

At eighteen, Samira Makhmalbaf is the youngest filmmaker ever to show a feature in competition at the Cannes Film Festival. Set in her native Tehran, *The Apple* is based on the true account of a father who, in an attempt to shield his twelve-year-old

Samira Makhmalbaf, director of *The Apple* (2000, Iran) at the Festival de Cannes press conference. Photo © Liza Béar.

twin daughters from anything he perceives as threatening to their Islamic faith, had kept them under a sort of house arrest—feeding them only rice and refusing to bathe them—since birth. After seeing a local news report on the family, Makhmalbaf cajoled child welfare authorities into letting her make a semi-fictional sequel to the story and then convinced the father and daughters to play themselves. The result is not only an indictment of extremist patriarchal values, it's a chance for the girls to reclaim their lost childhood.

"I wanted for *this* father and for *these* daughters to have to change their lives," says Makhmalbaf, who drew convincing, natural performances from her cast. At the outset, the girls could barely speak.

Makhmalbaf herself is emblematic of Iran's emerging feminist spirit: having grown up watching her father, award-winning Iranian director Mohsen Makhmalbaf (*Gabbeh*) on the sets of his movies, she dropped out of high school at fifteen and persuaded him to teach her filmmaking. "It was harder to order people older than me around," she says, "but only for the first five minutes."

Originally published in *Elle*.

SAMIRA MAKHMALBAF

Blackboards

When we are wandering, we have to carry what we need with us. In our minds, too, ignorance and pain are baggage.

Samira Makhmalbaf, 2003

Samira Makhmalbaf's second film, *Blackboards,* a highly original story about itinerant Kurdish schoolteachers, was shot in the forbidding mountains of Iranian Kurdistan. Shown in competition at Cannes, like *The Apple,* the film won the jury prize.

Makhmalbaf is the elder daughter of director Mohsen Makhmalbaf. He co-wrote and edited *Blackboards* and *The Apple,* and if that's an argument for a return to the apprentice system or a testament to family values, so be it. Now aged 22, Makhmalbaf lost her mother in a fire at the age of eight, and quit Islamic high school at 15. The film school, Makhmalbaf Film House, started by her father at Samira's instigation, coproduces features by Mohsen, Samira and her stepmother Marziyeh, as well as short subjects by siblings Hana and Maysam.

That both of Samira Makhmalbaf's films center on education is no coincidence. When *The Apple* was released in 1998, its success in Iran turned Makhmalbaf into a role model not only for women there but for all young people. In *Blackboards,* the obstacles to education are not religious beliefs bu the vagaries of the terrain and of recent historical events.

Full of strikingly poetic images and rich in allusions, the film is set near the Iraqi border and features an almost all-Kurdish, non-professional cast.

NO FRIENDS BUT THE MOUNTAINS

An estimated 20 million Kurds, most of whom are Sunni Muslims with their own language and cultural identity, live in a contiguous mountain region that straddles the borders of Armenia, Iran, Iraq, Syria and Turkey. The 1920 Treaty

Production still from Samira Makhmalbaf's second feature, *Blackboards* (2002, Iran) about itinerant schoolteachers in the mountains of Iranian Kurdistan. Courtesy of Photofest.

of Sèvres, which carved up the former Ottoman Empire into the modern states of Iraq, Kuwait and Syria, was to have included a state of Kurdistan, but it was never created. The Kurds have had and still get rough treatment at the hands of their host countries. As a Kurdish saying goes, they have "no friends but the mountains."

Blackboards begins with a dozen or so Kurdish trained teachers, heavy blackboards strapped to their backs like an unwieldy carapace, discussing the previous day's unsuccessful hunt for pupils.

Two teachers, Said (Said Mohamadi) and Reeboir (Bahman Ghobadi, the director of another Kurdish-Iranian film, *A Time for Drunken Horses*) decide to go their separate ways, splitting the film's narrative in two.

Said eventually meets a group of 100 or so old men accompanied by a woman and child. The men, who in 1988 fled their homes in Iraq to escape a poison-gas attack that killed their fellow villagers, are now trying to return to their birthplace to die. Reeboir, meanwhile, meets up with a group of adolescent boys smuggling goods across the border to Iraq.

Makhmalbaf met both groups while shooting the film and included them in the script. In addition to dire living conditions and hazardous terrain, the Kurds face the threats of bombardment from helicopter gunships, the avalanches and the uncertainty of mountain weather.

For the filmmaker, the mountains offered a dramatic landscape and color palette. But the weather presented a tremendous logistical challenge.

"I had a very good connection with the weather," said Makhmalbaf during an interview at the Cannes Film Festival. "I wanted a certain look for the film, so I was waiting for the right weather: fog." The fog arrived, but the crew had other ideas, she recalled.

"The crew came to me and said, 'We are not going to shoot.' 'Very good,' I answered, 'We are going to shoot.' We had to drive for two hours; I was chasing the fog."

Makhmalbaf said she had to work hard to shoot the day's scenes before the fog dissipated, for the sake of continuity.

"All I had to work with were these simple people, the mountains, and nature," said Makhmalbaf, "so I had to make the most out of it visually. I decided that all the colors of the people's costumes should merge with the landscape."

Makhmalbaf had to persuade the actress who marries Said in the film and gets his blackboard as a dowry that her clothes should not be brighter than anyone else's, because she already stood out as a woman. "I was often caught between humanistic and artistic decisions," the director said.

> "In this film there's a thin line between the imagination of art and the reality of life. To me, when reality and imagination make love, that's the moment that art or metaphors are born."

For Makhmalbaf, language did not present a special problem because the Iranian Kurdish dialect is close to her native Farsi. She was able to communicate directly with the cast in Farsi and double-check with bilingual assistants from the area and, by the end of the shoot, she says, she understood all the Kurdish dialogue.

"You need to make things easy for yourself when you are a director," said Makhmalbaf, who has been on the set of her father's films since she was eight. "Although I like to shoot in continuity, I shot the two groups, the boys and the old men, separately. Sometimes I had to decide on the exact sequences and precise shots the day before to take advantage of the weather."

For the Kurds in the film, basic survival needs trump the acquisition of reading and writing skills. It's hard to imagine a more dramatic setting for teaching and learning than the situation in which they live. But the story's narrative momentum is reinforced by the roles the blackboards play: they serve as defensive shields, shelter against the elements, stretchers, partitions, and a marriage dowry; one is even broken up to make splints. They act as a visual storytelling device that reinforces the two principal lines of action.

While the historical context is important, Makhmalbaf says the image of the blackboard was central in her concept of the film and that she was more interested in its metaphorical references.

"When we are wandering, we have to carry what we need with us," said Makhmalbaf. "In our minds, too, ignorance and pain are baggage. Desire, pain, and everything. Also happiness."

Makhmalbaf explained that for the old men in the film, the burden was the memory of the Iran-Iraq war and of the homeland to which they wished to return.

"Knowledge can be a heavy burden to carry," said Makhmalbaf, who's now in Afghanistan working on a new movie. "In this film there's a thin line between the imagination of art and the reality of life. To me, when reality and imagination make love, that's the moment that art or metaphors are born. The reality in this film is smuggling, poverty, wandering, being a refugee. But my choice as an artist is to show them visually and beautifully. Art is imagination."

Originally published in the *Boston Globe*.

FERNANDA MONTENEGRO
Central Station

Montenegro is a Brazilian icon, comparable to Gena Rowlands, Melina Mercouri or Vanessa Redgrave . . . She's also a human rights activist who's participated in the movement against dictatorship and against all forms of repression. She had the courage to take on an unglamorous role with no make-up, no veils.

Walter Salles, director, 1999

March 14, 1999—For Fernanda Montenegro, the initial drama of the news has not worn off. It may never wear off.

"You can't imagine how happy I am," said the doyenne of Brazilian stage and screen and now Academy Award nominee, in a telephone interview from Los Angeles.

Montenegro is the first Brazilian to receive a Best Actress nomination—for one of her rare wide-screen roles as the cranky Dora in Walter Salles's road movie *Central Station,* itself nominated for Best Foreign Film.

Although Montenegro is no stranger to awards—her performance as Dora has already won acting honors from the Berlin Film Festival and the Los Angeles Film Critics Association, she said the experience of receiving the Oscar nomination was "strong, beautiful and unexpected—like a dream."

A surfeit of happiness is not exactly the plight of the disgruntled Dora, the *Central Station* role written for the veteran stage actress by Salles. To round out her measly teacher's pension, Dora works as a public scribe in the train station lobby, writing letters for illiterate commuters with inordinate faith in the power of the word. She stuffs the letters in a drawer without mailing them. Then, very grudgingly, she takes 10-year-old Joshue (Vinicius de Oliveira) under her wing when a bus in front of the station kills his mother, one of her clients. The film turns into an odyssey for these unlikely traveling companions when Dora accompanies Joshue in the search for his father across the somber landscapes of northeastern Brazil. Bit by bit, she regains her zest for life.

In an interview before her nomination, Montenegro—at 69, svelte, chic, debonair, full of joie de vivre and radiating contagious energy and warmth—appeared the polar opposite of the fatigued, battle worn and vulnerable Dora. But as a second generation Brazilian, most of whose family came from Sardinia in 1897 during a huge migration, Montenegro said that she could relate to Dora's occupation as a letter writer because her own maternal grandmother, an Italian immigrant, was illiterate, and as a child, she used to read to her.

For Salles, the collaboration with the veteran actress was a coup and the fulfillment of a 10-year ambition. "Montenegro is a Brazilian icon, comparable to Gena Rowlands, Melina Mercouri or Vanessa Redgrave," said Salles. "She's not only the most respected stage actress in Brazil but she's also a human rights activist who's participated in the movement against dictatorship and against all forms of repression. She had the courage to take on an unglamorous role with no make-up, with no veils," he said. "She also understood that the boy was a little warrior who was fighting for his voice in such an honest manner that she very generously set aside her 40 years of Stanislavski technique to find a common denominator with him."

Montenegro, who still puts on plays with her husband, actor Fernando Torres, said her 50-year career "feels like 100 years because I'm always working in theater and TV at the same time. Double track."

Apart from a 5-day break at her coastal Ipanema, Rio de Janeiro, home, Montenegro said that since November she had been working nonstop to promote *Central Station.*

And what will *Central Station's* two nominations mean for Brazilian cinema?

"For our cinema: wonderful," said Montenegro, "because we are now showing that we can make films. It is not easy to make films in Brazil, because we don't have an [established] industry. Far from it. So each film is a great proof of love, of a vocation. Each film that crosses our borders and makes it abroad is a great [triumph] . . . a great possibility for the future. And I think *Central Station* has this humanistic quality which is recognized internationally. Movies are the first and foremost way of showing your country to others."

As for winning an Oscar, Montenegro hesitated to say whether her life would change.

"Ah . . . I think so," she said, "but not too much. I don't think about it any more because I don't want my expectations to get too high. Just being nominated is so wonderful."

Montenegro said she hopes Torres, her son Claudio, a theater director and set designer, and her daughter, Fernanda, also an actress, will fly to Los Angeles from Brazil for the ceremony.

Should it come to an acceptance speech, Montenegro said she would rely on the inspiration of the moment for her list of thank-yous. For now, she prefers to enjoy the moment.

"My home is full of flowers and telegrams and calls and visits, constantly," said Montenegro, "In the streets, too. I have never had [an experience] . . . like that. Today I thought, I am like an old Cinderella."

CATHERINE BREILLAT
Romance

There's a very direct and frontal aspect to my films. I shoot actors and actresses with an attention and an acuity that's almost entomological. I want to register the most minute tremors of emotion . . . I see women as both very aggressive and also very vulnerable.

Catherine Breillat, 1999

August 14, 1999—Part sexual farce, part gender revenge fantasy, *Romance* is the first of Catherine Breillat's six resolutely irreverent films, made over a 20-year-period, to get a U.S. theatrical release, opening nationally in October.[1] What took so long? After all, the films—*Une Vraie Jeune Fille, Parfait Amour, Tapage Nocturne, 36 Fillette* among them—are noted for their frank depictions of sexual themes, an approach which won so-called mainstream "soft core" success for *I am Curious Yellow* (1967), *Emmanuelle* (1974), and *Last Tango in Paris* (1972). Even in Europe, *Une Vraie Jeune Fille* (1976) took 23 years to be released. Maybe it is Breillat's own insolent blend of French metaphysics, Kieslowskian visual syle and a no-holds-barred approach to subject matter (a 14-year-old girl is determined to lose her virginity in *36 Fillette,* for instance).

Entirely told from the woman's point of view, her latest, the ironically-titled *Romance* tracks the sexual odyssey of 22-year-old elementary schoolteacher Marie (Caroline Ducey), whose live-in boyfriend Paul (Sagamore Stevenin) has not had sex with her for three months. (The script makes Paul a fashion model, supposedly to underscore his self-absorption.) Rather than fine tuning her seduction strategy, Marie defiantly goes on the prowl, abandoning herself physically to all comers. Her heart, though, still belongs to Paul. (That Cartesian mind-body dualism is still engrained in the French psyche.) She soon ventures into shady terrain. After rough sex (cunnilingus plus violent sodomy) with a street pick-up,

---

[1] This year the Rotterdam Film Festival showed a retrospective of her films.

Caroline Ducey and Sagamore Stevenin in *Romance* (1999, France), directed by Catherine Breillat. Courtesy of Photofest.

spread-eagled on the apartment stairs, she gravitates to stud Paolo (Italian porn star Rocco Siffredi) who is visibly better hung than Paul, but does not love her, alas. Initially, her nocturnal flings are accompanied by a diaristic voice-over, so we know that she retains her lucidity even as her physical self goes to pieces and that it's all *her choice,* the official feminist bottom line. Fortunately, Breillat spares us the obligatory neo Freudian child abuse flashback sequence à la Hillary Clinton, blaming current depravation on earlier experiences. Opting for existential tableaux rather than the cause and effect thing, Breillat nevertheless manages some deft segues. In a hilarious classroom scene, Marie's increasingly dissipated appearance flags the attention of school principal, Robert (François Berléand of *Seventh Heaven*), a bondage aficionado who initiates her into the twin thrills of S&M and caviar. Who better than your employer? We never see her again in the classroom after that.

Framing its frontal nudity in a Good Housekeeping, all white décor, its set pieces an elaborate bondage sequence and an in-your-face childbirth scene, its denouement packing the retaliatory violence of a Valerie Solanas, *Romance* aims for sacrilege while idolizing the profane.

White in *Romance* is by turn bridal, clinical, sacrificial, ultimately seraphic. Transposing from religion for the purposes of parody the love of ritual and self-degradation, Breillat clearly has her roots in Catholicism and post-existential French literature (Georges Bataille's *Blue of Noon*) as well as in the Marquis de Sade. (At the ages of nine and ten, she and her sister, sequestered by their parents because of early puberty, were nevertheless allowed to devour the adult section of their local library in Nyors, a small town south of Poitiers in the French provinces, also home to Georges Clouzot. At 13, her bedside reading was Lautréamont's *Le Chant de Maldoror*.)

Although boyfriend Paul is finally turned on by Marie's hard won sexual ecstasy (think Emily Watson in *Breaking the Waves* sacrificing her sexual integrity for her man's titillation), Breillat presumably has no interest in dramatizing the very common predicament of the passive-aggressive sex partner. The last straw for Marie is that Paul makes her pregnant from preseminal fluid, which sparks a drastic, final response from Marie; nevertheless, the film plays more as a deadpan minimalist spoof on sexual mores than as a relationship film.

"There's a very direct and frontal aspect to my films," said Breillat. "I shoot actors and actresses with an attention and an acuity that's almost entomological. I want to register the most minute tremors of emotion . . . I see women as both very aggressive and also very vulnerable."

Breillat said she had written the role of Marie for a 30-year-old woman. However, when she tried to cast the part, she realized she needed someone much younger.

"There's a sadomasochistic side to Marie's character and in a 30 year-old that would seem perverse," said Breillat, 50, mother of three (26, 19 and 7) by different fathers. "I wanted Marie to be like an angel, heroic. There's this fiery excess to her. Young girls can drag themselves through the mud yet remain very pure. There's a kind of rapture, of idealized purity, which you can only find on a young girl's face. A woman may stay adolescent much longer than her physical appearance. But since cinema deals with physical appearances, I cast a really young actress."

Appealingly slender, pert, small-breasted and slightly cross-eyed, Caroline Ducey has exactly the right louche aspect for the role of Marie, never losing her sang froid and delivering a courageous performance in potentially compromising scenes, such as the lengthy bondage sequence which is almost totally shot in real time. Gagged, bound and tied (with white rope, of course) to a window, the scene is played out in macro detail to show that Marie sexually enjoys the proceedings, at least until she breaks down. Fortunately, the actress only had to go through it once.

"I like to feel the vibrations, the small losses of actor control," said Breillat. "The longer the scene, the more tension and violence it contains. It took us a while to find out how to tie the rope. I wanted to make a figure of a cross as in a Mondrian painting, with the same proportions. The act of tying had to look simple and clean for the purposes of the film, not too fast and not too slow. The rehearsal take was the one we used," Breillat said, "because I was struck by the strangeness and beauty of the scene. Caroline looked as though her soul was leaving her body, as though she was living a kind of death. Then I burst into tears because I thought maybe I'd gone too far [with her]. The scene was like a death and then a redemption."

While other feminists may vehemently strive to deny any soupçon of victimhood, Breillat, enfant terrible that she is, reinstates the pursuit of extreme sensation, even at the pleasure-pain threshold, for its own sake, and stages it cinematically with a quasi-religious fervor.

"Romanticism is dark, somber," Breillat said. "For the purposes of marketing, they've made it pink and blue. I think you have to accept your passions and understand them . . . Cinema for me is a leap into the void. You mustn't be afraid of putting yourself in extreme danger."

Breillat explains that she wanted to use explicit scenes in her film so as to reclaim sexual representation from the pornography industry, and to restore some dignity to the portrayal of human sexuality.

"The 'pornography' in *Romance* has nothing to do with the institution of pornography," Breillat said, "but is an attempt at a humane representation of sex. Cinema must film human functions in a noble manner. It's our duty."

Originally published in *Bomb*.

HAYAO MIYAZAKI

Princess Mononoke

One of the major themes I had to confront once I decided to make a film based on historic Japan was how to free myself from the grip of restrictions that Kurosawa had [established]. Although most of the characters in *Princess Mononoke* have not been "the main actors" in Japanese history, they are the people who have supported and carried its history forward on their backs.

Hayao Miyazaki, 1999

October 28, 1999—Meteorologically speaking, with the recent spate of earthquakes, hurricanes and floods around the ever-warming globe, this could hardly be a more apt time for the release of *Princess Mononoke,* which explores the archetypical conflict between man and nature. Set in a virgin forest and loosely based on Japanese folklore, this anime feature by master animator Hayao Miyazaki depicts funky, feisty female protagonists, giant bristling supernatural monsters and rival factions all vying for supremacy in an almost mythical, wooded landscape.

Mononoke introduces archer Ashitaka (voiced for the film's English incarnation by Billy Crudup), who brings a curse upon himself when he is wounded by a boarlike monster that was threatening his village. After killing the beast, Ashitaka learns that it was a god that protected the forest. As he travels across the mountains in search of a cure for the infection that is spreading over his body, he gets drawn into a raging battle between warring clans. He then has the arduous task of convincing a ferocious young woman warrior, San (Claire Danes), aka Princess Mononoke (*mononoke* means half-wolf, half-human), to adopt the peacemaker role and stop the carnage.

The Japanese animation house Studio Ghibli, cofounded in 1984 by Miyazaki and Isao Takahata, created the film. (An aficionado of Italian culture, Miyazaki named the studio after an old Italian airplane he was crazy about.) Ghibli's output is notable for its intensity, detail and superb craftsmanship and is revered by many American animation heavies, including John Lasseter (*A Bug's Life, Toy Story*). The serious-minded *Mononoke* has been hailed as the studio's crowning technical achievement.

Miyazaki, 58, is utterly forthright, with a wry sense of humor that casts his uncompromisingly bleak view of the future into sharp relief. He's also refreshingly low-key about his role in creating the second highest-grossing movie in Japanese history, trailing only *Titanic*. "I don't really know why *Princess Mononoke* was such a monstrous hit in Japan," he says, speaking through an interpreter. "But I imagine that the film awakened something that was long slumbering inside people's hearts."

Miyazaki found inspiration in the film's 14th-century setting. "That is the age during which Japan as we now know it was formed," he says. "Broadly speaking, during the 14th and 15th centuries, there was a power shift. Up until then, the gods had had more power; after the 15th century, humans had more power. In our own times, the balance of power has shifted again. [We are trying to] escape from a nature that can no longer regenerate itself. Historically speaking," he concludes, "our situation is hopeless."

The Tokyo-born animator was obsessed with drawing by the time he attended Tokyo University as an economics major. "[Drawing] became a duty," he recalls. "I would study just enough to keep from flunking out, and all the rest of the time I drew." But Miyazaki's career epiphany came when the 18-year-old college student saw *The Legend of the White Serpent* (1956). "It's actually a very simple, straightforward romantic love story," Miyazaki recalls. "But for me it was salvation." He began his professional career in animation by drawing *manga* (Japanese comic books); in the succeeding years, he worked at different animation studios. His career breakthrough was *Nausicaa of the Valley of the Wind* (1984), his own adaptation of his graphic novel about industrial pollution.

"My aim is to draw the world that the characters inhabit as fully as possible," says Miyazaki. "To be as sensitive to the seasons, the light, the rain, the history of that world as to the characters themselves." During the creation of more than 144,000 cels for *Mononoke*, Miyazaki supervised a team of 50 full-time and 30 part-time animators. "The computer was used only to manipulate some of the images," he says. "Basically, every picture was drawn. My job as a director is to look at all the drawn images and refine them."

Samurai, peasants and feudal overlords are notably absent from *Mononoke*'s legion of characters. Instead of depicting a traditional Japanese social hierarchy, Miyazaki focuses on strong female protagonists (also hallmarks of his earlier films) and craftsmen who manufacture arms in a fortresslike iron works on the edge of the forest.

In the film, Miyazaki combines an egalitarian social philosophy—a desire to set the record straight—with a Faustian view of man's nature. "One of the major themes I had to confront once I decided to make a film based on historic Japan was how to free myself from the grip of restrictions that Kurosawa had [established]," says Miyazaki. "Although most of the characters in *Princess Mononoke* have not been what you would call the 'main actors' in Japanese history, they are the people who have supported and carried its history forward on their backs."

On the heels of a contract between Disney and Studio Ghibli's distributor, the Miramax-distributed *Mononoke* is the first Japanese animation feature to be released theatrically in the U.S. by a major studio. Although sometimes-gruesome battle scenes earned the film a PG-13 rating, the brutality is anything but titillating. And Miyazaki takes a clear stand on violence: "I do not approve of any kind of film, video games, any kind of media, Japanese or otherwise, that tries to make a buck by depicting violence or that sells a film on the strength of the violence." He also has reservations about the effects of animation on children. "[In Japan,] animation gobbles children for breakfast and robs them of their time and their freedom. I realize that I belong to that [problem]," he concedes. "I think one great animated film per year is plenty for a child."

Originally published in *Time Out New York*.

ZHANG YIMOU

Not One Less

I personally like very strong characters. Only with strong characters can you create drama. And in China you have to have a strong character in order to get anything done.

Zhang Yimou, 2000

Wei Minzhi, a 13-year-old schoolgirl who needs money, takes on the job of substitute teacher in an isolated mountain village school while the regular teacher cares for his sick mother. Rural families are so destitute that the mayor is more concerned with keeping the kids in school than with her teaching methods in the one-room school-house; Wei Minzhi is promised an extra 10 Yuan if not one child has quit by the end of the month. When the class troublemaker takes off for the city to seek work, the other kids rally to Wei's support and help her get to the city to look for him. In this moving, thoroughly engrossing story, a smart, often hilarious script and first-rate performances offer a sympathetic but scathing look at the state of rural education in China.

January 29, 2000, 9 A.M.: Breakfast at the Mayflower Hotel, Central Park, New York. Norman Wang translates from Mandarin.

Liza Béar: What were you doing in Las Vegas?

Zhang Yimou: I went to Las Vegas to see the production of Cirque du Soleil, because I'm planning to do an opera.[1] I've been to Las Vegas three times. I don't like to gamble nor do I like to drink. So every time I go there, I get very annoyed and stay in the hotel room while my friends gamble. This time I noticed that they have agent representatives from the casinos, just to handle Asian clients

---

[1] Zhang Yimou directed an international coproduction of *Turandot* at the Forbidden City of Beijing in 1999. He will direct *First Emperor* at the Metropolitan Opera in New York in 2008.

Zhang Yimou, director, at the Mayflower Hotel, New York, during an interview for *Not One Less* (1999, China) a story about a 13-year-old substitute teacher in a village school. Photo © Liza Béar.

because there are so many. For Chinese people, the image of gambling is very recognizable, how it can change your fate. But even though I'm not a gambler, it's something I like to appropriate.

LB: *To Live* is a portrait of China in the '40s, '50s and '60s. Is *Not One Less* in some sense a portrait of China in the late '90s? Is this the new China?

ZY: First of all, I can't say that one film represents the new China, because China is so complex and so big.

LB: But one element of new China.

ZY: *Not One Less* can only point to the life of poor, rural China, village life, particularly in the school. It's also attempting to show the differences between city and villages.

LB: But the outspoken feistiness of the children, and especially the girls in the class—seem very fresh and modern.

ZY: I personally like very strong characters. Only with strong characters can you create drama. And in China you need to be strong in order to get anything done.

LB: The 13-year-old substitute teacher has the stubbornness of Qiu Ju, in *The Story of Qiu Ju*. Beyond strong, she is obstinate.

ZY: Definitely. Because in China human interventions create obstacles to your plans. To overcome them, you need a very strong personality. Just like in moviemaking. We have to deal with economics, the market—and also with censors. If we don't insist on what we believe in, then it's very hard to make films.

LB: How hard was it to make *Not One Less*?

ZY: The biggest challenge of this film was how to work with these non-professional actors. The selection process went on for months and months. After we found them, we had to find a way to communicate with them. The story was filmed chronologically. We didn't give them a script but told them what might happen—common incidents from real life that they are familiar with. Instead of feeding them lines, we wanted them to use their own words. To make this kind of film, I have to create an atmosphere for the crew and for the cast that is very relaxed. What is filmmaking? You can't let the kids worry about how much celluloid costs. It costs more than what they make a year. And everyone has to be relaxed except me. I'm the one who needs to make choices . . . But I cannot show my stress. If I show it, then people can feel it and it would affect the whole thing. If you had visited our set, you would have imagined it . . .

LB: I wish!

ZY: . . . to be a very relaxed set, but for a director, it's far more stressful than shooting a traditional fiction film.

LB: I can imagine. Would you like to eat? We can take a break.

Translator: He says he can eat while I translate. Once he's in the mood he likes to talk.

LB: You started out as a still photographer?

ZY: I started shooting still photography in my twenties when I was working in a factory. By chance one night, a cousin of mine who likes photography—we had taken some pictures together in the past, just for fun—that night, my cousin took me to his darkroom. He was in charge of the whole [developing] process, controlling the contrast, the exposure and all that; my job was to put the print into the other solution to stabilize it. That's all I did. He wouldn't let me touch [the developing fluid]. For my cousin, it was routine. But for me, that night changed my life. I suddenly became intrigued by photography. That's how I got into the Beijing Film Academy.

LB: Did you get your own camera?

ZY: At first I borrowed my cousin's camera. It was an Hwassan, a Chinese camera, named after a mountain in that region. It cost 8 yuan, about $1, and tiny. At first I didn't know what I was doing. Then I saved 5 Yuan each month and after two years I had enough to buy my own camera—one with two lenses. But I had nobody to teach me so I stole books from the library and copied them so I could study from them. At that point, I decided to start taking pictures. I liked to try out different compositions. And when my friends got married, they would ask me to take their wedding photos. My wedding photos were not traditional. I would take them to the seashore, to the bamboo grove; I would treat the sun as though it were the moon. I wouldn't make money but they would take me for a meal. And my photo would be displayed on the wedding day. Last year, some tv station went to the factory where I worked and interviewed an old colleague of mine. They saw my photos, because I had taken his wedding photos.

LB: What kind of factory?

ZY: Textile, in Shaanxi. I made 40 Yuan a month, about $5. It was in the '70s. I would keep my expenses, like food, to the minimum, to $3 a month. I would save $2 to buy celluloid in order to take pictures. Eventually, my photographs got the attention of the propaganda department of my factory. At that time there was a lot of unrest among the workers. I was given five rolls of film to document the uprisings in the factory. I would use three and save two. I was working the nightshift. So whenever I was taken off work for two days or so to photograph, I was very pleased, because I didn't like working the nightshift. This continued for seven to eight years.

LB: Quite an apprenticeship!

> "I was very quiet, very shy. After two years, I decided to drop out. What use would it be for someone like me to get into film? My friends agreed. They said, yes, you should quit, but get a diploma. So I asked the school for a diploma ... But the school said no, so I ended up staying there."

ZY: So when the Cultural Revolution was over, I was still in the factory. In 1978, the schools restarted. At the time, I had no idea there was a film academy or what cinematography was. A friend of mine said, look at this ad in the newspaper. It was a tiny ad for admission to the film school. I applied, but there were obstacles. For one thing, I was 28 years old and the age limit was 22. Eventually, after many detours, I got in. And honestly, I found the film school quite aristocratic [elitist], not for me. With my background, I had very low self-esteem there. I was very quiet, very shy. After two years, I decided to drop out. What use would it be for someone like me to get into film? My friends agreed. They said, yes, you should quit, but get a diploma. So I asked the school for a diploma. At the time, my dream was to return to the factory town where I'd worked, and to become a newspaper photographer. And I'd already contacted the newspaper. The newspaper said, as long as you have a diploma, we'd let you.

But the school said no, so I ended up staying there. And I guess this is why in my films, there's fate and accidents, everything changes overnight.

LB: Yes, it does. So did you grow up in a village like the one in the film?

ZY: I grew up in the city of Xi'an in Saanxi province in Northwest China. Basically, my knowledge of rural life comes from the Cultural Revolution days, when I was sent to the countryside for three years. And the village I was in was near the border of the province.

LB: The young girl who plays the teacher—she must have been really hard to find. She's a real gem.

ZY: About 40,000 girls were screened.

LB: Forty *thousand?*

ZY: The assistant director found all these faces in the age group that he thought were appropriate. I would line everyone up and videotape them. When we watched the tapes I would pause and say, I like that face. Out of the tapes I chose 150. Then they went through a series of tests, one of which was to sing a song in front of a large public. Out of that there were two girls. Wei Minzhi, [the actress chosen], came in second, not first. There was another girl who was even better. I didn't choose the other girl because when she was asked to run, I noticed her body was becoming adolescent, no longer a child. But I gave a final test. The two of them went into the city and had to yell into the street. Under my direction the number one girl could never do it. The other girl could. Later, she told me, 'I knew I got the job, because you were laughing.' These kids are very bright. The selection process was also filmed and shown in China. It was very popular.

> "I don't write my own scripts. I am involved with the script-writing process, even though my name is not on the credit. What I found is that if you write your own stories, there's a tendency to have a theme prior to the writing. And that would make the writing more conceptual."

LB: All of your films are adapted from Chinese short stories or novels. Are you very in touch with contemporary Chinese literature?

ZY: I know a lot of writers. I myself am interested in literature. But that's not the reason why all my work is based on literature. It's the principle. I don't write my own scripts. I am involved with the script-writing process, even though my name is not on the credit. What I found is that if you write your own stories, you tend to have a theme prior to the writing. And that would make the writing more conceptual. So for me, if I read a lot of literature, it's like browsing through a shop. You suddenly see something that you find interesting, that stimulates you and that inspires you to do something else. I want each of my films to be different. Also, not all the work I do is based on famous novels.

For instance, *Not One Less* is based on a novel written by an older man. It's about an older man who's a substitute teacher. And it talks about the wages, the life of this teacher, less about the search. But when I looked at this story, I got inspired.

LB: Everything in the script is set up so that you're always surprised at the turn of events . . . For instance, a lot of attention is paid to the box of white chalk that the old teacher leaves for the substitute. And you don't find out the dramatic implications until later. Was that all in the novel?

ZY: No, it's something I devised. The novella provided a framework. However, when we filmed it, I filled in the details. What happens is that details like the chalk add up and at the end you see a larger picture. That's very traditional Chinese aesthetics. From one drop of water, you can see the sky, the sun.

LB: First-rate screenwriting.

ZY: That's also something I attempt to do with the second film, *The Road Home*, the one that's going to Berlin next month.

LB: *Not One Less* also seems to be very positive about a more life-based kind of education. It's really touching to see how the kids' math skills improve when they have a real problem to solve, like calculating the number of bricks they need to move [to raise enough money for a bus ticket to the city]. And they work together as a group quite naturally. Exactly the opposite of rote learning.

ZY: I myself also believe in this kind of educational system. When I was filming the last scene of the film, I told everyone that they should write whatever they want on the blackboard, as long as they don't repeat [each other]. The only one I told what to write was the little boy; I asked him to write *way-lo-shay*, which means "teacher away." (I thought about asking them to write a paragraph or a sentence, but I realized that was a more adult idea.) And it was a long shot, because I knew that I was going to use it for the end credits. I got everybody to leave the set and the children were the only ones in the room. The only sound you hear is the chalk on the blackboard. And that process was so moving. I remember as a child, it was exactly like that, learning how to read and write these difficult Chinese characters. I felt very happy with this ending. Some of my crew members were in tears.

LB: How are we doing for time?

Translator: The next one is here. Last question?

LB: This film feels very upbeat. Are you optimistic about the future of filmmaking in China?

ZY: You can't link the ending too much to the reality of China. Many people criticize me for the ending. Because 80 percent of these missing children who go to the cities will never return. Bad things happen to them. However, I also use the end credits to give the statistics, so there's some space for the imagination to think about what's happening in contemporary China. That's my way of dealing with it.

LB: Still. The film as a whole gives a sense that problems can be overcome.

ZY: A Chinese audience might not see it the same way. They are very serious, very sad at the end of the film. It leads to a lot of discussion.

FRANÇOIS OZON

Criminal Lovers

My goal is to dig deep into a story to the place where it hurts, as Fassbinder did in his films. Not to stay with the nice, superficial side of things. . . . That's what I want from cinema—to be perturbed. I want my ideas to change . . . to be faced with a worldview that's different from my own.

François Ozon, 2000

French satirist François Ozon has been acclaimed as much for his formal ingenuity as for the hoary topics excoriated in his films—incest, murder and cannibalism among them. In New York recently to receive the Gay/Lesbian Festival Best Film Award for his latest outing, Water Drops on Burning Rocks, *an inventive adaptation of an unproduced play by the 19-year-old R. W. Fassbinder, the very suave and urbane Ozon, Parisian born and bred, now tests American theatrical waters with another foray into adolescent turbulence. Ozon's second feature,* Criminal Lovers, *is a tabloid horror story recast as a psychosexual fairy tale in which a teen couple, at the girl's instigation, kill a classmate, run off into the woods and get picked up by an ogre.*

Liza Béar: How do you find U.S. audiences?

François Ozon: Well, at the Gay/Lesbian Film Festival they're certainly not puritanical, but let's say they are very politically correct. In general, walking down the street in New York, I find people seem well-meaning. *Voilà.* Whereas in France, people are more perverse.

LB: In your mind, is there still a bourgeoisie to shock?

FO: It's true that my first film *Sitcom*, a satire of the conventional family, was seen as provocative, but that wasn't my intention. My goal is to dig deep into a story to the place where it hurts, as Fassbinder did in his films. Not to stay with the nice, superficial side of things, but to get to the point of suffering. Which means violence. The spectator may not always want to be upset, but that's what I want from cinema—to be perturbed. I want my ideas to change . . . to be faced with a worldview that's different from my own. That's what I find interesting and that's what I try to do in films.

LB: The opening sequence of *Criminal Lovers,* where Alice is sexually taunting her boyfriend Luc with S&M games, is already disturbing . . .

FO: Because Luc is blindfolded and the spectator must accept the blindfold for himself. Yes, it's an aggressive start and I like to play with the spectator, testing how far you can go. Hitchcock did that too. However, that wasn't how the script began originally. If I recut it I would start with the classroom scene where Alice reads a poem and stares at her classmate Said's back, because that scene is about desire and the fear of desire. That's the crux of the story. If she could accept her desire, there wouldn't be all these problems . . .

LB: Uhhuh, [murder as] an extreme form of sublimation. In the second part of the film they face the consequences of their action. However, they don't submit to "justice" in the traditional sense.

FO: No. What I wanted to show was that these kids—they're teenagers—like the little children in fairy tales, despise society and think they can control it. That's especially true of Alice's character. Luc is in love with her and follows her. In the woodsman Alice discovers that there's a force stronger than her in the world, and she accepts that by dying like a heroine. Whereas Luc accepts the "law" in a different way by allowing the woodsman to have sex with him—that's where the film is really perverse.

LB: Well, it's certainly very revealing.

FO: For me, in the story, the woodsman replaces "society." He's a symbolic character just like the witches and ogres in traditional fairy tales which are there as obstacles for the main characters to overcome. For Luc the woodsman's dictates are sexual, but then that's how Luc's own desires are revealed.

LB: In both these films—*Water Drops* and *Criminal Lovers*—there's an adolescent, apparently heterosexual couple, in which the guy is not able to make love to the girl, and for whom sexual initiation comes from an older man. What's interesting is that you don't stay within a gay context. You accept bisexuality. Is that a wish to rectify the place of homosexuality in the world of cinema, which is mostly heterosexual?

FO: Not consciously so, it's more a reference to my own past, I think. A reference to what I've been through, my own love relationships. But for example the parallel that you draw between *Water Drops* and *Criminal Lovers,* I hadn't thought of it because *Water Drops* is a Fassbinder play, not my personal history.

LB: But you chose it.

FO: Yes, because I found myself in this play. In *Sitcom* it was very clear, I really did want to attack the classic heterosexual bourgeois family. I use a rat symbolically to show that things [family relationships] are not as simple and straightforward as they appear. But it's true that at the same time I don't want to just make gay films. Since both times the protagonists are adolescents I want to show how fluid and open sexuality is at that time in your life, in relation to exterior events and what you are exposed to. With reference to homosexuality— I don't want to be confrontational. These are not militant films. I try to make films that are close to how I feel.

LB: I understand you started out in Super 8.

FO: Yes, I made 30 Super 8 films while at film school mostly because it was cheap, 10-, 15-minute films with my parents, brothers and sisters. In one of these films my brother kills my father, my mother and my two sisters and takes the bodies into the living room, puts himself in the middle and takes a portrait. It was very morbid. I called it *Family Photos*.

LB: What did your parents think?

FO: My parents thought that in art anything is possible. They were very tolerant of artistic practice, strict when it came to homework. Punishment was not being allowed to watch movies.

Originally published on *edificerex.com*.

FRANÇOIS OZON

Swimming Pool

Creativity is not something that just happens, that falls on you from the sky, but something very concrete. At times there are false trails, you have to work out problems, and you have to allow enough time for your idea to mature on its own.

François Ozon, 2003

Cannes, France, and New York—Sarah Morton, the frosty London mystery novelist in François Ozon's latest film, *Swimming Pool,* may be stuck in a rut, but it's hard to imagine Mr. Ozon himself in that situation. Even on two hours' sleep, Ozon is good-humored, quick-witted, and radiates boundless energy.

Having turned out one film a year since 1998, Ozon has established himself as one of France's outstanding young auteurs. His elegant, deliciously subversive films—notably *Sitcom,* a farcical satire of a middle-class nuclear family, and the Fassbinder adaptation *Water Drops on Burning Rocks*—are characterized by superb craftsmanship and irreverent camp humor.

"The success in France of my last three films, *Under the Sand, 8 Women* and *Swimming Pool* has given me a lot of freedom," says Ozon, who was interviewed at the Cannes Film Festival and later in New York. *8 Women,* which starred Catherine Deneuve, Isabelle Huppert, and other leading French actresses, was among the Top 10 French box office hits in 2002. "I could have made a very big film," says Ozon, "but instead I made a low-budget film with two actresses in a location that didn't cost much."

The location for *Swimming Pool* was an idyllic red-tiled and blue-shuttered Provençal house with a sumptuous pool in the chic reclusiveness of the Luberon, next to a house owned by director Ridley Scott, and not far from the former Marquis de Sade's château in Lacoste, which was used in one scene.

Charlotte Rampling, François Ozon, and Ludivine Sagnier at the Festival de Cannes press conference for the psychothriller *Swimming Pool* (2003, France), directed by François Ozon. Photo © Liza Béar.

Tired of churning out her popular Inspector Dalwell series, Sarah Morton, played by Charlotte Rampling, takes up her publisher's offer to stay at his house in southern France, hoping to draw inspiration from a change of scenery. But the pastoral calm is soon shattered by the unexpected arrival of the publisher's nubile teen daughter Julie (Ludivine Sagnier, who appeared in *8 Women*), an uninhibited party girl who makes good use of the pool and brings home a different man every night. Gradually, the two polar opposites learn to accommodate themselves to each other's routines. And when evidence of foul play shows up, Sarah is well qualified to investigate the matter.

The filmmakers drew on authors Ruth Rendell and Patricia Highsmith for Morton's character, but a particular favorite of Ozon's in this genre is the lesser-known Elizabeth Atwood Taylor, a 1957 Vassar alum who helped raise the status of crime fiction among literati.

"I chose a mystery novelist as Sarah's profession," says Ozon, "because crime fiction is a minor genre that is a bit like screenwriting, in that you have to sow clues along the way. I thought it would be amusing to draw a parallel between the two."

Shot partly in English, *Swimming Pool* is a Hitchcockian intrigue about the creative process with a novel twist. "What I wanted to show in this film," says Ozon, "is that creativity is not something that just happens, that falls on you from the sky, but something very concrete. At times there are false trails, you have to work out problems, and you have to allow enough time for your idea to mature on its own." *Swimming Pool* reunites Ozon with co-screenwriter Emmanuelle Bernheim and Rampling, both from *Under the Sand*.

Ozon, who says he prefers to direct women, approached Rampling before the script of *Swimming Pool* was written. "I asked her if she wanted to play an English writer in a bad mood," says Ozon. "She did, and we took it from there."

Ozon is not afraid to tackle difficult subjects. *Under the Sand*, a study of grief, provided Rampling with a career-defining role as a woman who's in denial over her husband's drowning. "My last film, *Eight Women*, a musical murder mystery, had been rather hard to make," says Ozon. "I'd lost some of the pleasure of shooting a movie and needed to recharge my batteries by working with two actresses I knew well."

Originally published in the *Christian Science Monitor.*

ABBAS KIAROSTAMI
The Wind Will Carry Us

The goal of a film like *The Wind Will Carry Us* is not really to reach any conclusion or to map the development of the character per se; in a sense, it's sort of like a journey whose goal may not be so much getting to the end as the experience of the journey itself.

Abbas Kiarostami, 2000

New York, July 21, 2000—The wandering and wondering mood of late July could hardly be better suited to the relaxed tempo of Abbas Kiarostami's wonderfully serene films. The automobile is avowedly Kiarostami's favorite location, and the films are full of driving scenes that wind through dusty rolling hills and past roadblocks. As they drive, his characters pose questions from the absurdly literal to the metaphysical—with plenty of double-entendre. The series[1] revives the master director's superb Koker trilogy, *Where Is My Friend's House?* (1987), *And Life Goes On* (1992) and *Through the Olive Trees* (1994); it also includes *Close Up* (1990), a story about a cinematic impostor based on a reported incident, and Palme d'Or winner *A Taste of Cherry* (1997), about a middle-aged man seeking an accomplice for his planned suicide. *The Wind Will Carry Us* (1999), about a man from Tehran on a secret mission, also opens today[2] at the Quad and Lincoln Theater.

The Koker trilogy was shot near its namesake, a village 350km north of Tehran devastated by the 1991 earthquake, a premonition of which occurs in *Where Is My Friend's House?*, a straightforward story about a boy trying to return his friend's exercise book so as not to incur their teacher's wrath. But the film is also an immensely subtle and captivating portrait of growing up in rural Iran, balancing simultaneous and contradictory parental commands such as "rock the baby" and

---

[1] Screening Room, New York City, July 28–August 3, 2000.
[2] July 21, 2000.

"bring in the laundry" with "do your homework." Kiarostami is able to cull not only poignant humor from such seemingly slight situations but also real dramatic tension in the relationships between children and adults, or between the educated and the illiterate.

"If every road goes somewhere, then what's a dead end?" an 8-year-old boy asks his filmmaker dad in *And Life Goes On*. In *Through the Olive Trees*, a film about the fictitious and real rapport of a rural couple acting in an episode of *And Life Goes On*, the driver is a woman, a no-nonsense assistant director in a black chador who's responsible for negotiating the transport of actors and props.

As with their often domestic settings—little pockets of intimacy in forbidding, desolate landscapes—Kiarostami's films also work together as a "family" of sorts through linkages; an element in one film will help to spawn a later film. For example, a scene in *A Taste of Cherry* with a Kurdish soldier morphs into *The Wind Will Carry Us*, which is set in a Kurdistan village.

Dubbed "the Engineer" by the local townsfolk, the protagonist in *The Wind Will Carry Us* is a semi-balding TV producer from Tehran who must await the fate of an elderly invalid before he can accomplish an undisclosed mission. He's always going up to the cemetery to take calls on his cell phone because that's where he gets the best reception. The film is in part a continuation of Kiarostami's inquiry into the rapport between filmmakers and the subjects that they film, shot through with ironic, self-reflexive observations.

Homayon Ershadi as Mr. Badii in *Taste of Cherry,* aka *Ta'm e Guilass* (1997, Iran), directed by Abbas Kiarostami. Winner of the Palme d'Or at the Festival de Cannes, 1997. Courtesy of Zeitgeist Films.

Reinforcing the general secrecy of the Engineer's objective, what you *don't* see is exploited to Chekhovian effect in this cunning film. Kiarostami, speaking at a recent New York screening at NYU's Cantor Cinema on 8th street, said the film had 11 characters that were all hidden from the camera. (There is also a priceless scene in which the Engineer goes to fetch milk from an underground cave where the head and face of the woman milking the cow are hidden from view, a reference to Islamic convention.)

Rather than being coy or arbitrary, Kiarostami intended this cinematic secrecy as a comment on the nature of the viewing experience. In such academic settings, he is invariably asked to characterize "the protagonist's arc" in a story, but Kiarostami took the inevitable question in a playful spirit.

"It's your bad luck to have me sitting here to answer questions like this," he said, "but if I were to answer it, then I would have to fill in that half of the story which ideally the audience should be answering. The goal of a film like *The Wind Will Carry Us* is not really to reach any conclusion or to map the development of the character per se; in a sense, it's sort of like a journey whose goal may not be so much getting to the end as the experience of the journey itself."

While Kiarostami first thought about making this film 23 years ago, he said the time difference had not given him a different perspective on the material because historical events like the Iranian Revolution have not affected internal family dynamics of a Kurdish village.

And as for Kiarostami's extended cinematic family? Three of Kiarostami's former assistants have won the Caméra d'Or at Cannes: in 1997, Jafar Panahi for *The White Balloon,* and in 2000 Hassan Yektapanah for *Djomeh* and Bahman Ghobadi for *A Time for Drunken Horses,* both of which were shot in Kurdistan.

Originally published on *edificerex.com*.

ABBAS KIAROSTAMI

ABC Africa

A recipient of the UN's Fellini medal in 1997 for his humanitarian work in film, Abbas Kiarostami was invited by a UN agency[1] to sensitize the world to the plight of Uganda's orphans—in any way he chose. ABC Africa, *Kiarostami's poignant and poetic response, is his first full-length documentary since* Homework (1989), *his first digital video feature and first film to be shot outside Iran.*

A travel diary shot over a 10-day period, in visual style ABC Africa *is deceptively low-keyed. But, much as in the earlier* Life and Nothing More, *shot in the wake of the 1990 Koker earthquake, its keynote is human adaptability in the face of tragedy. Armed with two digital video cameras and a still camera, Kiarostami and his assistant Seifollah Samadian (plus sound person and production coordinator), crisscross some 300 miles of the lush countryside outside Kampala, driving past billboards promoting safe sex, and stopping in villages notably devoid of men.*

The filmmakers turn a compassionate eye on the surviving widows and orphans. Long, handheld verité takes show children jumping rope, reciting English in outdoor classrooms under a tree's huge canopy, joyously singing in chorus—and mugging for the camera. Women at work, playing volleyball or seated on the ground pooling their savings show the resourcefulness of the caregivers. Local AIDS relief workers explain how mothers and grandmothers, all volunteers, take care of orphans through a savings/credit system. Under the auspices of the Uganda Women's Efforts to Save Orphans (UWESO), they first form groups of five, then larger clusters of 50 to engage in small income-producing activities. With 1.6 million orphans registered at the 1991 census, the logistics are daunting: one 72-year-old woman who lost all 11 of her children to AIDS now takes care of 20 orphans.

Throughout there are telltale signs of the bigger picture—not far from the well-stocked fruit and vegetable stalls and the You and I *barber shop, an outdoor lumberyard*

---

[1] International Fund for Agricultural Development (IFAD).

churns out an endless number of coffins; the smug portrait of Pope John Paul hangs next to signs advocating virginity.

Two disturbing scenes offset the film's general ebullience and high spirits. The crew visits a crowded hospital ward for terminally sick children in Masaka, the epicenter of the AIDS epidemic. There, a buxom, white-uniformed nurse jokes with a colleague, then bundles up the still limp corpse of a dead child into a flattened cardboard box that is wheeled away on a bicycle.

Later, in a powerful blackout sequence—electricity is routinely shut off after midnight—the filmmakers stumble in the dark for several minutes looking for their hotel rooms while the camera records their dialogue. Over a totally black screen, occasionally lit by the flame from a match, Kiarostami comments on the terror that Ugandans must feel of dangers lurking in the dark, in particular of the large mosquitoes bearing malaria, yet another fatal disease.

This interview took place at the Festival de Cannes where ABC Africa *premiered; it was translated from Farsi and French.*

Cannes, May 12, 2001.

Liza Béar: When this invitation to make a film in Africa came from the UN, at what point were you in your life?

Abbas Kiarostami: I must say I was going through a not particularly happy period. For a year I hadn't been able to walk too well, and so my morale was low.

Production still from *ABC Africa* (2001, Iran/France), directed by Abbas Kiarostami. Courtesy of Photofest.

I received the invitation in the spring and right away it lifted my spirits because it offered a change of scene.

LB: And of mindset?

AK: And of mindset. It's not that I wasn't able to travel. The fact that the film would be about Africa and children helped me to decide. And I remember being truly delighted and really wanting to go. What's more, the fourth day after arriving in Uganda, I noticed that I was beginning to walk normally.

LB: There's a wonderful overhead shot of a black road snaking across the red soil of Africa . . .

AK: Uhhuh.

LB: In Iran you were exposed to disasters such as the Koker earthquake, for instance. But even so—what was the hardest thing to get acclimatized to in Uganda, either in terms of environment or psychologically?

AK: The first four days, we weren't authorized to go inside the hospital in Masaka. But once we stepped inside the hospital, a big change took place in each of us. Our fear turned into sadness. [We were afraid] because although we had been vaccinated against malaria, we'd nevertheless been warned about the risk of AIDS if we cut ourselves or were stung by insects. But once we were able to see for ourselves the conditions in the hospital wards, we felt that AIDS was some-how outside of us. AIDS as experienced in the U.S. or in Europe is different from the AIDS experienced in Africa. What's shocking is that in Africa it's a disease of poverty, whereas in the West it affects the middle classes and the intellectuals.

LB: Did you choose a different crew from your normal one for this trip because of the demanding nature of the project?

AK: Initially, we weren't going to Uganda to make a film, but merely to scout locations and do research. We went with a really reduced crew, just four people. And we took two digital cameras. It wasn't my normal crew. For instance, my assistant [Seifollah Samarian] was a photographer, and I took him with me be-cause he likes to travel and he travels well, so he's a good traveling companion. After we looked at our footage, we decided we had enough to make a film. I shot 30 hours myself.

LB: Did you have a plan? How did you decide where to go and what to shoot?

AK: No. I just wanted to be completely open to impressions and to film as we traveled. From Kampala we drove about 300 miles through the surround-ing countryside to small villages. And we only discussed our itinerary with the people who had invited us, to get some practical information.

LB: Suggestions as to who to visit?

AK: Right.

DAILY NEWS

Tuesday, October 1, 2002

Visa flap roils N.Y. film fest

By LIZA BEAR
SPECIAL TO THE NEWS

Global politics trumped esthetics yesterday at the New York Film Festival.

Finnish director Aki Kaurismaki announced that he will not travel here to promote his movie "The Man Without a Past."

Kaurismaki's decision, as relayed by fes-
tival director Richard Peña, is a protest over the U.S. government's denial of a visa for Iranian director Abbas Kiarostami, whose film "Ten" is also in the fest.

"Under the circumstances, I am forced to cancel my participation. ... As a private citizen of Finland, I accuse the U.S. government of violating the Geneva Convention," wrote Kaurismaki in a letter read by Peña. "If international cultural exchange is prevented, what is left?"
Peña described the visa denial as "unjust, extraordinarily shortsighted and a snub to a major Muslim artist."

"As for the Kaurismaki response," said Peña," it's very brave. It hurts the festival but it also hurts Kaurismaki. It's hard for me to say I support it, but I respect it enormously."

"The Man Without a Past" won the Grand Jury Prize at Cannes this year and is scheduled for a spring release in the U.S.

Clipping of metro news item written for the New York *Daily News*. Courtesy Liza Béar.

LB: Do you think of going back to Uganda to film there again, something else?

AK: Yes, I think about it a lot. Especially to take photographs. I took some extraordinary photos while we were there. The people are really beautiful. And very often they don't know that you are shooting them, so they don't change their pose in front of the camera. That gives me time to change vantage point, even to change lenses.

LB: *ABC Africa* focuses very much on the sheer exuberance and joie de vivre of the children and the women that you filmed. Was that your main objective, so that people would realize the enormous loss, seeing them so happy? When, in reality, 1,600,000 children are orphans and risk dying of starvation.

AK: Yes, it was. I had seen several films [about Uganda] on television, where the children are completely covered with flies. There's so much misery shown that you end up thinking that AIDS is perhaps a blessing in the sense that it would liberate them from this miserable existence. On the contrary, when you see them as they are, beautiful and happy, clean, well-dressed and totally civilized—and I must tell you, they had so much respect for the law that when we were driving on the road, those who were on bicycles or mopeds, would ride on the dirt paths at the roadside so as not to obstruct the cars driving on the highway. Whereas, *boum,* it would have been much easier for them to pedal on the tarmac. These people are really disciplined. And it's this contradiction that makes you regret that they will die. That's when you feel the pain of their death.

The film shows the disaster by means of statistics and during the ten minutes we were allowed to film in the hospital, when a child dies in front of the camera. But when you see how beautiful and happy they are alive, that's when you realize the immensity of the tragedy. You cannot infer the disaster by just showing the disaster.

WONG KAR-WAI
In the Mood for Love

Set in the straitlaced and gossipy Hong Kong of the early Sixties, In the Mood for Love, *Wong Kar-wai's latest masterpiece of suave innuendo stars Maggie Cheung and Tony Leung as two married neighbors who share a contagious secret. Recent émigrés from mainland China, Mr. Chow (Leung), a journalist, and Mrs. Chan (Cheung), a secretary for a shipping company, have rented adjacent boardinghouse rooms in the close-knit Shanghainese section of Hong Kong.*

Left stranded by their absent spouses, Chow and Chan slink past each other on the stairs on their way to the noodle shop, and initially their casual encounters remain quite formal. Eventually, through a slow, undeniable accumulation of clues, the two surmise that her husband and his wife are having an affair, and their own burgeoning rapport acquires an erotic charge. (The erotic tinder of secrecy is ignited by the sexual nature of the secret.) The rest is left up to the viewer.

Known for his unique visual flair, Wong Kar-wai, whose career began as a graphic designer and screenwriter, here abandons the impressionistic flamboyance of his earlier award-winning films, Days of Being Wild, Chungking Express *and* Happy Together. *In this oblique, sensuous, divinely crafted portrayal of shame and yearning, Wong Kar-wai has tossed the moral card clean out of the pack, caring not a fig about the pros or cons of adulterous passion and glorifying neither marital fidelity nor betrayal. Rather, he opts for a phenomenological approach to the imperceptible flowering of desire, meticulously refracting each telling glance, movement or gesture through the diamond prism of his lens.*

In the Mood for Love *received a Best Actor award for Tony Leung and, for its sublime art direction, the Grand Prix de la Technique at the 2001 Cannes Film Festival, where this discussion took place in the gardens of the Grand Hotel.*

Liza Béar: How was the story of *In the Mood for Love* constructed? I heard it was a very long shoot because of the way you work, in blocks.

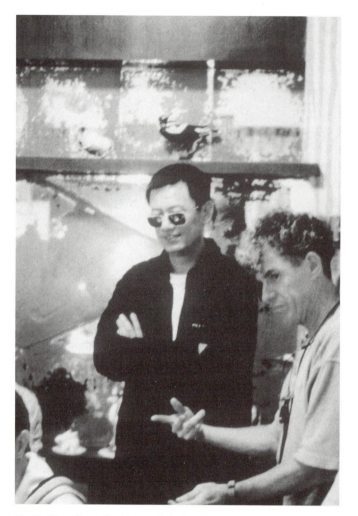

Director Wong Kar-wai on the set of *In the Mood for Love* (2000, Hong Kong). USA Films, courtesy of Photofest.

Wong Kar-wai: Yes. Well, at first we called this film, *Story about Food,* and there were three stories in it. In fact, *In the Mood for Love* is only one of the three original stories. It's about two people who meet each other because they're neighbors, and they're always buying noodles. So in the film we had noodles, the staircase, the restaurant and the house. And I realized that this story of the three was the only reason I wanted to make the project, so I expanded it. First I had to build the apartment, because I think the film is like chamber music—all the scenes should take place in the apartment. And so we spent a lot of time defining this apartment, and then we built it. But later on I changed my mind and thought, well, we should go outside and see something else. In Hong Kong now, it's difficult to find streets or locations that are the same as the old Hong Kong. So we moved to Bangkok, and we shot all the street, taxi and Singapore scenes at the end of the film there.

LB: So were you changing the story during production?

WK: Yes, it's like we started in a McDonalds for a quick lunch, but then it became a big feast.

LB: Did you shoot on a sound stage?

WK: We shot in old abandoned buildings where nobody lives anymore. The hotel in the film is a military hospital in Hong Kong. Now it's gone.

LB: How would you compare the making of *In the Mood for Love* with your previous films?

WK: At the beginning I thought this would be an easy film because it is only about two people. At the end I realized it's much more difficult than my previous films, which have ten or five or four characters. You had to put more details in it. Originally the story took place from 1962 to 1972, and in the editing room I decided the film should stop in 1966, which is the film you see now.

LB: What made you set the story in Hong Kong in the early Sixties?

WK: Well, I always wanted to make a film about this period, because it is very special in the history of Hong Kong. Right after 1949 a lot of people came from China to live in Hong Kong, and they still had their traditions and their dreams about their lives in China.

And so, like the Chinese communities in the film, there are people from Shanghai who had their own language, and they had no contact with the local Cantonese. They had their own cinema, their own music, and their own rituals. So they were actually building Shanghai in Hong Kong. I'm from that background, and I wanted to recreate that world. At that time we had neighbors, we knew, who were living next door to us, on the other side of the wall. And there was a lot of gossip and it was fun.

LB: What did your parents do?

WK: My father worked in a nightclub as a manager. Before that he was a sailor. And my mother was a housewife. My sisters and brothers stayed in China, so I was the only kid with them at that time. It was a special period for me, too. But actually, *In the Mood for Love* was the most difficult film of my career, and not only because it took almost two years to make. During the production we had the Asian economic crisis. We had to stop the production, because the film's investors all had problems. We had to find new investors. Also, at the end of the film, during the editing we realized we could go on editing this film forever because we fell in love with it. And so we decided to enter it in Cannes, because that meant a deadline, and it was about time to say good-bye, and that's it.

LB: When did you decide to enter it?

WK: Just before Cannes printed the catalogue. I always wanted to call this film *Secrets,* something about secrets, but Cannes said no, there's so many titles about secrets already. So we were listening to the music of Bryan Ferry, a song called "I'm in the Mood for Love," and I said, "Why not call the film *In the Mood for Love?*" Actually, the mood of the film is what drives these two people together.

LB: To some people the emotions you displayed on screen may seem strangely Latin—a yearning that never really gets consummated physically. Does that come from your previous experience working in South America?

WK: No, no. I like Latin American literature a lot, and I always think Latin Americans and Italians are very close to the Chinese, especially the women— the jealousy, the passions and the family values. And the Latin music in the film, actually, was very popular in Hong Kong because the music scene at that time was mainly from the Philippines and all the nightclubs had Filipino musicians, so they got Spanish influences there. Latin American music was very popular in the restaurants at that time, that's why I put it in the film. And I especially like Nat King Cole because he's my mother's favorite singer.

Maggie Cheung as Mrs. Chan and Tony Leung as Mr. Chow in Wong Kar-wai's *In the Mood for Love.*
© USA Films. Courtesy of Photofest.

LB: Your other films have a more freewheeling style. This obviously is quite the opposite.

WK: We're going to get a sunburn.

LB: What was it like trying something new?

WK: Actually, it makes you more anxious when you're not so lazy as before. We get used to certain types of style, and people say this is our label or trademark. And whenever we go to a new location, we see things as before; we know the camera should be here and there, and that becomes very boring. When you try to do something else, you have to see things afresh, in a different perspective. And for *In the Mood for Love* my cameraman, Chris Doyle, was away during the film, because he had to shoot another film, so we had to use another cameraman, Mark Li Ping-bin. I could not be as lazy as usual, because in the past I could rely on Chris for lighting, framing, technical aspects like that. This time I had to control all those things myself. But by engaging in this process I discovered I could control more of the film, and the style of the film could be more attached to the content.

> "I like American literature a lot, and I always think Latin Americans and Italians are very close to the Chinese, especially the women—the jealousy, the passions and the family values."

LB: Can you tell us more about the cinematography and specifically the use of colors, which seem very saturated?

WK: We always put something in front of the camera because we wanted to create the feeling that the audience was one of the neighbors and was always observing or watching these two people. And the color is so vivid because everything from memory is vivid—it's beautiful because it's very close to your mind.

LB: Everybody has been admiring the look of the image. There's an incredible correlation between the wall texture, the costumes, and the upholstery fabric. How did you work with the art director?

WK: I must say I'm very happy because I have a very good art director. William Chang Suk-ping has worked with me since my first film, and basically we are from the same background, so he knows everything by heart. We seldom discuss anything about the film, because the way we work together is very organic. He's not serving me, he's trying to create his own idea and capture all the details in the film, and he's also the editor of the film, so sometimes he cuts things he doesn't like. All the clothes in the film are tailor-made, and it's a painstakingly long process. And because the film was made over a two-year period, when Maggie [Cheung] gained weight, or became slimmer, we had to change the fitting of her clothes. And as for the hair, Maggie had to spend six hours everyday before shooting.

LB: How did you develop Maggie's look? It's very iconic.

WK: Because that look was very popular. All the women looked like that in the early Sixties.

LB: Tiny little sleeves, very tight fitting.

WK: There were very minor changes during all those years. In '62 you have sleeves, in '66 you don't have sleeves, the dress length got a little shorter. We didn't have to do research because our mothers dressed like this.

LB: It looks like you chose to describe the passing of time, days or hours, through the changes of costume. Tony Leung's character is basically wearing a similar costume, but Maggie's character changes constantly.

WK: We had 20 to 25 dresses for Maggie for the whole film, but the time period of the film was very long. Originally the film covered from 1962 to 1972, and the clothes were repeating themselves. But when we cut the film short, the costume changes became like a fashion show. And my purpose at first was to make the film very repetitious—we repeat the theme music all the time, we repeat the angle of a shot all the time, always the clock, always the corridor, always the staircase, because I wanted to show that nothing changes except the emotions of these two people. So we tried to show the changes only through them. But because we cut the film short, the repetition is not so obvious in Maggie's clothes.

LB: In a way, it's quite natural for a woman to change her clothes.

WK: Yeah, and she's a working lady.

LB: But also a person who's attracted to someone tries to make herself appealing, so she's very conscious of what she's wearing.

WK: That's why there are comments from the neighbors: why is she dressed like this to buy noodles?

LB: We never see this pair's husband and wife. Were their characters much more developed in the longer version of the film?

WK: Well, actually the film is not about having affairs, and I thought it would be more interesting for Maggie and Tony Leung's characters to play the leads, because they are the victims of that relationship between their spouses, and then later on they move beyond this affair. So I didn't think we should meet the other husband and wife. We're not saying who's right, who's wrong, it's about a process—how people treated secrets.

LB: What's the role of suspicion in the film? How much of the thrill comes from the neighbors' suspicion?

WK: I think these two characters are drawn together by this suspicious gossip and they bond. They have a secret they don't want other people to know. They have each other to share it with, because they cannot share it with anyone else, because they want to be decent, they want to be respectable. They can talk to each other and that draws them together. And because there are so many things about the secret that are unknown, there's a lot of imagination on their side too.

LB: Maggie Cheung said she had difficulty with her character because it was too perfect. Is that how you remember your mother?

WK: Of course my mother is perfect. When my father worked as a sailor he didn't come home very often, so most of the time I was with my mother. She was the one who took me to the cinema and to music concerts, so to me she's always perfect. But she's not very much like Maggie. Maggie's character represents a modern woman at that time, because she's a working woman and she has her own space. My mother was more like a housewife, very traditional.

LB: For several years now in Europe and in the United States we've witnessed the great success of Asian cinema. From your perspective do you see it as the rebirth of Asian cinema, or is it just that Western countries are now discovering a film industry that has always been producing a lot of interesting films?

WK: Well, we all need stories and what happens in our daily lives changes our stories. You can see the Italian cinema and also the French New Wave in the Sixties was the first generation after the Second World War. So that gave them a new perspective. And for the last two years Asian cinema, even Korean and Taiwanese cinema, have become very, very strong because they have their problems and they have new stories in their lives, which gives their films energy. So they are not repeating the same old stories. And the young filmmakers there, their thinking is more global, they are not very local, so their films are more accessible to Western audiences.

LB: And that's a recent change.

WK: Yes.

LB: You are a model now for young filmmakers. When they ask, what do you tell them about filmmaking?

WK: You have to be very patient. You have to wait. That's my advice.

LB: Can you tell us about *2046*, your new project?

WK: Well, we were supposed to finish the *Mood for Love* in August last year, because of various problems we had to stop production, and we started shooting *2046* at the same time. *2046* is about a promise because in 1997, the Chinese government promised Hong Kong 50 years and change. So I thought, well, I should make a film about promises. So it is a futuristic film, but it's not a science fiction film. There are three stories in the film, and each one adapted from a Western opera—*Madam Butterfly*, *Carmen* and *Tannhauser*. The cast will be

Faye Wong from *Chungking Express,* Carina Lau and Chang Chen, and also Tony Leung, and we have a Japanese actress named Takuya Kimura. We are shooting in Bangkok and for the third story we'll shoot in Korea.

LB: Can you get financing from Europe and the U.S. now?

WK: Years ago we sold films to traditional markets. Now we can get the financing not only from Asia but also outside Asia.

LB: Could you, at this stage, be financed exclusively by the West?

WK: I think it's not so easy as you might expect, because normally if you want to work with European distributors or you need joint ventures, they want to have scripts, but I don't have scripts, so that's a problem. So you have to find someone who understands you well and has confidence in you; otherwise it's very, very difficult.

LB: At the Cannes press conference, you said that in the Sixties, everybody made their living in Hong Kong by writing.

WK: Yes. I am very interested in these writers because nobody treated them as serious writers. They wrote every day for the newspaper, a lot of articles about food, about horseracing, about women, about football, about novels; they wrote for a living. Even now the people in Hong Kong are all educated people from China. Because of the war they came to Hong Kong, and they have nothing to do there. The only thing they know how to do is write.

Originally published in *Bomb.*

ALEJANDRO GONZÁLEZ IÑÁRRITU

Amores Perros

I like weak characters that through a painful process can really learn a lot of things about life and about love.

Alejandro González Iñárritu, 2001

For Alejandro González Iñárritu, the 37-year-old director of the Oscar-nominated *Amores Perros*, shooting a car commercial rather than the ferocious car crash that launches his impassioned feature debut might seem a bit like a step back. But clearly he's making the most of it.

"It's very, very hard," says Iñárritu, reached by phone at the Mexico City airport where he is directing a new Ford campaign.

"I have [mixed] feelings about advertising," he says. "On the positive side, with a camera and two actors you always learn something. Also, it keeps you humble. You don't consider yourself so very important.

"On the other hand," he adds, "you're dealing with clients who think the slightest choice is a metaphysical decision."

The accolades for *Amores Perros*, a 153-minute psychological drama whose three storylines intersect via an atrocious car crash, began with three awards at last year's Cannes Film Festival and have continued unabated on the festival circuit.

Iñárritu, who initially wanted to be a rock star, got an early start in show business. In his teens, his sonorous bass voice was noticed at a casting, and by 23 he had become producer and head DJ for WFM, Mexico's top-rated rock station.

"For 5 years I was a DJ playing music and talking all day long about my feelings," said Iñárritu. "I was happy to do my therapy in public," he said, "but I got bored and went into advertising. I was very lucky. I directed hundreds of commercials from my own ideas. I was training to write and shoot, make a lot of mistakes and learn."

Jorges Salinas in *Amores Perros* (2000, Mexico), directed by Alejandro González Iñárritu. Courtesy of The Kobal Collection/ Alta Vista.

During these shoots he discovered an actor who went on to star in *Amores Perros:* the now London-based, English theatre-trained Gael García Bernal who portrays Octavio, a young punk drawn into dogfighting. Bernal is a standout in a cast that includes Emilio Echavarría, Vanessa Bauche and Goya Toledo.

Although he directed one TV film, it wasn't until he read novelist Guillermo Arriaga's original script for *Amores Perros* that Iñárritu felt impelled to make a dramatic feature.

"It was like finding a lost brother," said Iñárritu. He spent three years with Arriaga, revising the complex screenplay 36 times, with some pages being rewritten as many as 300 times.

Even with a polished script, making *Amores Perros* was risky in many ways, not only because of the film's length. "The complexity of the script for a first-time director was very risky," he says.

Told sequentially, the three stories depict characters from different generations and different social backgrounds.

"The accident acts as a centrifugal force that spins out into all their lives," says Iñárritu.

"The first story was the hardest. Arriaga's characters expressed a lot of things I have felt," he adds. "Being young and innocent, discovering your sexuality and suffering. I had a tough adolescence."

When Alejandro, the youngest of five siblings, was five years old, his ranch-owning father was suddenly dispossessed and became a fruit and vegetable buyer for Mexican hotels. For a time, the family lived in a rough neigbborhood.

"In that kind of environment, proximity creates promiscuity. More than explicit violence," says Iñárritu, "[the film] is an exploration of psychological violence, intrafamilial violence. How the father's absence in the first story creates anarchy; in the second story, the father leaves the family, and in the third the father tries to return."

What Arriaga's story captured about Mexico City, Iñárritu said, is the fragility of human existence and the feeling that anything can happen.

"What we are living here is civil war," says Iñárritu. "With 21 million people we have 1,600,000 assaults a year."

The fact that *Amores Perros* has been critically acclaimed for its emotional depth may in part be due to Iñárritu's experience of violence, both growing up and even during the film's production.

"When we were scouting locations in the house where the dogfights take place," Iñárritu said, "we were assaulted by two fourteen-year-old boys with guns who took our equipment. The crew said, let's get out of here, but the weird vibe in that house was something I wanted to use in the film. The kids didn't want money. They wanted 'respect.' So we negotiated with them to protect us from other gangs while we were shooting."

The shoot was difficult in other ways, too.

"My characters were very risky. I like weak characters that through a painful process can really learn a lot of things about life and about love, and at the end, with dignity, they are better."

As for the prevalence of dogs in the film—a fighting Rottweiler, a pet Maltese terrier, and a slew of strays—Iñárritu said he was disturbed about the disparity between canine and human relationships.

"[Some] people are often taking more care of dogs and animals than human beings," said Iñárritu. "That's very scary for me. I love dogs, but I really love human beings more than animals. So then this movie reflects how intense a relation between dogs and human beings can be. Chivo has a family of dogs, but in the end the love for his daughter is more important than the dogs."

Originally published in *The Boston Globe*.

Agnès Varda

The Gleaners and I

I saw an old woman bend down with a lot of difficulty to pick up an orange [off the ground]. It was like a vision—the orange passing across her black coat—but what really touched me was the imbalance between the effort and the result—so much for so little. That was the emotion that launched the film.

Agnès Varda, 2001

Against all odds, a spirited portrayal of people who live on other people's leftovers seems to have hit a nerve. Since the release of *The Gleaners and I,* Agnès Varda is in demand around the world.

Jumping up repeatedly from the breakfast table of her hotel suite to the desk phone, Varda takes four calls in five minutes before asking the receptionist to stop further interruptions.

But then the creator of *The Gleaners* is no novice, having made 30 films over five decades. Her seminal first feature, *La Pointe Courte* (1954), a love story with parallel subplots shot in a declining fishing village near Sète in southern France, where she grew up, had few viewers at the time. Among her landmark films are the real time drama, *Cleo from Five to Seven* (1961), in which the title character travels through Paris while awaiting the result of a cancer test, and *Le Bonheur* (1964), a stylized melodrama about the possible consequences of adultery. The film was noted for abstract characters and pictorial compositions, and made Varda the point person for the Nouvelle Vague.

Apart from the later *Vagabond* (1985), starring Sandrine Bonnaire as a homeless woman, the majority of her dozen dramatic features shared the adventurous sensibilities of the 1960s. In 1962, she married Jacques Demy, director of *Umbrellas of Cherbourg.* The couple traveled to the United States where she produced shorts, among them *Uncle Yanco* (1967) and *Black Panthers* (1968). Her many documentaries, such as *Mur Murs* (1980) show a concern for people and the environment. The play on words in her titles indicates that her approach to form tends to be diverse and highly personalized. For instance, *Mur Murs* is pun for murmurs in French (*mur* is the French word for wall, and the film is about murals in L.A.).

Agnès Varda, director, in *The Gleaners and I* (2000, France). Courtesy of Zeitgeist Films.

Describing herself as neither a mainstream nor fringe filmmaker, she is clearly elated by the extraordinary public response to *The Gleaners and I* in France and at international festivals. It will be shown today [April 22, 2001] in the Women's Film Festival at the Brattle Theatre in Cambridge.

"I have never had such a response in my life," said Varda. "But it's to the authenticity of the gleaners and the people who eat out of garbage cans that audiences are responding. They are grateful to me for being their vehicle."

At 72, in her long-sleeved black polka-dot dress and bobbed hair, framed by large bowls of pink tulips and azaleas, she's mindful of her image—after all, she worked for 10 years as a photojournalist. A fast and voluble talker, Varda brings a Gallic thoroughness and intensity to the table.

Varda had not made a film since *The World of Jacques Demy* in 1995, the second of two documentaries devoted to her late filmmaker husband. In the year 2000, everyone in the media seemed to be celebrating aspects of society. She chose a contrarian approach.

"I'm aware of statistics proving that the food produced in the world could feed the entire world's population, but I didn't want to start from a theory and then find examples to illustrate it. I took exactly the opposite tack."

The real trigger, what gave her the desire and the inspiration to make the film, was a chance observation after an outdoor market on the Place de la Bastille in Paris had closed for the day.

"I saw an old woman bend down with a lot of difficulty to pick up an orange [lying on the ground]," she said. "It was like a vision—the orange passing across her black coat—but what really touched me was the imbalance between the effort and the result—so much for so little. That was the emotion that launched the film. I also recognized the gesture as being the same antique gesture of gleaning."

Varda began to go to other Paris markets with her mini-DV camera during the half-hour interval after the merchants have stowed their tables and before the street is swept and hosed down, to film the people who pick up fruit and vegetables that have fallen off the stands.

Another compelling image, of a handsome farmer discussing the merits of his state-of-the-art combine on French television during the 1999 harvest, prompted her to explore the countryside of Beauce between Paris and Chartres, a farming region known for its wheat.

"Now I had the city and the country," said Varda. Because of the efficiency of the new combine there was not a grain of wheat on the ground, but other equipment left behind plenty of corn, cauliflower, and potatoes. She chose the potatoes for her research.

"My inquiries before filming made me understand," said Varda, "that we live in a society of formats. Everything is standardized. Potatoes of four centimeters by seven centimeters in five kilo bags are sold in the supermarkets. Everything bigger or smaller is discarded. One single cultivator who grows 4,500 tons of potatoes will throw out 30 tons."

While she was doing research with her mini-camera, she chanced upon some heart-shaped potatoes. She took them as a cue on how to proceed.

"I saw their shape as symbolic for the film. I found them very sensual. I took them home. You can make [grand] statements about the economy but, in a sense, among the waste I found the heart.

"I felt we would find people in the dregs, but that they would nevertheless have heart, and that's what we should look for."

To a greater extent than some of the earlier hybrid films such as *Daguérreotypes,* about neighbors, and *Jane B. par Agnès V.* (1987), a portrait of an actress, *The Gleaners and I* is a fluid merge of the documentary and the personal essay film.

"That was the big challenge," said Varda, who at one time had wanted to be a museum curator. "I worked very hard in the editing to show [that] not only am I a woman drawn by 'social issues,' as you say in the U.S., but by paintings and by the pleasure of taking walks. Also, I wanted to show what fun it is to make a documentary, and to show myself as a gleaner in a metaphorical sense. The real work was to introduce play into a film about a serious subject, the distribution of goods, a subject much bigger than me."

The people in the film pick not only from potato fields and vineyards but also from oyster beds that have moved. They refurbish refrigerators and retrieve outdated food from supermarket trash bins.

"Those people were so calm and so lucid," said Varda. "They were very grounded. Not one of them was pathetic or melodramatic."

One man Varda questions in the film about the possibility of contracting germs from the trash bins tells her that he uses his common sense, his nose and his mouth to tell him if the food is good in spite of the expiration date on the package.

"The man in the caravan who's had too much beer," Varda said, "could neither read nor write. Yet he could speak well." She says she was lucky to find people who were intelligent and even had a sense of humor. "They managed to find the right words. And it's their sincerity that pushed me to be sincere myself."

"*Vagabond* is a somewhat clinical study of woman who said no to everything, even to the community of other marginal people like herself," said Varda of her 1985 film. "So much so that she dies. The people in *The Gleaners* also have nothing, but they say 'yes' to others. The man who fixes broken appliances gives them away if he cannot sell them."

Originally published in the *Boston Globe*.

BARBET SCHROEDER
Our Lady of the Assassins

Colombia may be the most Catholic country in the world, but it's also the most violent.

Barbet Schroeder, 2001

Sunday, September 30—Barbet Schroeder has always been a risk-taker, both as a film producer and, later, as director of such provocative works as *Barfly, Reversal of Fortune,* and *Single White Female.*

But in his new film, *Our Lady of the Assassins,* which opened Friday, he took personal risks to realize a lifelong dream: to make a movie in Colombia.

He lived in Bogotá from the ages of six to ten, traveling with his engineer father in Cali, Cartagena, and Medellin. "Those are the important years of childhood and they marked me very much," he said during a recent interview.[1]

His sister married a Colombian, while Schroeder himself wound up in France, where he worked with some of the leading European directors of the '60s and '70s. Visits to Colombia every year or two enabled him to keep pace with the country's piecemeal unraveling under warring drug cartels.

"Colombia may be the most Catholic country in the world, but it's also the most violent," he said. "Bit by bit, everything became more difficult. Now it's impossible to take a car or even a small plane between Bogotá and Cali because it could be taken hostage."

Schroeder knew he wanted to feature Colombia in a film. The challenge was finding a Colombian writer to work with.

His cinematic ambition was realized when, on a friend's recommendation, he read all the works of Fernando Vallejo, including *Our Lady of the Assassins,* set in Medellin after the reign of terror waged by drug kingpin Pablo Escobar.

---

[1] The interview took place at the Sundance Film Festival.

Barbet Schroeder, director, *Our Lady of the Assassins* (2001, France/Colombia).
© Gary Indiana.

With its searing candor, the 1994 semiautobiographical novel shook the Hispanic literary world. It charts an impossible love affair between maverick writer Fernando (played in Schroeder's film by Germán Jaramillo), returning to the nation after a 30-year absence, and the divine 16-year-old former gang member Alexis (Anderson Ballesteros), a latter-day exterminating angel (à la Bunuel) who offs anyone irking the couple. Immediately seeking out the Mexico-based Vallejo, Schroeder expressed his desire to work with him. "The same thing had happened with [Charles] Bukowski when I read *Barfly*," said Schroeder.

When Vallejo suggested adapting *Our Lady*, Schroeder initially refused. "There were too many people being killed in the book," he said. But then he reconsidered, persuading Vallejo to reduce the number of deaths.

"I had just been making Hollywood movies that were about other movies, that were variations in genre," said Schroeder. "Those films were the results of huge fights for me to make them the way they are. But the new film would look like nothing else. It was very exciting to me to make a movie based on a real phenomenon."

Still wrestling with the legacy of Escobar, the mid-'90s Medellin pictured in the film is a city of derelict streets lined with sumptuous High Church architecture, filled with crack addicts prostituting themselves. Flamboyance and utmost deprivation share the same frame. Yet despite its uniquely terrifying context, the love story strikes a delicate balance between romance, humor, and dread.

"During the adaptation process, something very interesting happened. Everything Vallejo writes is in the first person," said Schroeder. "The book is like an imprecatory monologue. But in writing the screenplay, suddenly the boy in the love story was becoming an important character. In the book his voice was never heard."

In working on the dialogue, the boy came to life. "The exchange [between the two men] was very moving," he added. "The writer had gone there to die, and instead he met love and an unbearable pain worse than death. And through that pain you could feel the pain of a whole country."

Even for someone with Schroeder's exceptional production savvy, the making of *Our Lady,* shot in high-definition digital video under the protection of armed guards, posed an enormous challenge, especially since no insurance company would cover the film. Members of Schroeder's cast, nonprofessional actors such as Ballesteros drawn from the streets of Medellin, narrowly escaped being killed by a real gang member during the filming.

"The minute we started shooting, the risk was very high that people would understand what we were doing, and that I too would receive death threats and be forced to leave town. I had my backup plans. Luckily, things went OK.

"One of the big problems shooting in Medellin is the very high unemployment," Schroeder explained, "and the many people in the street waiting for something interesting to look at. At times I had to organize a fake shooting with clowns and homeless drug addicts. My production manager would direct this other movie to attract the crowds. In the meantime, we were a few feet away shooting the real movie, which of course was much less entertaining than the fake one."

He added, "The Colombians use humor as a defense mechanism in the most gruesome situations, and I tried to do the same. . . . That's very different from becoming anesthetized to violence. I lived very intensely, and I was having more fun during the shooting of that movie than in many other moments of my life."

Originally published in *Bomb.*

JACQUES RIVETTE

Va Savoir

RIVETTE PUTS ACTORS' LIVES CENTER STAGE IN *VA SAVOIR*

New York, September 2001—Not wishing to talk in the dark, smoke-filled bar of Jacques Rivette's hotel and denied access by authority to the totally empty dining room, we settle for a small window table in the lobby overlooking Central Park.

"It could have happened in any country," says Jacques Rivette as I apologize for this inhospitable predicament. At 73 a frail, delicate man, he rewraps his red plaid scarf carefully around his neck as protection from the draught. Having first come to New York with the wistful *Céline and Julie Go Boating* (1974), this is his first visit in 20 years—to a very new New York. The occasion is the opening of his latest film, *Va Savoir,* a virtuoso romantic comedy about a French actress who returns to Paris to perform an Italian play. The story combines astute character study with some fancy plot flourishes—even on second viewing, an unexpectedly delightful film for these not so delightful times.

"The starting point for the story was Jean Renoir's *The Golden Coach,* which I absolutely did not intend to remake," said Rivette. "It's about a troupe of actors from one country who go to perform in another country. What I took from it was the idea of an actress and her relationship with three very different men." The three men are an impetuous Italian man of the theatre (Sergio Castellito), a stiff intellectual pedant, (Jacques Bonaffe) and a suave con man (Bruno Todeschini).

Why three? Because, Rivette explains with an anecdote, as Renoir told Truffaut in a very long interview for *Les Cahiers du Cinéma* (which Rivette at one point edited) "three is the magic number in theatre."

With this rather vague idea in mind, Rivette sought out the Rome-based Castellito after seeing him act in several films, seconded by his cinematographer who had previously worked with the popular Roman actor/director.

Jeanne Balibar in *Va Savoir* (2001, France) aka *Who Knows?* Directed by Jacques Rivette. Photo by Moune Jamet, courtesy of Photofest.

It was Castellito who suggested *Come Tu Mi Voi*, the Pirandello play that the actors in *Va Savoir* perform. He went on to play Ugo, an actor, director and the husband of lead actress Camille (Jeanne Balibar) in the film.

Actors and the theatre have been a recurring theme in Rivette's films from his earliest *Paris Belongs to Us* (1961), in which actors rehearse Shakespeare's *Pericles,* juxtaposing the mystery of the creative process with the physical realities of artistic survival.

"It's significant," says Rivette, "that Camille's character in the Pirandello play is known in Italian as *l'ignota*—the unknown."

With a so-so box office and Paris audiences for Pirandello fluctuating, Ugo applies himself by searching for an unpublished Goldoni manuscript, *Il Destino di Venezia,* which may be in a private library in Paris. A typographical error in the title complicates the search and also provides the perfect set-up for the film's festive ending.

With a strong Italian anchor for the scenario, other Italian plot links followed. "From the moment the Italian troupe acting Pirandello was in the story," Rivette explains, "I wanted Ugo, this Italian director in Paris, to have his own thing going. She [Camille] comes to Paris terrified about seeing her former lover, a philosophy professor, from whom she'd fled because she felt trapped by him. To offset her anxiety, I wanted to give Ugo hope—the hope of finding this unpublished Goldoni manuscript which he'd read about in a biography."

While Rivette and his coscreenwriters invented the details, he said that Ugo's trajectory in the film was inspired by historical fact—Goldoni's financial struggles for much of the last 30 years of his life spent in Paris.

"He barely survived," said Rivette.

An earlier film of Rivette's *La Bande des Quatre* (1989) addresses another kind of survival, artistic survival, amongst young actresses.

"The two films, *La Bande des Quatre* and *Va Savoir* are polar opposites," Rivette said. In *La Bande des Quatre,* they're learning the process. Three-quarters of them will never make it to the stage. In *Va Savoir*, it's exactly the opposite. They're all experienced actors with a play that they've already performed in Italy . . . In *The Gang of Four*, I tried to show how the demands of their work affects these young actresses' private lives, what they must sacrifice if they are to succeed. They got a severe ethics lesson as well as acting training."

The light playful tone of his latest film allows Rivette to make fun of an abstruse philosophical text like the German Heidegger, whose writings inspired Jean-Paul Sartre's much better known *Being and Nothingness,* at least in France. And to make fun of academic staples such as the thesis. As the epitome of academic frivolity, a supporting character in the film, Do (Hélène de Fougerolles) is writing her own thesis on the history of the brooch through the ages. Rivette credits the idea to his co-screenwriter, who once worked in the costume department.

Born in Rouen, Rivette said his parents did not approve of his cinematic ambitions. His father owned a pharmacy on one of the main squares in the city, and the family lived above it. In 1940, he recalls, when the Germans arrived in town, the whole neighborhood burned down.

"My father had already been called up by the army. My mother, my sister and I were part of the exodus to the country and we found ourselves in a part of France called La Vendée with my grandparents. However during the bombings of 1942–43–44, at the time of the liberation, we were in Rouen and we spent a lot of time in caves waiting for the sirens. Once we were in a makeshift shelter and a bomb dropped 15 meters from our house, which was blown to bits. During the raids as many as several hundred people might be killed in one night."

Speaking of his own start in cinema, "The desire to make films grew bit by bit," said Rivette, "but someone who had enormous influence on me unknowingly was Jean Cocteau. I was studying French literature and classics at Rouen University but not doing very well in Latin and Greek. So I started going to the cinema. Rouen had been ravaged by the war so there were only two or three theatres left in 1944–45. Cocteau's *Beauty and the Beast* was screened. But what especially impressed me were the diaries Cocteau kept during the making of the film, from the very first day of shooting, which were published when the film came out. It's one of the most beautiful books about cinema ever written. This was an extremely difficult shoot because at the end of the war France was still very impoverished."

At 21, Rivette headed for Paris and within two years started to work at *Les Cahiers du Cinéma* along with François Truffaut, Claude Chabrol, Eric Rohmer, and Jean-Luc Godard.

"We were writing while we waited," Rivette said. "We had absolutely no desire to be critics for the rest of our lives. We only wanted to make films. At the same time it was interesting to discuss what we admired or disliked about the French cinema of that period."

As for Rivette's views on the state of current French cinema, he says it has certainly become easier to make films in France then it was 20 years ago.

"I've had the luck not only to work with the same producer, Martine Marignac, for the past 20 years," said Rivette, but I also like to work with the same key crew people who know my ways of working. That really helps a lot. You really don't want to start from scratch with each crew. Forty years ago I didn't mind, but now I don't want to any more. Actors, now, that's another thing."

"What has changed over the years," he added "is that I've become more and more interested in the actors themselves, and the production stage of the film, the actual time on the set, which I used to dread, I've come to value more and more because that's the time when you are really working with actors. That's what counts, the actual moment when you are shooting."

Originally published in the *Boston Globe*.

MOHSEN MAKHMALBAF

Kandahar

What sort of an impact has *Kandahar* had when bombs can easily be dropped on Afghanistan but humanitarian help cannot get to where it is most needed?

Mohsen Makhmalbaf, 2002

When Mohsen Makhmalbaf set out to make the movie *Kandahar,* little did he or anyone else anticipate that a city in southeastern Afghanistan, the former headquarters and spiritual home of the Taliban, would become a household word. He had simply wanted to focus on the plight of women and the pervasive human misery under an oppressive regime.

"I've never in any of my films before been touched by such a deep tragedy, a pain that's burning inside me about the subject," said Makhmalbaf, interviewed at the Cannes Film Festival where the film premiered. "The whole world is concerned about the destruction of the Buddhas but no one is paying attention to the problems of Afghanistan."

Then came September 11. And, ironically—considering *Time* magazine's choice of New York's former Mayor Rudy Giuliani over Osama Bin Laden as the person who has most affected the media in 2001—*Kandahar* heads *Time*'s best film list for the year.

Now 44, the head of Makhmalbaf Film House, apart from directing 17 highly regarded films, has acted as mentor and written screenplays for his daughter Samira (*The Apple* and *Blackboards*) and on *The Day I Became a Woman,* directed by his wife, director Marzieh Meshkini. He's also no stranger to hardship, having worked from the age of eight in a poor Tehran neighborhood to support his family.

Produced under almost impossible conditions and, like all Iranian films on a very modest scale, *Kandahar* has had a White House screening, distribution in 40 countries and has outperformed *Moulin Rouge* in France and Italy.

Regardless of its acute relevance to contemporary viewers, *Kandahar* transcends the plight of individuals and, like Makhmalbaf's earlier *Gabbeh,* works

Film still of wedding procession from Mohsen Makhmalbaf's *Kandahar* (2001, Iran). Makhmalbaf Film House, courtesy of Photofest.

poetically: it achieves a wrenching emotional impact mostly by surreal images that evoke the permanent results of violence—like mutilation—rather than violence itself.

One such unforgettable scene (shot in slow motion) is of billowing parachutes dangling artificial limbs high above men on crutches racing across the desert below to retrieve them.

"This was based on something I'd seen," said the director, whose films have often seamlessly melded strands of documentary and fiction, once casting a policeman who had arrested him in *A Moment of Innocence* (1996).

"Here, what I saw being dropped by parachute, were meals, not legs. Whenever I'm making a film I leave a window open for what the wind will bring—an idea or some interference from reality."

A desert odyssey across a treacherous mine-filled landscape, in which Kandahar the city is an unreached destination, the semi-documentary film is based on the real-life predicament of Afghan-born, Canadian journalist Niloufar Pazira, who recounted it to Makhmalbaf in Iran four years ago and eventually became the film's leading lady. In the interim, Makhmalbaf wrote a 47-page essay based on his United Nations research on Afghanistan and clandestine trips into the country [see www.makhmalbaffilmhouse.com].

Armed with a tape recorder, a fistful of dollars, and her sister's letter, the film's English-speaking reporter, Nafas, deplanes in Afghanistan, dons a burka and sets off to find her sister, who has lost both her legs to a land mine and has threatened to commit suicide before the next solar eclipse in three days' time. For Nafas, a single woman on a perilous voyage through Taliban-controlled territory, male traveling companions are de rigueur. She initially persuades a family headed for Kandahar to take her on as a fourth wife.

Apart from International Red Cross workers and a shadowy African-American doctor, Hassan Tantai, whom Makhmalbaf recruited on the spot, the rest of the cast were all Afghan refugees living in camps in Iran. Another of Nafas' guides is a young boy who has been expelled from a *madrassa* [Taliban school] for misquoting the Koran and tries to sell her jewellery stolen from a corpse.

Although Makhmalbaf made an earlier feature film, *The Cyclist* (1988), about an Afghan refugee in Iran, that was before the Taliban took over. Finding an area to shoot *Kandahar* in 1999 proved a nightmare.

"Afghanistan and Iran share a 500-mile undefined frontier and there are maybe two and a half million Afghan refugees living in Iran. But only about 50,000 of those have any kind of ID," said Makhmalbaf. "I had crossed the border to scout locations, but conditions were so difficult that I decided to shoot in Niatak, about a mile from the border, in Niatak, one of the Afghan refugee villages about a mile in on the Iranian side of the border."

Nonetheless, the proximity of the Taliban and of armed opium smugglers forced the crew to be on the run themselves. "We had to change locations every single day," said Makhmalbaf, who grew a beard and wore Afghan clothes as camouflage.

The lack of security was not the only difficulty the filmmakers faced.

"The biggest other problem was the lack of cooperation from the Afghan [refugee] community itself," said Makhmalbaf. "The Afghan women, despite the fact that they are living in Iran, even under full cover, were reluctant to participate in the film.

"Another problem in Afghanistan is ethnicity," said Makhmalbaf. "The country's various ethnic groups—Hazarah, Pashtun, Tajiks—are unwilling to work together, or even to be together. Most of the people where we were working had not even heard the word 'film' before. We offered to set up a temporary movie theater to show them a film on a video screen, just to introduce them to the concept, but we had difficulty seating these people together, so we finally had to agree to have different times for different ethnic groups to watch the film."

Then there were other demands.

"Every day as we were working in the desert near the border, we would discover a group of famished people who had escaped from Afghanistan," said Makhmalbaf. "They were considered illegal refugees in Iran. For example, from one group of 40 people who had managed to escape, 20 of them had died on the way, either from disease or hunger.

"The other 20 who had reached the Iran border were also dying because they could not go and get help from the government, since Iran is sending the refugees back home. They had to resign themselves to an almost animal-like existence, hiding in the desert area . . . Each time we would come across these people, we had to stop filming and instead try to rush to the help of the dying. And that was a very sad scene."

Still, the difficulties of filming *Kandahar* have not prevented Makhmalbaf from undertaking another film about Afghanistan. In fact, since September 11, his efforts have acquired a fresh urgency. The film, *Afghan Alphabet,* is sponsored by UNESCO and was shot in October in Zahedan and Zabol, two border towns near Afghanistan. It will premiere in Paris on January 14. The director, reached again a few days ago via e-mail, wrote that in addition to making a film, he has focused on fund-raising in Europe to facilitate the education of Afghan children.

"When you see [*Afghan Alphabet*]," said Makhmalbaf, "you realize that the root cause of terrorism is in the economic and cultural condition of a people. . . . Right now, I am trying to get from Iran to Herat, in Afghanistan, to help establish schools for the education of Afghan children. But my own government does not allow me to do so, because they say they have closed down the border for fear of appearing to have terrorists escape to Iran and give the U.S. a pretext to attack Iran too.

"What sort of an impact has *Kandahar* had when bombs can easily be dropped on Afghanistan but humanitarian help cannot get to where it is most needed? I feel more responsibility as a human being than as a filmmaker."

Originally published in the *Boston Globe.*

Wang Xiaoshuai

Beijing Bicycle

BEIJING BICYCLE TOURS CHINA'S LATEST REVOLUTION, CLASS CONFLICT

A mountain bike—stolen from a courier and then bought at a used bike lot by a prep-schooler—becomes not only the object of a tug of war but an emblem of class conflict in Wang Xiaoshuai's *Beijing Bicycle*. A stark, fresh look at the fallout from China's recent economic reform, the film won the 2001 Berlin Film Festival's Silver Bear Award for its suspenseful drama and a New Talent Award for its teenage actors, Cui Lin (as Guei, the courier) and Li Bin (as Jian, the student).

The film portrays the city as having huge construction projects alongside ancient courtyards and, surprisingly, high school brats decked out in posh uniforms. "There is a new class of cool kids springing up in Shanghai, Juanjo and Beijing," says the 36-year-old Wang. "They're not afraid of anything. They're always watching MTV, playing on the computer and wearing the latest fashions from New York and Hong Kong. And I really feel an inherent distance from these kids.

"This is the first generation with a completely different lifestyle from the one I had when I was their age." The fact that Guei, a lower-class Beijing resident fresh from the countryside, has his bike stolen spells disaster—the only reason he has a job is because of the bike, which he was paying for out of his earnings. "For Guei, it's a means not only of transportation but also of survival," says Wang. When the stolen bike is anonymously put back on sale, Jian (one of the "new class"), legitimately buys it—albeit with money he swiped from his father—so he can gain status with his friends. "For Jian, it's more a plaything," says Wang. "But it's still an equally important and necessary part of life in his social stratum." Against all odds in a city of nine million cyclists, Guei finds and takes back his bicycle from Jian, who, with help from his gang of friends, pursues Guei in a seemingly unending war of nerves until the boys work out a time-share plan—a quixotic solution that aptly illustrates the uneasy relationships formed by China's emerging economic class system.

Beijing Bicycle will be the first of Wang's five features to have a broad theatrical release in the U.S.; ironically, none of his films have been shown in China. A graduate of the Beijing Film Academy, in 1993 Wang made his first film *The Days*—about a deteriorating personal relationship between two artists—on his own without the required official studio backing. (*The Days* and *Frozen* [1995], about a performance artist who freezes himself to death, were banned in China; the 1999 Cannes selection *So Close to Paradise* [1998] passed the censors after three years of re-editing.)

The course of his own rocky filmmaking career has spanned more than a decade of turbulent social change. "*The Days* was made around the time of the June 4 Tiananmen Square incidents [in 1989]," he says. "After that incident, there was a feeling of desperation and we didn't know where we were going or what we were going to do. People were rushing to get out of the country. No one even talked about computers in 1989, let alone wanting to buy an automobile or a computer or their own house. But economic reform, this capitalist fervor that struck in the last few years, was so radical that everybody, even artists, now has the means to buy cars and computers."

And how does the director get around his newly affluent hometown? "My last bicycle was stolen six years ago," he says. "It made me crazy, and I promised myself that I would never, never buy another bicycle. Three years ago, I bought a car—a coproduction between China and Citroën."

Originally published in *Time Out New York*.

TSAI MING-LIANG
What Time Is It There?

We groan under the weight of information and spoken language. Hsiao Kang and Miao Ten may be pokerfaced, but their lack of expression gives them a mythical quality which I find more beautiful.

Tsai Ming-liang, 2002

Although his Chinese peasant immigrant father witnessed Tsai Ming-liang's successful career in theatre and tv drama in the '80s, he died in 1992 and never got to see his son rise to international movie fame as a second-generation Taiwanese director with his debut feature, *Rebels of a Neon God* (1992).

Austere, searingly honest and sexually bold, *Rebels* set the tone for Tsai's subsequent films, all of which have earned acclaim on the festival circuit and among art-film fans.

His work is distinctive: movies that wittily explore the vicissitudes of solitary characters clinging to their humanity in dilapidated, often waterlogged buildings amid the urban desolation of post-economic boom Taipei, one of the much-vaunted Pacific "Little Tiger" economies.

What many have in common is an impassive, riveting young actor named Lee Kang-sheng, the director's muse and alter ego, who appears in *Rebels* as well as in *Vive L'Amour* (1994), *The River* (1996), and *The Hole* (1998).

The actor's nickname, Hsiao Kang, provides the name of his character in Tsai's latest film, *What Time Is It There?*. And the actor's experience led the director to make the film, and to turn to his own family history in the process.

It wasn't until Hsiao Kang's father suddenly died a few years after his own that Tsai decided to make a film about mourning and time that would honor both deaths.

"I was very close to Hsiao Kang's father. He taught me a great deal, and actually he played a passer-by in *Vive L'Amour*," said Tsai, interviewed at Cannes in 2001. "So when he passed away it was also a great shock for me. But it happened while we were busy making *The Hole*. Hsiao is always very pensive and melancholy, so it wasn't until things had quietened down and we were on a plane together after the

Lee Kang-sheng in *What Time Is It There?* (2001, Taiwan) aka *Ni neibian jidan*. Directed by Tsai Ming-liang. Photo Winstar Cinema, courtesy of Photofest.

film was finished that I noticed how unhappy he had become. It was as though I saw a double image of myself a few years ago when my own father passed away."

> "My cinema is the perfect mirror reflection of my own experi-
> ence . . . the more I travel the more lonely and adrift I feel, knowing
> nothing about the places I go. Not knowing your actual space and
> time is the way I wanted to portray time in the film."

Taking compassion and deadpan humor to new directorial heights in Tsai's unique vein of absurdist cinema, *What Time Is It There?*, shot in Taipei and Paris, is at once droll, grave, tender and strangely moving.

After a 3-minute, deliberately-paced opening scene, filmed in a single master shot, in which the father (Miao Tien) serves a plate of food for his son and then walks through the kitchen to smoke a cigarette on the balcony, Hsiao Kang is seen carrying his father's ashes in an urn to the columbarium for a Buddhist ceremony.

From then on, mother (Lu Yi-Ching) and son Hsiao Kang cope with the incomprehensibility of permanent absence in radically different ways, one no more logical than the other. She furbishes an enticingly red-lit altar with food and drink and sets his place at dinner, awaiting reincarnation; and forces her son to pee into bottles and plastic bags lest using the toilet at night disturb his father's spirit.

For his part Hsiao Kang, who makes his living as a watch vendor on a Taipei esplanade, is badgered into reluctantly selling his own dual-time watch to a persistent young woman (Chen Shiang-Chyi) on the verge of leaving for Paris. In order to keep a link with her, he sets the hands on his watches, and on all the clocks he comes across around town, back seven hours to show Paris time.

"My cinema is the perfect mirror reflection of my own experience," said Tsai, who spent a month in Paris after completing *The Hole*. "For the last few years I've been travelling a lot as a director attending film festivals, which has brought me an acute awareness of time zones. Also, the more I travel the more lonely and adrift I feel, knowing nothing about the places I go. Not knowing your actual space and time is the way I wanted to portray time in the film."

While Hsiao Kang's clock-changing is a playful attempt to show psychological continuity between two characters in different countries, the notion gets a further twist when Hsiao Kang changes the time on his own kitchen clock, leading his mother to believe that his dead father has returned and changed the clock so that they can be "on his time"—thereby achieving continuity between characters in this world and the next.

Tsai treats place as he does time to achieve conceptual continuity in spite of spatial dislocation, thus emphasizing Chen's loneliness in a foreign country (she doesn't speak a word of French). Unlike most filmmakers shooting in foreign cities who use establishing shots of recognizable landmarks, Tsai works in the opposite manner, from inside out. Chen, for example, is at first shown in anonymous interiors or underground spaces—hotel room, corridor, café, telephone kiosk, the metro. It's not until later in the story that outdoor Paris emerges.

Born in the small town of Ku Ching (which means town of the pet) in Sarawa, eastern Malaysia, 44-year-old Tsai was raised by his grandparents who ran a noodle stand and were ardent movie buffs.

"Since I was three years old I've been a serious moviegoer," said Tsai. "My grandparents would take turns to take me to the theatre, sometimes to see the same movie. On average I watched two films a day, and never completed any homework assignments. This was a very happy golden era for me because I learned to love watching movies."

He moved to Taipei to attend university, only to find the school did not offer a film department. Tsai studied drama and discovered the French and German New Wave Cinemas of the '60s and '70s mostly through bootlegged video copies.

"This was a very important time for me because through their films, I had the eye-opening view that to be in touch with your creativity you had to be totally free," said Tsai.

In *What Time Is It There?*, a cameo scene with Jean-Pierre Léaud in the Père Lachaise cemetery, for instance, pays homage to Francois Truffaut, which is reinforced by a scene of Hsiao Kang in Taipei watching the 14-year-old Léaud drinking from a stolen bottle of milk in *The Four Hundred Blows* on a rented video.

Using a spare visual style, static camera, long takes, flawless composition, with no music and very little dialogue, Tsai's wonderful comic timing in part derives from the Zen-like meditative space he induces around his core group of actors.

"We groan under the weight of information and spoken language," said Tsai. "Hsiao Kang and Miao Ten may be pokerfaced, but their lack of expression gives them a mythical quality which I find more beautiful. You can read infinitely more into what they are thinking, and there's more interaction with the viewer."

First published in the *Boston Globe*.

Laurent Cantet
L'Emploi du Temps [Time Out]

I've never thought of myself as an activist, far from it. I have a sort of left wing sensibility but my films are a way of exploring the complexity of things rather than offering solutions.

Laurent Cantet, 2002

A taut psychological thriller about a laid-off worker's precarious existence and the web of deception he spins to hide the fact from his family, Laurent Cantet's *L'Emploi du Temps* sparked an electric response when it premiered at the Venice Film Festival. But the 40-year-old wiry silver haired French director hasn't had time to get excited.

"A few days ago I was still in the editing room," said Cantet just after the Venice screening. "This is the first time I've seen the film screened and been able to gauge the public reaction."

The critical reaction was just as positive, the film winning the Golden Lion of the Year Award.

Cantet's first film *Human Resources,* a gripping drama examining the impact of the 35-hour workweek on labor and management, climaxes in the firing of a veteran blue-collar father from a factory by a management team that includes his own son.

With unemployment in France hovering around 9%, it's not surprising that a talented, thoughtful French filmmaker would find working conditions to be a rich source of material for character and story, rather than a documentary, U.S.-indie style.

"I've never thought of myself as an activist, far from it," said Cantet, "I have a sort of left-wing sensibility but my films are a way of exploring the complexity of things rather than offering solutions."

Cantet was born and raised in Niort, a small town near Poitiers in western France, and although he graduated from IHDEC, a film school in Paris, and now lives in a Parisian suburb near Montreuil, he says he still feels provincial. He started out as a cameraman then made two well-received short films, *Tout le Monde à la Manif* (*Everyone to the Demonstration*) and *Jeux de Plage,* which enabled him to meet his current producers, Haut et Court. They proposed that he make a television film, *Les Sanguinaires,* for Arte in an international series called *2000 Seen By* . . . Arte went on to produce *Human Resources.*

In *Time Out,* set in the nebulous world of high finance, the protagonist, a consultant, has already lost his job when the film opens. Slumped on the front seat of his car in a parking lot with his cell phone, he's on his own time now. (The French *L'Emploi du Temps* means both how time is spent and schedule or timetable.)

Cantet co-wrote *Time Out* with Robin Campillo, his long-time editor and best friend.

"The script is a little vague on the reason for Vincent's lay off," said Cantet. "It was a little of his own making. He explains that driving from office to office was the favorite part of his job, he was no longer going to meetings, he preferred to stay in his car, and finally he's quite happy not to be there anymore."

Vincent (Aurelien Recoing) zealously keeps the fact of his lay-off a secret from his wife Muriel (Karin Viard), his three young children, his parents and his friends. While he tools around in his car, he pretends he's working at a more prestigious United Nations job in Geneva, developing managerial training programs in African countries to make them ripe for foreign investors.

"He lies to his wife because he's afraid she won't buy his logic," said Cantet, "and also because he wants to lie. If he were truthful, they would have to change their lives. He doesn't want to. He wants to free himself from the constraints of working, but he doesn't want to jeopardize his nice cozy family life. As we wrote the script, we thought of this story as a very ambiguous escape attempt in which the prisoner acts like he's still in his cell."

"Vincent could almost be Frank's older brother," said Cantet, referring to the college-educated son in *Human Resources.*

CHARACTER STUDY

In casting the part of Vincent, Cantet said that Recoing was the first actor that he had tried out for the role, having seen him play a short part in another film. Recoing is primarily a well-known theatre actor and director who formed his own troupe.

"I was immediately attracted by his solid physique and the soft round contours of his face," said Cantet. "And his ability to suddenly close up and become very troubling. We worked very hard on the confused incoherent nature of his character, someone who can seem totally lucid in social milieus but when he's alone, summons up all the anxiety that he engendered for himself through his behavior."

A crucial role was played by Serge Livrozet, an author and former safebreaker who went to jail for the crime. He plays Jean-Michel, a smuggler with whom Vincent becomes involved.

Baby-faced, crinkly-eyed and balding, Recoing's physiognomy somewhat resembles the thumbprint internet photo of the noted criminal Jean-Claude Romand, whose life inspired the character. For 18 years, Romand, a failed medical student, managed to sustain a false identity as a doctor doing research in cardiology and officer of the World Health Organization in Geneva while he defrauded his friends of millions of francs.

"The comparison stops there," said Cantet. In 1996, when Romand's secret was revealed, he killed his wife, his children, his dog and his parents and attempted to commit suicide by setting fire to the house.

"Rather than a killer or a psychopath," said Cantet, "I wanted to create the most commonplace character possible, so that the viewer could identify with him . . . What interested me about the Romand case was how a man could for so long write another parallel life for himself, so to speak. Everyone dreams at some point of changing his life. [Vincent] actively lives that dream."

Having a character most of whose life is a fabrication made his work especially difficult as a director, Cantet said.

"It was very difficult to know whether to make the lies very flagrant," he said, "or whether to go for the overall sincerity of the character."

After several months of rehearsal with Recoing and the other actors, all of whom were non-professionals except Viard, Cantet said they felt they were getting close to the right tone.

"Although it may seem paradoxical to cast a theatre actor with amateurs, in fact it worked out well," said Cantet. "Film actors are afraid of rehearsals, because they're used to being spontaneous. Rehearsals don't scare a theater actor, and amateurs definitely need them too."

"In fact," Cantet added with a tongue-twisting flourish worthy of Gilbert and Sullivan, "the professionals professionalize the non-professionals," he added, "and the non-professionals deprofessionalize the professionals."

First published in the *Boston Globe*.

FABIÁN BIELINSKY

Nine Queens

Street swindlers can be extremely kind to you as they are robbing you. I tried to maintain this duality [in the script].

Fabián Bielinsky, 2002

Although a set of rare stamps worth half a million dollars figures prominently in Fabián Bielinsky's caper film *Nine Queens,* set in his native Buenos Aires, the affable soft-spoken director did not collect stamps as a child: in fact, he was already making Super 8 movies at the age when many small boys are avid hobbyists.

In *Nine Queens,* his focus is on street swindlers. The angelic-looking Juan (Gaston Pauls), the rookie of the two principals, is trying to raise cash to get his dad out of jail; no such noble filial sentiment inspires his partner Marcos (Ricardo Garin), who is just looking for a sidekick to help him go after bigger game.

"I was always fascinated" by con artists, said Bielinsky. "It's an old tradition in Argentina. I knew a lot of them, I'd read a lot about them, and finally I had them in my head."

With street smarts as their weapons of choice, the film's swindlers, or *estafadores callejeros,* are unusually charismatic and amiable.

"Street swindlers can be extremely kind to you as they are robbing you," Bielinsky said. "I tried to maintain this duality" in the script. Over the course of a longish day, the pair work their way from the barrios to a posh hotel, where Marcos' imperious sister works as manager, in an attempt to pull off the sale and resale of the forged Weimar-era stamps to a Venezuelan collector. Gradually, it seems the entire cast of characters is implicated in a maze of crosses and double crosses.

Bielinsky traces his longtime fascination with swindlers to having heard stories about attempted fraud told by his father, an insurance broker who was also a film critic for some small cultural newspapers.

On the set: Fabián Bielinsky, director of *Nine Queens* (2000, Argentina) aka *Nueve Reinas*. Photo Silvio Benitez, courtesy of Photofest.

"All their lives both my parents were really involved in art," said Bielinsky. "My sister is a painter. They really encouraged us to go for it, whatever we wanted."

As a teenager Bielinsky Jr. joined a film group at Buenos Aires' oldest and most prestigious university-run high school. Then he won a festival prize for his film school short, *L'Espera,* an adaptation of a story by Jorge Luis Borges. Bielinsky, though, waited nearly 20 years before directing his first feature.

"I wasn't ready, and I didn't have a story to tell," said Bielinsky. "I preferred to work in the industry, to continue learning."

His position as a first assistant director—the AD, the man in charge of the set—on hundreds of commercials and on several features by Argentinian directors—taught him to be very organized, at least in his professional life, said Bielinsky. But it also affected him in another way.

"Having all this experience as an AD meant I was in trouble," said Bielinsky, 43. "You get to be on automatic pilot, and nothing excites you any more. That's the moment you have to move forward. And that's when I decided to make a film."

When Bielinsky sat down to write the script in 1997, Argentina was in turmoil. "The entire '90s in Argentina was a [period] of high corruption, high cynicism, immoral and obscene displays of wealth" by government officials, he said. "Not only did they suddenly increase their wealth, but they showed it. [It was] indecent exposure in every state-owned company. And then the economy exploded completely."

"THE SOCIAL SMELL OF THE TIMES"

"At the time, believe me, I wasn't trying to do any social commentary," he said. "But as I was writing, what was going on in the country, the social smell of the times, passed through me into my story. I was really concerned with telling the story in the best way possible, to make it enjoyable for the audience. Then, the script became a little more than I thought it was going to be."

The wait paid off. Acclaimed for its meticulous detail, nimble plotting, and engaging performances, *Nine Queens* won a script award that got it a producer—and seven national Argentinian awards when it was released.

"On one hand, the experience as AD helped me a lot, because the set of a film was already a very familiar place for me," said Bielinsky. "I knew what was happening around me, and what every member of the team was doing. I was able to plan, with much precision, everything that I wanted to do and concentrate on the most important things, without losing time. But the bad thing was that in the first few weeks of filming, I continued thinking like an AD, preoccupying myself with logistics and organization, without realizing that [directing] is something more. When I was able to put those thoughts aside, I felt liberated and very comfortable in my role as director."

Audiences told Bielinsky that they saw the film as a reflection of their society, but he now sees it differently.

"I don't think it's a portrait [of Argentina]," he said. "We are not crooks. We are not swindlers. A con man story does not represent us. All it represents is a mood, the feeling that everybody is a son of a bitch. Not a reality."

Bielinsky said that there were times when he had felt that everyone, even a little kid or his grandfather, would lie, cheat, rob, do whatever he had to do to survive. "But we still have working people, very nice people, honest people in our country," he said.

Street swindlers were understandably loath to come forward to assist him in his script research, but victims were legion and more than willing to share their experiences. A scam in the film—ringing apartment doorbells and pretending that Juan is a long lost relative in need of a loan—was reported by the director's aunt.

"In my research I came across 50 different tricks, all beautiful, and I used maybe four or five in the film."

When the crooks finally sell the stamps and rush to the bank for the cash, they arrive to find people pounding on the bank's locked doors. It seems like a premonition of more recent news reports.

"Bank closure? That happened in my country for years," said Bielinsky. "What is happening now is not just a sudden explosion . . . Banks closing their doors, that happened every three, four, five years in my country. That scene was describing reality."

First published in the *Boston Globe*.

JUAN CARLOS CREMATA

Nada

My film is called *Nothing,* but really it means *everything.* We were looking to put our finger on the Cuban reality exactly.

Juan Carlos Cremata, 2002

The stylish and cosmopolitan Juan Carlos Cremata, whose debut feature *Nada* has already been fêted in his native Cuba, will now have the chance to saunter on the Croisette and to test the waters at the world's élite film venue when *Nada* screens at this year's Directors' Fortnight, a Cannes Film Festival sidebar where entries from Turkey, Syria and Mauritania and all four corners of the world are on an equal footing with those from Cuba's largest neighbor.

A slightly trimmed version will enable the Directors' Fortnight to list *Nada* as a world première, although the original cut premiered at the Festival of New Latin American Cinema in Havana in December 2001.

"For many Cubans, a very important [aspect of] the film is the relationship between Cubans in Cuba and Cubans out of Cuba, and what it means to be Cuban, anywhere," said Cremata, interviewed at his home in Havana. "The story of my film could make you cry from beginning to end, because it's pretty serious—the immigration problem and the political problem between the United States and Cuba. But we try to laugh, to think about it in a positive way. Even in the worst situation, you have to be able to find things that are beautiful." *Nada,* a romantic comedy, has a strong vein of bureaucratic satire in its portrayal of the workplace.

"Bureaucracy is a universal sickness," said Cremata. "I found it in Germany, Holland, the United States, everywhere. It's the closed mind. [In *Nada*] I wanted people to laugh and think at the same time. If that is dangerous for somebody it's not my problem."

This lighthearted approach masks the sting of *Nada*'s social critique.

"My film is called *Nothing,* but really it means *everything.* We were looking to put our finger on the Cuban reality exactly."

Foto: Ismael Almeida

Portrait of Juan Carlos Cremata, director of *Nada*, which premiered at the
Festival of New Latin American Cinema in Havana, 2000. Courtesy Liza Béar.

Nada stars Cuban leading actress and dancer Thaïs Valdez as the free-spirited,
dreamy, zen-like Carla, a post office worker whose parents have emigrated to
Florida and have entered her name in the U.S. immigration lottery. A fish out of
water amongst her more frenzied, officious colleagues, an accidental coffee spill
on the mail she is sorting suddenly opens up a world of suffering amongst letter writers, and an opportunity to embellish their correspondence with her own
input. Once she warms to the task—and to a co-worker—winning the lottery presents her with a difficult choice.

"I was in love with Thaïs Valdez since she made her first film," said Cremata.
"She's a muse, she's divine, she's completely natural." The veteran Cuban actress

Juan Carlos and Thaïs Valdez on the set of *Nada*. Courtesy Liza Béar.

Daisy Granados, one of her co-stars, calls Valdez "the Cuban Garbo," according to the filmmaker.

While Valdez portrays Carla as quiet and compassionate, in the film Cremata wittily blends animation and special effects for comic exaggeration and to convey Carla's inner world and point of view.

In cinematic terms, Cremata was able to convey the light and the dark side of life in Cuba by making his film both in color and black and white. The bulk of the images in the final print are black and white, but occasionally objects appear in color, such as the yellow flower on Carla's desk.

Cremata's training and prior filmmaking experience prepared him to undertake such an audacious, technically challenging feat.

After graduating in theater from Havana's Art Institute, Cremata (whose full name is Cremata Malberti, after both parents), made award-winning children's series for Cuban television, where his mother still works. He attended Cuba's international film school at San Antonio Los Baños, and subsequently taught editing and directing at two film schools in Buenos Aires. His experimental short films have been widely shown in international festivals and earned him a Guggenheim Fellowship in 1996, after which he spent time in New York.

Enigmatic, irreverent and occasionally caustic, Cremata is an arresting figure with a panama hat, sunglasses and harlequin bells sewn into his clothes. In spite of appearances, he plays neither the court jester nor the enfant terrible; he treads lightly in a climate where a filmmaker is dependent on local support from the

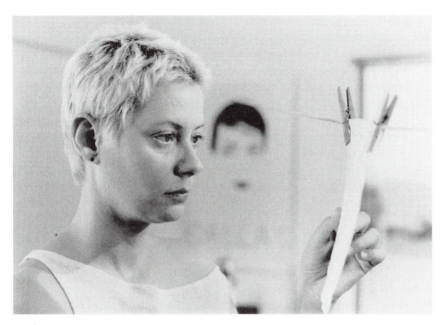

Thaïs Valdez, as Carla the postal worker, reading a letter in *Nada*. Courtesy Liza Béar.

Cuban Film Institute (ICAIC) for equipment and crew and must secure foreign co-production financing.

Few of the films made under such conditions ever see wide U.S. release—the 1995 Oscar nominee *Strawberry and Chocolate* is a notable exception—but many are screened at art film venues and on the international festival circuit. *Life Is to Whistle,* a more recent depiction of political and economic anxieties in contemporary Cuba, also received a limited run in U.S. theaters, and even played the 2000 edition of the Miami Film Festival, despite protests from the Cuban exile community.

The prospects look good for *Nada,* which has been five years in the making. After a false start with a New York restaurant owner/producer, Cremata hooked up with French producer Thierry Forte.

"It was very hard to raise the money, and to make the film in black and white and color," said Cremata. "The French producer helped me a lot. I think in France producers are different than in the rest of the world. They look for artistic pieces. That was my opportunity."

Forte was able to bring Italian and Spanish co-producers on board, and the highly skilled postproduction work, which required transfer from film to digital video and back to film, was performed in Spain and France.

Cremata's frequent travels—which most recently included participating in a screenwriting workshop for Latin American filmmakers run in Mexico by the Sundance Institute—have not rendered him immune from long waits and bureaucratric hassles to secure the necessary letters of transit. So it's not surprising he's sympathetic to the tortuous procession outside his Havana house.

A stone's throw from Cremata's balcony is a small park crammed with several hundred people waiting to apply for visas from the U.S. Interests section. The visas are mostly for permission to visit their relatives in the U.S., not for permanent emigration.

"It's very funny that I live here," said Cremata, "because *Nada* is about the people who are waiting over there [across the street]. Every morning they wake me up with their problems. On the other side is a funeral parlor where the most famous people in Cuba lie in state—artists, politicians. They call this park the Park of Hope—you wait for one place or the other."

Originally published in the *So. Florida Sun Sentinel.*

ELIA SULEIMAN
Divine Intervention

A young West Bank woman flouting a military checkpoint in broad daylight could have triggered yet another disaster in the Israeli-Palestinian conflict. But the woman was the intrepid Ramallah journalist Manal Khader and her act of defiance instead became the inspiration for a friend's film.

Divine Intervention, directed by Palestinian filmmaker Elia Suleiman, evokes the absurd side of the Israeli occupation through a series of farcical vignettes that erupt into violence. The semi-autobiographical story tracks the movements of E.S., a seemingly car-bound filmmaker played by Suleiman himself, as he visits his

Elia Suleiman stars in *Divine Intervention* (2002, Palestine) which he also directed. Suleiman continues his exploration of tensions in the occupied territories. Festival de Cannes, courtesy of Photofest.

dying father in a hospital, meets with his lover in a parking lot, and blows up an Israeli tank with an apricot kernel thrown from his car window.

The checkpoint crossing is wittily recreated with the road as a fashion runway. Wearing a clinging pink dress and high-heeled strap shoes, Khader stares down the soldiers, makes them drop their guns and causes the watchtower to collapse.

"Unfortunately it made me hate my job as a journalist," said Khader at the Cannes Film Festival of her newfound freedom as an actress. Playing themselves, she and Suleiman mutely reenact their former real-life rapport as lovers, caressing each other's hands in silent reproach of the verbal and physical harassment they regularly witness. The film burlesques the hassles endured by Palestinians at the checkpoints. Israeli soldiers strip a driver of his jacket, make other drivers switch cars, arbitrarily stop some from passing through the checkpoint, and quiz a Muslim about his social life during Ramadan. A drunken soldier seizes another Palestinian by the shoulder, forcing him to sing Israeli marching songs in lockstep.

"The only place [Manal and I] could meet was the parking lot next to the Al Ram checkpoint on the road between Jerusalem and Ramallah," said Suleiman, 42, who lived in Jerusalem for five years while he set up a film department at Bir Zeit University. "One day she was very late. She said they'd blocked the checkpoint and told everybody to go back. She decided to cross. They raised the machine guns, saying, 'If you go one more step we'll shoot.' She said, 'Shoot,' and continued walking. She's tough."

Suleiman was born in Nazareth, which falls within the pre-1967 State of Israel borders, so he carries Israeli identification, although he rejects the label Arab Israeli. Life for him and his brothers growing up in Nazareth, he says, consisted of street games, small-town boredom and hushed voices. At the time the ruling

Manal Khader and Elia Suleiman meet in the parking lot next to Al Ram checkpoint in Suleiman's *Divine Intervention*. Courtesy of Photofest.

Labor Party's Shin Bet, or Domestic Security Agency, had instigated strict control of Palestinians.

"We were all monitored very closely," he says. "A lot of phones were bugged, and some [people] were expelled because of their political views."

Divine Intervention is dedicated to the memory of his father. When Suleiman was 14, his father was accused of being a Palestine Liberation Organization supporter and imprisoned for three days. In 1948, he had been tortured to a comatose stage by the Israelis for refusing to denounce a Palestinian political leader, then thrown off a cliff and left for dead.

The young Suleiman was fascinated (as an outsider) by gangs and by the Communist Party, a cultural force in Nazareth that screened films and provided a social venue for teenagers.

Livelier than his impassive screen persona suggests, Suleiman has either charmed or been lucky with his neighbors. These have included an undercover cop in Nazareth who tipped him off to a pending arrest for allegedly being a gang member at age 17. Within 24 hours, Suleiman fled to a London life of dishwashing and attractive French girls.

There he met Marxist art critic John Berger whose book *Ways of Seeing*—about the primacy of the image over the word in our understanding of the world—greatly influenced him. *Divine Intervention* and his first film, *Chronicle of a Disappearance* (1996), rely more on visual gags and set pieces than on dramatic action.

During stays in New York between 1981 and 1993, Suleiman lived near Columbia University and met Palestinian author Edward Said and producer James Schamus who became mentors. Schamus recalls standing on a bluff in Devonshire, England, on the set of Ang Lee's *Sense and Sensibility,* fielding questions from Suleiman who was phoning him from Bethlehem.

TURNING ON EACH OTHER

Chronicle of a Disappearance explored the filmmaker's feelings as an expatriate on his return to his hometown after a 12-year absence. The neighborliness shown in that film is not apparent in the Nazareth of *Divine Intervention*. The strain of second-class citizenship has taken its toll. Neighbors develop feuds, curse each other under their breath, throw garbage in each other's yards, obstruct roadways, and even beat each other up.

"Palestinians are confined to very little space," says Suleiman. "Many are low paid laborers or unemployed, with no cultural venues. They build on top of each other because the rest of the land has been annexed. It results in the total disintegration of social harmony. Instead of facing the real enemy, they clash among themselves."

Miranda Sissons, a Middle East researcher at Human Rights Watch in New York, says that Palestinians in Nazareth are suffering from lack of access to land and discrimination in social benefits, as well as higher unemployment rates compared with those of Jewish Israelis.

"The perception is that the bureaucracy at best doesn't care," Sissons says, "and at worst is working actively against them."

Coinciding with the start of the latest Intifada over two years ago, the filming of *Divine Intervention* was harrowing. Suleiman said the crew would constantly have to strike the set and change locations to avoid gunfire. "As we packed to go to Nazareth, 11 people were killed," he says. "And they were bringing in the dead to the hospital while I was location scouting."

Schamus says the great thing about Suleiman is that he has disregarded most of Schamus's advice. His ambitions have always far exceeded what any rational person would say a Palestinian filmmaker could accomplish," Schamus says. "And he achieves the impossible."

"It was a long, difficult adventure," says the film's veteran French producer Humbert Balsan, the only producer Suleiman approached who did not ask him to remove the Ninja sequence from the script because it would absorb 30 percent of the film's budget.

First published in the New York *Daily News*.

Manoel de Oliveira
I'm Going Home

VENERABLE DIRECTOR MANOEL DE OLIVEIRA BRINGS
A LIGHT TOUCH TO A TRAGIC TALE

Portuguese maestro Manoel de Oliveira no longer uses his garage to develop film negatives in or the family billiard table to edit his films on, as he did in the early '30s, but at 93 his passion for filmmaking continues unabated.

Gaining international notice in the '70s with a slew of salon dramas satirizing romantic love and social pieties, Oliveira has made at least a film a year in the last two decades, creating a unique body of work. It includes the ambitious *Vale Abraao,* his 1993 adaptation of *Madame Bovary,* and exquisite journeys like the Marcello Mastroianni valedictory *Voyage to the Beginning of the World* (1997), and the Proustian road movie *Oporto of My Childhood* (2001), which he narrates and in which he has a cameo as a thief. His movies frequently reveal his taste for the unexpected, and even the odd practical joke.

In town briefly with his grandson Ricardo Trepa on the first lap of a promotional tour for his first U.S. theatrical release, *I'm Going Home,* the famously mischievous director couldn't resist stealing a march on the publicity machine, showing up unannounced in the lobby of the Mayflower Hotel and proposing we take the stairs to his 11th-floor suite.

I'm Going Home, which opens at Film Forum on Wednesday, is set in a sparkling, millennial Paris. Frenchman Michel Piccoli plays an esteemed theater actor who is performing the lead in Eugene Ionesco's tragic farce *Exit the King* when he learns that his wife, daughter and son-in-law have been killed in a car crash. Nursing his grief privately and taking care of his orphaned 6-year-old grandson, he copes with the ups and downs of daily life in Montparnasse and with pressures from his agent.

Oliveira's longtime producer, Paolo Branco, introduced Piccoli to Oliveira for a role in *Party* (1996), which was shot in the Azores.

Michel Piccoli in Manoel de Oliveira's *I'm Going Home* (2003, Portugal). Courtesy of Milestone Films.

"He was marvelous," said Oliveira. "I really wanted to work with him again."

He offered Piccoli a small role as the older Padre Antonio Vieiria in *Word and Utopia,* Oliveira's 2000 biopic about the radical 17th-century Jesuit, orator and Portuguese national hero who emigrated to Brazil during the Inquisition and fought slavery. But Piccoli was busy with his directorial feature debut.

"When Piccoli turned down the part," Oliveira continued, "the famous Italian actor I invited at the last minute simply could not memorize Vieira's long speeches in Latin. He fluffed his lines three times and finally just said, 'I'm going home,' and left."

HUGE SECRET

Oliveira saw the potential in this episode for his next film. "It was tragic for this to happen to a name actor," he said, "but what I saw here was not so much a character as human vulnerability. We are all headed for disaster. And I was inspired to make a film which would end in exactly this way, with the actor saying, 'I'm going home,' using the elements from the real-life situation but transposing them."

It was, he noted with a touch of glee, "a film that Piccoli could not resist."

"This film is based on a huge secret," said Piccoli. "It's about what you don't see or talk about, which finally becomes an extraordinary trap. Occasionally a door in the movie will open up onto a farce"—like the scene of the actor talking to his agent with the camera on their shoes—"so as to avoid tragedy. To me, the film is about suffering and the modesty or reticence that goes with it."

Piccoli says that Oliveira is "a man of great culture, great secrets, great age, who acts younger than everyone else."

The son of an Oporto industrialist who took him to the movies as a child, Oliveira began to make films in his 20s when he was also a champion pole-vaulter and racecar driver. In 1931, he directed his first film, *Douro, Faina Fluvial*, a silent short chronicling the harsh conditions endured by workers on the River Douro. Two years later, his fame as an athlete got him an acting role in the first Portuguese talkie.

"Sport put order in my life," said Oliveira. "It helped me do things that were good for my health."

It was in Oporto nightclubs and cafés where he began to observe life, he says, and where he met future artistic collaborators such as Rodrigues Freitas, whose short story inspired a feature about ghetto children, *Aniki Bobo* (1942). Oliveira took a forced break from movie making during the Salazar dictatorship to run the family business, returning to filmmaking in 1956 with one of his lyrical documentaries.

Branco, who distributed Oliveira's *Ill-Fated Love* in 1978 and has produced 18 of his 22 films since 1981, says his job as a producer is easy because Oliveira simplifies his images.

"Each film is a surprise, even for me," Branco said. "But there's never any doubt that Manoel knows exactly what he wants. The biggest challenge of [*I'm Going Home*] was to cull a life lesson from such a little story and touch on very serious matters with an incredible lightness of spirit—and with a smile."

First published in the New York *Daily News*.

DENYS ARCAND

Barbarian Invasions

Emotion's not my trademark. My trademark is irony, blistering satire. If you don't have perfect pitch on this subject . . . you're a dead duck.

Denys Arcand, 2003

The premiere of Denys Arcand's sizzling, poignant new film, *Barbarian Invasions,* at the Cannes Film Festival this year wrenched equal parts tears and laughter from its audience.

The film is about reconciliation between a father and his son as the father is dying. It examines generational friction, euthanasia, the state of Canadian hospital care, the plight of religious artifacts, and the vagaries of the narcotics squad, all of which are deftly woven into the plot.

The film brings back most of the cast from Arcand's *Decline of the American Empire* and adds two striking newcomers, Stéphane Rousseau as the son and Marie-Josée Croze as a heroin addict who administers the coup de grace. It won Cannes' Best Screenplay Award and Best Actress award for Croze at Cannes. Before the screening, the French-Canadian director was unusually nervous. His previous film, *Stardom,* reflecting his own take on celebrity, had bombed.

"Emotion's not my trademark," says Arcand. "My trademark is irony, blistering satire. When I had tears in my eyes while we were shooting, I said, 'If we miss on this, we're going to be savaged.' Because if you don't have perfect pitch on this subject . . . you're a dead duck. 'I have a twelve-gauge gun waiting for you. All right Canada goose, fly in front of me and I'm going to shoot you down.' So the fact that we pulled it off has put me in a blissful state."

Pulling it off wasn't so easy. Ever since his grandfather, father and mother died within a five-year period more than a decade ago, Arcand had wanted to make a film on the theme of loss.

"I was mulling it over," Arcand says. "But I couldn't come up with the right idea for a script for a long, long time. I wrote four or five drafts that I left on the shelf because they had a heaviness to them that I hated. My ultimate hero, or heroes, are people like Chekhov, people like Luis Bunuel, who talk about something extraordinarily serious with a smile, with a sort of slight detachment. I always try to emulate that. So that was the thing I couldn't get in my first tryouts. Some person's going to die, but yes, we're all going to die."

In the meantime, when Arcand was 55, he and his domestic partner adopted a Chinese baby girl. He describes the experience as a kind of Proustian epiphany.

"It wasn't until I was taking care of my daughter that I remembered things from my own childhood—my mother giving me a bath in a very cold bathroom with an electric heater. And how much my parents had loved me," says Arcand, who grew up in a small village in Quebec until the age of 11. "I was never able to give that love back, in [their] life, to tell them how much I loved them. So films are made also to repair the past. In this film I could make the son say that to his father."

Another breakthrough in the writing process was when Arcand decided that one of the four main characters in *Decline*—Remy (Remy Girard), a history professor—should be the father. The original Remy had two children. "What's an old socialist's worst nightmare?" he asks. "To have a young ambitious, puritanical capitalist son. And since I knew people exactly like that I molded his character on these young turks."

In the film, Remy's son Sébastien is an international financier working in London, and estranged from his father. He comes to Montreal at the request of his mother to orchestrate his father's last days. Thanks to Sébastien's deep pockets, he is able to minimize his father's discomfort by securing him a private room. The film becomes a celebration of life, friendship and filial love.

Arcand's witty observation of academic mores and verbal jousting has long roots; he received a degree in history at the University of Montreal and has many friends among academics. He numbers books, along with golf clubs and tennis racquets, as his favorite possessions. "I have a life outside filmmaking," he says. "There are long gaps between my films because I enjoy living."

After auditioning him twice, Arcand cast stand-up comedian Stéphane Rousseau as Sebastien. "He called me an hour after the audition," says Rousseau. "I never thought Denys would come and get me for one of his films. But I had a feeling that role was meant for me." His 20-year career as a comedian began at 13, after his mother died. "I made my mom laugh all the time, because she was very sick for the last five years of her life," he says. "So I was always getting into costumes. And my mom would tell me, 'You're going to be a stand-up.' So obviously, I couldn't be anything else."

First published in *The Christian Science Monitor*.

RA'ANAN ALEXANDROWICZ
James' Journey to Jerusalem

Cinema is a shallow medium in many many respects but what it can do stronger than most media is show you the world though someone else's eyes.

Ra'anan Alexandrowicz, 2004

In a startlingly upbeat fiction feature debut, Ra'anan Alexandrowicz presents a contemporary odyssey through the seamy underbelly of Israeli society.

James (Siyabonga Shibe), a young Christian from South Africa sent by his village on a mission to the Holy land, gets a rude wake-up call in Tel Aviv on his immediate arrest at the airport. In a shady deal with the authorities, the immigrant jail doubles up as a source of cheap manual labor for Shimi (Salim Daw) who whisks him off to prison-like digs, takes his passport and forces him to work as a cleaner. But James' magic touch soon earns him a better job tending the garden of his boss' father Salah (Arie Elias), under whose tutelage he gradually wises up to the rules of the game. Being a quick study, James sets up his own scam hiring other immigrants. While never losing hope, his search for Jerusalem becomes subverted by the lure of economic gain. With his sagacious wide eyes and radiant smile, Shibe's apt performance as a modern Candide breathes a joyousness rare in political entertainment.

At once a rueful comedy of manners and a scathing satire of a certain strand of Israeli society, the film's wonderfully light touch avoids both caricature and preachiness. Alexandrowicz springs ample plot surprises and to the film's many deliciously wicked ironies adds his own penchant for casting Arabs as Jews. I talked to Ra'anan Alexandrowicz on a windy afternoon at Cannes after the film's premiere in Director's Fortnight.

Liza Béar: Tell me how you came up with this highly original story—is it your story?

Ra'anan Alexandrowicz: It is. Five or six years ago I knew a 45-year-old Nigerian man named James. He lived in Tel Aviv on a long-expired tourist visa. He

Salim Daw as Shimi and Siyabonga Melongisi Shibe as James in *James' Journey to Jersualem* (2003, Israel), directed by Ra'anan Alexandrowicz. Photo by Y.R. Morad, courtesy of Zeitgeist Films.

hoped to reach Canada one day. And once he told me how he had imagined my country before he came. In Nigeria people are very religious—the Holy Land has a clear image, straight from the Bible. And he imagined it as this amazing— beautiful, calm and happy place where the Chosen People live, very virtuously. And when he got off the plane and he smelled the air of the Holy Land, he began to cry. He didn't come to be a tourist, he came . . .

LB: On pilgrimage?

RA: No, to stay and work. What people can make in Israel doing hard labor is a lot of money for where they come from. From the contrast between his expectations and the reality of his life, I felt something very strong, like the beginning of a film . . . I just knew that the tension between these two, the Holy Land one dreams of and the Israel one finds, was something that I should explore. And then I began to write the story. I created this basic situation of someone who comes for a pilgrimage and then ends up as a migrant worker.

LB: So in the script you changed the nationality of your character from Nigerian to Zulu.

RA: Right . . . The nationality here is not really highlighted. In Israel there's been this new black community for about ten years now. It's mainly from Nigeria and Ghana, but also from many other countries, including South

Africa. So in the end I chose to place James from South Africa because of the actor I was working with. But I don't have a vision of Africa as a place where everything is so different regarding how people are with each other, and regarding the influence of money on people's lives. And since I've researched, I know that there are remote places in the African continent where people still live a very different life, and a life that is less influenced by these strong forces of materialism that have infested our social behavior to a great extent. So James in the story comes from this place that's the furthest you can go from Western society.

LB: Sounds idyllic—a place of innocence and naiveté. You must have been thrilled when you found Siyabonga Shibe because he's the perfect actor to convey that . . .

RA: I think so.

LB: How did you find him?

RA: We worked with a casting agency in South Africa and saw about 20 actors on tape. We narrowed it down to two. I went to South Africa to work a couple of days with each of them and decide.

LB: I know around the world immigration regulations have tightened up. How realistic is it that in Israel people are slammed into jail the minute they get off the plane?

RA: There's a slim chance. People are [eyeing Israel very critically] now. Just like when you make an American film about someone who goes on death row without being guilty: it's a horrible statistic, but . . . you're more likely to find yourself in a car crash.

LB: No, but the U.S. has over 2 million people in jail. It's one of the largest incarcerated populations in the entire world. And probably the most proportionately who undergo capital punishment.

RA: And this is why it's good to make films about it. So in Israel if you don't get a visa you *might* get deported. And someone *might* bail you out and give you a permit to work. Legally, the situation is possible. How common it is, I have to say I didn't check. By the way, in the last 5 years there have been amazing European films about this subject, the Belgian *La Promesse*, a stunning film . . .

LB: Yes, and *Last Resort* by Pawel Polokowski, in England.

RA: It's important for me to say this—because my last two works were documentaries. To study the community of migrant workers in Israel within a documentary film, their way of life and their problems, is very important. It's something that I ignored from the beginning with this script. I wanted to make a film that talks about other things, but also comes from within this world.

LB: What was charming and a revelation was how James absorbs the values of the culture. And it must have been thrilling when you came up with that turn in the script. This approach gives you a double insight . . .

RA: You're right. This was definitely the moment of happiness when I had the idea, I'm going to make this journey through our culture through these very naïve eyes—it's actually a bit of my own journey emotionally. I let James ask the question for me and for us. Cinema is a shallow medium in many many respects but what it can do stronger than most media is show you the world though someone else's eyes. And when you take it one step further, it can show you yourself through someone else's eyes. And this is a very strong experience for the audience. Again, I decided that if I want to put up this kind of mirror, I'd do it with humor. When I say "us," I don't mean only Israelis, or the many nationalities and religions that live in my country. The reason I made this film a fairy tale was because these traits apply to us as Israelis, but also to everyone who lives within today's ruling economic system.

LB: Whatever religion or ethnic group they are.

RA: Regretfully there are some levels of the film that may not be easily under-stood outside Israel. For instance, James's strongest connection in the film is with Salah, his boss Shimi's father. This character is actually an homage to a character in an old Israeli film, *Salah Shabati*, about an immigrant from an Arab country. Salah is an Arabic name. Salah is from Iraq. [As it happens] the actor who plays the part actually emigrated from Iraq in 1950. He knew how to do Shakespeare in Arabic. But once in Israel he was completely denied [his status] as an artist and as an actor because at the time Arabic was not accepted as a cultural language. So this man, the actor himself, in fact had a very difficult time immigrating to Israel. And the character that he's playing also has this his-tory. So the old immigrant from 50 years ago who has learned the tricks of the society and gained his own power, and also weakness, is now teaching the new immigrant who's just arrived . . .

LB: . . . the tricks of the trade. What's touching is that Salah's very attached to his backyard, this tiny plot of land that's about to be engulfed by huge, ugly build-ing projects, and he represents . . .

RA: James in a way represents the development of the Israeli dream, how we came with very idealistic and pure dreams, about how we were going to develop ourselves in the country. And at the moment it seems to us that somehow on the way to making these dreams come true . . .

A strong gust of wind blows down a tent pole, nearly hitting us.

We were saying . . . So James comes to the Holy Land with this very strong dream. And on the way to making it come true, he sort of loses his way. Now he's no longer dreaming of Jerusalem but he's dreaming of a new television. But he's still *talking* about Jerusalem. So he symbolizes for me our confusion with ourselves at the moment.

LB: Materialism.

RA: Materialism is the common denominator for all the roughness in human behavior now, whether it's so-called political problems, or any form of social interaction between people, between nations.

LB: How do you feel about what's happening in your country?

RA: My previous film, *The Inner Tour*, dealt with [the Israeli-Palestinian] situation. And that's why in interviews I felt I had the right to talk about it. And now, since the new film does not in any way deal with the subject, I sort of restrict myself to . . . but I do have something to say regarding the film. And it's about this concept of *frayer* [Yiddish slang]. The character Salah in the film is teaching James not to be a *frayer*. He's teaching him to be strong, to not let go of anything, just as he did his son. But afterwards his two sons, his own creations, turn against him, and he finds himself in a weak position in relation to them—his real son and his adopted son. At one point James tells him, look, you can get $1 million for your plot of land. Why don't you take it? Don't be a *frayer*, take it. It's the other way around now. If I take the money I'm *frayer*. What do I gain from it? This is perhaps something the Israeli consciousness should understand, that we are trapped now, into not being *frayer* in the situation. Perhaps our way out is through being exactly the opposite of what we believe, the opposite of being strong.

LB: This is what you can contribute to the discourse.

RA: Yes. And the change of James in the film from someone who's completely ready to be a *frayer* to someone who won't be a *frayer* any more, and then begins to make enemies and to hurt other people, comes to a point in the end of the film where James wakes up, where he finds who he was and what he is now. And this is something that I hope for us very much.

Originally published on *indiewire.com*.

ALAN MAK, ANDREW LAU
Infernal Affairs

I'm impatient and like to work very fast. Alan is more patient. So we balance each other out.

Andrew Lau, 2004

In the mind-bending Hong Kong psychological thriller *Infernal Affairs*, Yan (Tony Leung) is a faux gangster who's really a cop working undercover in the Triads, the Hong Kong version of the Mafia.

His opposite is Ming (Andy Lau), a fake cop trained in the Police Academy who's really a Triad gangster, driven by ambition, now rapidly scaling ranks at the police force.

The stylish tale of divided loyalties has attracted an extra measure of attention because it has already been picked for a high-profile Hollywood remake—set in Boston with Martin Scorsese directing Leonardo DiCaprio as the undercover cop and Matt Damon as the mob mole.

Infernal Affairs has one more double bill, co-directors Alan Mak and Andrew Lau.

"We tried to divide up the directing beforehand but couldn't," said Mak. "So we just went to the set and let it happen."

"I'm lazy and didn't want to talk," said Lau, who also shot the film. "So I let Alan talk to the actors while I set up the camera and the lights." Lau's dazzling mise en scène [he formerly shot for Wong Kar-wai] is big on rooftops and reflections.

"Besides, we're very different people," Lau said. "I'm impatient and like to work very fast. Alan is more patient. So we balance each other out."

Unlike the traditional Hong Kong genre film—in which fists and bullets dominate the action—Mak and Lau stressed the psychological predicament of the characters in their own private hells. The Chinese name for the movie, *Mo-Gaan-do*, means continuous hell, the lowest type of hell in Buddhism.

When a drug transaction and a drug bust go awry, both the Triads and the police realize they have been infiltrated. The moles are assigned to ferret each other out in a war of nerves.

Friend or Faux? In *Infernal Affairs* (Hong Kong, 2004), Andy Lau (left) and Tony Leung (right) struggle for the upper hand in Hong Kong's world of organized crime. Codirected by Alan Mak and Andrew Lau. Courtesy of Photofest.

"We wanted to put our eyes on the drama and the actors," Mak said. "Box office returns show that audiences are tired of fast action films. That's why I have details about character motivation, how the moles became who they are and what they face in the future."

In real life, the inner world of the undercover cop is notoriously hard to penetrate. But Mak, who spent three years writing the script, didn't have to go far for his research. He drew on his childhood memories. Both his father and eldest brother are policemen and as a youngster in Hong Kong he lived in police quarters.

"I heard many stories from my father about some of his guys who had disappeared from the police force," said Mak. "That's because they were going undercover . . . And when they finish their work and come back to the police force, after as much as 10 years undercover, they are not happy."

The uncertainty about who knows what when, and what they'll do about it, is not resolved until the final shot.

"The end was the most difficult scene to shoot," said Lau. "In Alan's script there was a fighting scene between Tony [Leung] and Andy [Lau] on the roof. But I was convinced that I just wanted pure tension, no fighting."

"We shot five different endings: in some both die, in others neither of them are dead and they become friends. And for mainland China we changed it again."

Originally published in the New York *Daily News.*

OUSMANE SEMBÈNE

Moolaadé

You have to transcend [the shock value] and prod the conscience. A good story touches people more when nothing degrading is shown.

Ousmane Sembène, 2004

Moolaadé, the new film by pioneering Senegalese filmmaker Ousmane Sembène treats the subject of female genital mutilation with sensitivity and even humor.

"Neither tradition nor religion justify this practice. It's a brake on the evolution of Africa," says the 81-year-old Sembène, whose films typically serve up blistering critiques of African society with kid gloves.

Moolaadé tells the story of a village woman who offers asylum to four small girls terrifed of being circumcised, and the violent power struggle that follows. The film's title means "sanctuary" in the West African language of Bambara.

A cruel, dangerous and illegal procedure, female genital mutilation—removal of the clitoris—is still being practised clandestinely in 38 of Africa's 54 countries; an estimated 90 million women have been harmed by it.

The female "cut and sew" procedure is performed by older women on prepubescent girls aged 7 to 10, supposedly in order to make them more marriageable. It interferes with normal physiological functions, especially childbirth. Infection from unsterilized tools poses a 10–30% risk of death.

Sembène's 1975 *Xala,* a stinging satire on postcolonial Senegal, used sexual impotence as a metaphor for official corruption. *Moolaadé* condemns arranged marriages, as well as the alleged purification rites, which dictate that women sacrifice their sexual pleasure at great cost.

"Given my age and biological education," says Sembène, "it's very hard to explain how we have become accustomed to seeking our own pleasure and not women's."

The film further shows how the blocking of women's access to information by burning their portable radios symbolizes the adherence to a repressive patriarchal society.

Fatoumata Coulibaly (right) as Colle Ardo Gallo Sy and Salimata Traore (left) as Amasatou in *Moolaadé* (2004). Courtesy New Yorker Films.

The movie is the second part of a trilogy Sembène is making about the hero- ism of daily life in Africa. The first part, *Faat Kine* (2000), is about a single mother who runs a gas station and becomes successful, despite being stigmatized.

A fisherman's son, Sembène worked as a mechanic and bricklayer before serv- ing with the Free French Army during World War II. He then worked as a long- shoreman and at a Citroën factory in Marseilles, where he was active in union struggles. He became a successful novelist, but seeking a broader African audi- ence, he started making films in the early '60s after winning a scholarship to study cinematography in Moscow.

In *Moolaadé,* Sembène's 13th feature, screams are heard but no graphic details are shown.

"You have to transcend [the shock value] and prod the conscience," Sembène says. "A good story touches people more when nothing degrading is shown, and it also opens up the discussion. I'm happy to hear my people talk to each other. But [the film is] only scraping the surface."

First published in the New York *Daily News.*

OUSMANE SEMBÈNE

Transcript

New York, January 2005—Ousmane Sembène is sitting on his hotel bed in his py-jamas. The tape recorder is propped on a notebook on the bedspread. We speak in French.[1]

Liza Béar: What a long trip. Did you come directly from Senegal?

Ousmane Sembène: Yes, from Dakar, where I still live.

LB: And your birthplace too. *Moolaadé* is a magnificent film . . .

OS: Thank you.

LB: . . . and very courageous.

OS: Why do you say that?

LB: [cringes] The subject gives me . . .

OS: Goose bumps.

LB: What prompted you to make this film?

OS: No, it's a natural choice because this is a daily problem for African men and women. And whether or not the majority of women are excised,[2] they have to go on working. But excision is a brake on the evolution of Africa. It no longer has a raison d'être. The reasons for this practice date from centuries ago. But it's become dangerous since we have the scientific knowledge of its harmful effects on women. So, we have to fight it. But it's an internal struggle.

---

[1] This is the original transcript of the interview from which the New York *Daily News* feature story was edited.

[2] Sembène uses the terms *excise, excision*, and *circumcise, circumcision* interchangeably.

Ousmane Sembène. Courtesy New Yorker Films.

LB: In what way?

OS: A struggle between African men and women. Not all of Africa carries out this practice. For instance, some cultures in Senegal do it and others don't.

LB: What reasons could there have possibly been to cause so much pain and take away women's sexual pleasure?

OS: We'll never know the original reasons. Because the practice goes back to when Egypt was black, to the time of Herodotus. He didn't know the reasons either.

LB: But you must have your suspicions.

OS: No.

Ousmane Sembène in his hotel room during the interview. Photo © Liza Béar.

LB: Oh. It has nothing to do with men's power over women?

OS: Maybe. There's so much *tiroli* [hot air] on this subject. To begin with, men have been circumcised since Abraham. In Jewish history there are debates between St. Paul and St. Peter 70 years after Jesus Christ. Jews who practised circumcision left for Europe. To distinguish one white from another, the Nazis made them drop their pants. The Jews were circumcised. But that's not my subject. As far as women are concerned, Egypt practices excision. Saudi Arabia doesn't. The Ethiopians do. Those are the most ancient cultures. The origin is lost in time. Now the practice continues and people say, oh, it's because of tradition or religion. Both [claims] are false. There are good reasons not to do it. Neither tradition nor religion justify this practice. In Egypt, the traditional method is condemned. You can go to the hospital or clinic to have it done. But it's still a criminal act.

LB: Was it hard to find this incredible village with the strange-looking mosque where you shot the film?

OS: What's strange about it?

LB: Because there's a huge anthill with big prongs jutting out of it, and next to it the mosque which looks just like a bigger version of the anthill.

OS: Why not? The mother of the first man who designed a building wasn't born in one. Maybe he was inspired by termite anthills. The land there is very flat. And these mosques are called "termitaries."

Pause. We both stare out of the hotel room's scenic window at Manhattan high rises.

OS: No difference.

LB: You found this village in Burkina Faso?

OS: Yes. We don't have termite mosques in Senegal. They belong to the Mandaingues culture . . . To human genius.

LB: How long did it take you to make the film?

OS: I don't measure time. It's difficult work that takes lots of patience. But you have to search. It took me a long time to find the village. I travelled throughout Senegal and Burkina Faso, until someone suggested the Banfora region. That's where I found this village. It was in its original condition. So I left it exactly as it was, didn't change a thing.

LB: What about the village inhabitants?

OS: They all took part in the film. They practise excision. What's unique about this village is that there's no cemetery.

LB: What do they do with their dead?

OS: They keep them home. Because now we are deep into African legend. The dead are not dead, they live on with us.

LB: True. Do they cremate?

OS: They don't burn, they bury.

LB: Underneath the house?

OS: Yes.

LB: But in *Moolaadé,* for the two little girls who drowned in the well.

OS: Well, they made a burial mound. That's because the act of dying in a well is condemned. When you die in a well, you're cutting off the source of water to the living. Here we are in a language of metaphors that's completely ignored by Europeans.

LB: The cast was made up of villagers but also some actors, like Colle?

OS: Colle, the three or four wives and the leading men are not professional actors but radio announcers. So they are in touch with people who accept modernity. Here I had to make them work with the villagers, rehearse for several months, figure out the camera angles and discipline everybody. Because Africans talk a lot. And when you're making a film, you have to have some respect for time. It's mathematical.

LB: You worked with or without a script?

OS: With a script that I wrote. But I let the actors make shortcuts in the dialogue. Sometimes a look is enough. You have to give actors that freedom.

LB: And there was no resistance, in the village, to treat a subject that's so uh . . .

OS: Oh no, we had to negotiate. Remember, this is Africa. We had to talk to everybody for a very long time and try to persuade them.

LB: What's interesting is that the film is not just about excision, it has many other themes, like . . .

OS: . . . liberty. The village itself hasn't changed. But the men [in the story] move. They arrive. They leave. For instance, the mercenary has been to war. This is happening right now in Guinea-Bissau with soldiers returning from a peace-keeping mission—their salary was stolen. They weren't paid and they rebelled. They nearly provoked a coup d'état. But the son of the village chief, we don't know what he did in Europe, but he came back with lots of ideas.

LB: He made money.

OS: So, that's important. For me that means that Africa can no longer seal itself off. Refusal. Africans know that now. Others bring us new ideas, which enable us to overcome . . . For instance, the water pump. OK, for Europeans that's a trifle but for us in the savanna it means we can get access to water. Water is life. *Voilà*.

LB: Apart from Colle, the woman who offers sanctuary to the little girls, the two men play a crucial role in the film. And both come from outside the village.

OS: Africa must open itself up. All countries, all cultures have borrowed from others and enriched themselves. I'm in New York, I learn things which I'll take home.

LB: At the screening I went to the audience was very surprised that it was Mercenaire who stopped the violence when Colle's husband whips her to make her say the word that will end the moolade.

OS: He intervenes because he's for peace. He's from another culture. The two men of the world, Mercenaire and Doukouré's son, always speak to each other in French although they both know the native languages, *bambara, mandingue*. As though speaking French adds something fresh to what they're saying.

LB: Still, that's a nice dramatic twist with Mercenaire—what a name.

OS: I named him after my wife!

LB: A business man who jacks up the price of bread . . .

OS: But he's also fairminded.

LB: Why doesn't the son of the village chief stop the domestic violence?

OS: No, he can't do that because here the movement [against excision] is led by women. Those who listen to the radio. It's their fight. Unfortunately even today in Africa, excision is not a concern for a large number of men. You accept the practice or you don't. But you keep your mouth shut. The village chief's son is offered an 11-year-old bride. In Senegal, like the rest of Africa, there are still arranged marriages. African men have to accept that women can lead the struggle for the common good. Men only know how to wage war. But in daily life, women's struggle is harder. It's heroic. I know all about it, the daily heroism of women.

LB: *Moolaadé* is part of a trilogy about women, right? First there was *Faat Kiné*, about a fortyish single parent who owns a gas station.

OS: I've written another script to be shot in Dakar, this time about a man and about problems of African society, *The Brotherhood of Rats*. There are film labs in Morocco and South Africa. I process my film and edit in Rabat. We can make entire films in Africa.

LB: So, the ostrich egg on top of the mosque?

OS: Represents the myth of creation. According to the *Mandingues*, the world originates from an ostrich egg. During the first conversions to Islam, they built these mosques with the termite architecture and they adhered to their cosmogony. Instead of the star and the crescent like the Arabs, the *Mandingues* kept these symbols. But this was at a time when ostriches lived in that region. Now you find them in South Africa. In Morocco they're starting to raise them for their meat. They make good steak. And ostrich eggs and feathers are very pricey. Another thing about the village where we shot was that it has no electricity. We used generators. And it's not the only one. Burkina Faso used to be Upper Volta and was under French rule.

LB: Is is true that 90 million women have been circumcised?

OS: Of the 54 African nations there are 38 that follow this practice, even today. There are laws against it in Senegal and Burkina Faso. So it's done clandestinely. It's going to be a long fight. But what's good is that women are leading the fight. But the men resist.

LB: But you think that men are so hooked on their own sexual pleasure that they want to deny it to women?

OS: I wouldn't go that far. But what do men know?

LB: Oh. They don't even know it's possible.

OS: Well, do they? That's the problem right there.

LB: They don't think women can experience . . .

OS: It's very hard to explain, given my age and biological education. We're accustomed to seeking our own pleasure and not that of the woman. Nothing is explained.

LB: Mothers don't talk to their sons.

OS: No. Because although the mothers suffer the pain, they're the ones who take their daughters to the excision ceremony. It's not the father. The father takes the son, the mother the daughter. If not, she's afraid that . . .

LB: The daughter will be *bilakaro* [unmarriageable].

OS: There's not only the excision [of the clitoris] but infibulation [sewing up]. There's no point in being shocked.

LB: I'm not shocked, it hurts me to think about it.

OS: It hurts everybody. That's what people should understand. I make films so that people can talk about this practice. There have been plenty of documentaries made by NGOs that show the graphic details of how it's done. But we have to transcend the problem and trigger people's conscience. And a good story is much more moving, and more discreet than [those documentaries]. *Moolaadé* helps women to get discussions started because they're the ones who screen it. In my opinion, nothing in my film shames the individual. That makes it possible to have a discussion. The question is always, why excise? I know that the subject extends far beyond me. This is my people's problem.

LB: Has *Moolaadé* been shown in Africa?

OS: Yes. It's still being shown.

LB: Did any African country refuse to show it?

OS: No. No one can prevent it being shown. It's the women who are doing it. Not me.

LB: Was the character of Colle based on a real woman?

OS: No. For years I did interviews and research on the procedure. I spoke to women. Five or six years ago when I started to write the script, I met a young couple. The woman explained the pains she had when she was with her husband, how difficult it was for her to have children. I met women doctors who took me to the lab and explained everything. Everyone knows I did really thorough, in-depth research. And although I'm happy that people like the film, I barely scratch the surface of the truth[3] about this crisis.

---

[3] The French expression Sembène used is "en dessous de la verité."

LB: The opposite would be what?

OS: To be above the truth. When you're above the truth you start to lie.

LB: At this point in history, there's a conflict between religious fanatics and humanists who believe in the values of the Enlightenment, reason, freedom of choice, and so on. But in the past few years religion is threatening to destroy those values.

OS: But is it religions or individuals?

LB: Individuals . . .

OS: Who claim to be religious. And to be prophets of doom.

LB: And to have a monopoly on truth. Intolerance.

OS: Those people aren't really religious. I made a film called *Guelwaar* which explored this topic in Africa. It was before Khomeini's time, I remember. I already anticipated this conflict. Because I'm from a very *maraboutique* family.

LB: *Maraboutique*?

OS: Yes, practising Muslims. From hearing debates, I could tell there was a real problem looming. And now we're in the throes of it. Europe went through it during the Inquisition. You had the man who said, and still it turns . . .

LB: Galileo.

OS: Men haven't evolved very much since then. And science should have helped us live better, to share, but instead there's this . . . It's very dangerous.

LB: You've been making films for 40 years and before that you wrote novels. What has changed for you, as a director?

OS: I'm a man like others. I'm responsible for what's being done on earth, good or bad. But I have children and grand-children. What kind of a future do we want?

LB: But I meant as a director.

OS: As a filmmaker, I'm happy to promote debate. It was the President of Senegal's wife, and the President of Burkina-Faso's wife who came to Cannes when *Moolaadé* was screened, and who hosted the reception. There was so many women there I was beginning to get anxious! It's part of this very very slow work that brings about social change.

MICHAEL WINTERBOTTOM
Tristram Shandy: A Cock and Bull Story

Known for his audacious treatment of tough and timely topics that skilfully blends documentary and narrative techniques in a variety of genres (Wonderland, In This World, Code 46, Nine Songs), *Michael Winterbottom's latest* Tristram Shandy: A Cock and Bull Story *is a wild, rambunctious double take on Laurence Sterne's* The Life and Opinions of Tristram Shandy, Gentleman. *Written by Martin Hardy, this is probably one of the funniest and liveliest adaptations of a historical novel ever made and the themes and form of the film (birth, the interweaving of life and art, storytelling digressions) mesh well with the literary original.*

Using a film-within-a-film structure, the film smartly captures the ribald comedy of Sterne's endlessly discursive eighteenth-century novel, hereto considered unfilm- able. An excellent cast headed by Steve Coogan (24 Hour Party People) *as Sterne's comic hero, features Rob Brydon, Keeley Hawes, Shirley Henderson, Naomie Harris, Kelly MacDonald, Jeremy Northam and a hilarious cameo by Gillian Anderson as Widow Wadham.*

Whether trading verbal barbs with his competitive co-star and vaguely look-alike Rob Brydon, or hung upside down in a giant artificial womb, Coogan is in top co- medic form here in his triple roles as Tristram Shandy, his father Walter Shandy and himself. Witty repartee, outrageous set pieces and a frantic pace tempered by genuine moments of tenderness as the overwhelmed new father tries to meet his obligations on and off the set are enhanced by superb cinematography and editing.

Liza Béar spoke with Michael Winterbottom last Fall [2004] while he was in town for his screening at the New York Film Festival. The film opens next week.

Liza Béar: I noticed that you're working on *The Road to Guantanamo*—sounds pretty intense.

Michael Winterbottom: Yep. It's a just a long journey about three friends, Muslims—two are 19 and one 23—from a small town in England and how they ended up in Guantanamo. It's based on the real life accounts of three friends who were released about a year and a half ago. We met them in London at their lawyer's, Garreth Pierce—he's a very famous human rights lawyer. Then we spent some months interviewing them. We had 600 pages of transcripts. In *Guantanamo* we're recreating parts of their experience using other people, but also retelling the story. So it's a mixture.

LB: Your first adaptation was Thomas Hardy's *Jude the Obscure—Tristram Shandy* seems a lot more ballsy and challenging.

MW: I first read it when I was about 17. But filming it was Frank Cottrell Boyce's idea originally, a writer I've worked with a lot. While we were working on the screenplay for *24 Hour Party People*, we talked a bit about *Tristram Shandy* being a similar shaggy dog story with no point to it, lots of digressions. Eventually I wanted to work with Steve [Coogan] again, so we thought we should do *Tristram Shandy* with Steve playing three roles.

LB: Switching fast between the parallel stories and the direct camera address, the comic timing really works.

MW: I did direct camera address in *24 Hour Party People* too. Steve [Coogan] is quite good at all that stuff. Having worked with him in *24 Hour Party People*, it was easier to imagine what he could do and couldn't do. . . . Obviously we tried to make the screenplay as funny as the book. But in terms of directing, I just observed, hoping what [the actors] were doing would be funny. Left the comedy up to them.

LB: It's very much told from the expectant father's point of view.

MW: Yes. In spite of the cleverness and the digressions, at heart it's a very domestic story. It is about a father trying to organize everything for the arrival of his son and all the things that could go wrong, do go wrong . . . So, yeah, I liked focussing on that aspect of the story. It seemed the most recognizable for a modern audience. It's unusual in the eighteenth century to find a father so worried about childbirth, labor, education and so on. As for the filmmaking story—it's not that I'm so interested in showing the filming process, it was more that since the book is so much about writing a book, we had to have some equivalent of that. Also it's a way of dealing with some of the same themes and characters and emotions in that section as well . . .

LB: The injury to the cock with the window sash . . . The material is really bawdy and Chaucerian.

MW: Exactly. In the book, nose and cock are interchangeable. He's worried about the size of his nose, he wants a big nose—it's full of cheap humor. Initially it wasn't a very popular book. Laurence Sterne was a small village vicar in his forties when he wrote it. No publisher wanted it. He paid for it himself. It became a huge popular success, Sterne became rich and famous and made his way down to London.

LB: Did you try to steer clear of bad taste?

MW: Well, it's hard to know where that is, really. [laughter] In the end you just decide, I like this, this and this.

LB: Are you a recent father?

MW: No, no, I've got two quite old girls.

LB: Did you show the script to your wife or your partner?

MW: Uh, no, not really.

LB: The birthing process in the film is incredibly protracted.

MW: During the labor scene, the women are commonsense and practical, while the men talk nonsense in the other room, out of touch with what's happening with the women. The reason it's protracted in both the book and the film is because the narrator wants an excuse to tell other bits of the story.

LB: So it's part of the digressions.

MW: Yes, it's more about storytelling than about the story itself. But hopefully the film has a similar tone to the novel, which is that in spite of all its silliness, you like the people. If you didn't, you wouldn't bother with it. Hopefully you become engaged with Walter and recognize the stupidities as the sorts of things that you would do.

LB: I like the opening music—ridiculously upbeat.

MW: All the music is from other film scores—Schumann from Bergman's *Fanny and Alexander*, Nyman from *Draughtman's Contract*. Then there's a lot of Nina Rota from Fellini. The Handel is from *Barry Lyndon*.

LB: [Steve's love interests] both having the same name, [Jenny and Jennie] is pretty fresh.

MW: The idea is that when Steve steps off set, he's got as many diffent things as possible distracting him from what he says he really wants to do, which is to be with his girlfriend and baby.

LB: What does Steve Coogan represent for the British public?

MW: He had a very successful TV series called Alan Partridge, which is now on BBC America. He plays flawed characters. So here Steve played a version of himself.

LB: Whereas Jeremy Northam was unusually low-keyed as Mark the director in the film.

MW: He wasn't supposed to be, but everybody else on the set thought he was being quite like me, letting the actors wander around.

LB: So now for you it's back to the orange suits and the shackles?

MW: All of that. We're halfway through. We've filmed in Afghanistan and Pakistan and now we're going to Iran to recreate Afghanistan, and also to recreate Guantanamo in Iran.

LB: Any problems getting in and out of Afghanistan and Pakistan?

MW: Pakistan's always a bit of a hassle, security services and so on. Kabul was fun. A lot of foreign presence, lot of troops, but we found a British bar.

First published on *indiewire.com*.

BRUNO DUMONT
Twentynine Palms

Bruno Dumont, a former philosophy professor, has made quite a name for himself with only two films: La Vie de Jésus *(1997), about the life of an unemployed youth, and* Humanité *(1999), about a self-questioning police officer who may or may not have killed a child. Shot in Dumont's unassuming, overcast home town of Bailleul in Northern France, both are powerful, stark, compassionate fables using nonprofessional actors in the tradition of Bresson and De Sica.* Humanité *made waves at Cannes when it walked off not only with the Grand Jury prize but also with awards for best actor and best actress.*

Dumont's new film Twentynine Palms *is set in the blazing heat of California's Joshua Tree National Park. A couple in the throes of a torrid love affair (David Wissiak and Katia Golubeva), driving a dark red Hummer, fuck and fight their way through motels, swimming pools, parking lots and some of the wildest, most bizarre landscapes of the Mojave Desert, in search of locations. There, another end greets them.*

The absolutist phrase "good and evil" has gotten a bad rap through its misuse by fundamentalists of all persuasions. Twentynine Palms *is even more of an allegorical fable than Dumont's earlier work, and his concerns seem genuinely philosophical rather than pseudo-moral. But I'll let him spell them out. The following is an excerpt from our discussion, conducted in French during Rendez-Vous With French Cinema, where the film had its U.S. premiere. Wellspring opens the film in New York and Los Angeles today.*

Liza Béar: This wasn't your first trip to the U.S., was it?

Bruno Dumont: No. I'd been here several times as a student and for the screening of *La Vie de Jésus* and *Humanité*. But in 2000 my producers took me out to the West Coast for the first time. I wanted to make a film called *The End*. It was a meditation on Hollywood cinema, which takes on its characteristics but then self-destructs. It's a bit naïve as a project, but I like the idea of challenging Hollywood on its own turf. It's important to do that.

LB: Sort of like culture-jamming.

BD: Exactly. You go into something and adopt its format, its look, key elements like the star system but your objective is entirely different.

LB: Do you think you did that in *Twentynine Palms*?

BD: No. *Twentynine Palms* was made as an experimental film while we were location scouting. I realized it would take ages to get *The End* off the ground and I wanted to shoot right away.

LB: You really liked this particular desert.

BD: Yes, much more than Death Valley, which did nothing for me. What I liked especially was that the trees gave a vertical element to a flat horizontal landscape. That's quite rare.

LB: They're also a weird shape.

BD: Yes, contorted, twisted.

LB: And the boulders look anthropomorphic and antediluvian at the same time.

BD: Absolutely. And they suddenly appear out of nowhere . . . Amazing.

LB: Yet the two lovers stark naked on the rocks are totally engrossed with each other, seemingly oblivious of their surroundings. You might say that their very lack of awareness or vigilance puts them in harm's way. It doesn't occur to them that others might be aroused by this overt sexuality or envy their freedom.

BD: Exactly. Good and evil are polar concepts—one can't exist without the other. If there was no evil . . . The couple is in the primordial human condition of sexual bliss, but with this threat of disaster that can spring from any quarter without reason and without cause.

LB: And for which the narrative offers no clues.

BD: No. My thinking was that today's spectator is so well-versed in film language that all theories about suspense, as argued by Dreyer and Hitchcock, on what makes you scared in cinema, can be ditched. It's the spectator, finally, who's going to construct the menace and the fear. In *Twentynine Palms,* because supposedly nothing is happening, it's impossible, something has to happen. What I discovered during the editing was that a dramatic tension emerged [between the scenes] that hadn't been there during the shooting.

LB: Yes, but that's partly the result of your very precise mise-en-scène.

BD: Maybe, but the more elaborate your narrative, the more the spectator shuts up and listens obediently. And if the filmmaker keeps quiet, the spectator will himself project his own assumptions and sentiments onto the screen.

LB: Had you wanted to make a horror film before you went out west?

BD: No. I decided to because of what I felt when I got there. I'd never been to a desert before and I had this profoundly metaphysical experience of fear.

LB: Not even the Sahara?

BD: No.

LB: Were you there at night?

BD: No, just in the daytime. But I knew I was in the USA where anything can happen.

LB: Well, in Europe too.

BD: Yes, but . . . no no no no no. There's a longstanding myth about the United States that is still very prevalent in Europe [despite recent developments]. Historically the "America" of this myth is an incredible human adventure and an experiment in political democracy. But at the same time, or so we're told, it's the land of extremes where the worst can happen.

LB: Yeah, but . . . What led to the casting of unknown actor David Wissak and the Russian Katia Gulebova?

BD: Mainly budget. My first choice was to work with only English-speaking American actors, but the financial partners in the film wanted 50 percent of the dialogue to be in French. I'd met Katia Golubeva in Los Angeles. She spoke very bad French. That she was Russian was incidental to the story—I had absolutely no geopolitical intentions. So, interestingly, the two of them could barely communicate.

LB: Except physically.

BD: Yes, which was great.

LB: To go back to this very erotic rapport in such a harsh location that's so exposed to the elements, sun, cold—was this in counterpoint?

BD: Well, I saw it as harmony rather than contrast. I saw the desert as a savage, even regressive place, where the human body is at one with nature—naked rocks, naked bodies. The couple are regressing precisely in their lack of awareness, of verbal language, everything that we think of as human and civilized—to try to revert to some instinctual state. You can't go further than being naked. And they're recharging their . . . they're taking the sun.

LB: The sex in this film is very much like the sex in your first film, *La Vie de Jésus*.

BD: Yes, raw, primal. Sex becomes violent when you eliminate all the sentiments . . . voilà, it gets crude. I wrote the script in two weeks flat.

LB: So the little narrative incidents, the lovers' fight, the dog with three legs—did those come up during the shoot?

BD: What's experimental about the film is that it stays clear of all the normal romantic conventions. It's about the banality of the couple. About boredom, anticipation, anger, reconciliation. All the so-called trivia, the details of a relationship, I made those the focus. I wanted to reduce the importance of the subject matter and change the figure-ground relationship. Have two tiny little figures against a vast backdrop. The best parallel I can think of is the transition from figurative to abstract painting.

LB: So with this very, very radical ending, do you think some people might not understand what you're up to?

BD: Perhaps the end of the film is too definitive and authoritarian, too violent even, by comparison with the first three quarters of the film, where the viewer is quite free to wander around in his imagination. But I knew I wanted to end up with total carnage.

LB: You knew that from the start?

BD: Of course. I wanted to show how one can arrive at that point. But I did ask myself a lot of questions about it.

LB: And you also left a lot of questions for the viewer.

BD: That too.

LB: How do you see *Twentynine Palms* in relation to your first two films?

BD: I see it as moving closer to formal art. My dream is that this film would be shown in museums, not in movie theatres. And that people should see it as individuals and not as a collective audience.

LB: Will your next film be shot here or in Europe?

BD: In Europe because it's less expensive. So I'm preparing something that I'll shoot in France when I get back . . . But the United States is such a potent political, cultural, and economic model in the evocation of the contemporary world, that to come here, select some elements from the prototype and rearrange them, that's really interesting artistically.

Originally published on *indiewire.com*.

Zhang Yimou

Hero

China, third century B.C.: *all war, all the time? Not if you allow Emperor Qin to unify feudal societies, build the Great Wall of China, and rule all the Warring States, supposedly putting an end to bloodshed and suffering for their folks. That seems to be the premise of Zhang Yimou's first martial arts movie* Hero, *in the eyes of its ironically named hero Nameless (Jet Li). Of course there's a bunch of assassins out there who don't agree, and he has to dispose of them.*

Trying to see things from an Emperor's perspective at a point in our own contemporary history when "empire" has again reared its ugly head, one may wonder at the red, white and blue coloration of Hero, *but it would be culturally presumptuous to read too much into it, especially on the basis of a very short interview via translator.*

Arguably the most internationally esteemed, versatile, and rebellious of Fifth Generation filmmakers, Zhang Yimou, whose unconventional wedding photographs won him entrance to the Beijing Film Academy as a cinematographer, clearly thrives on aesthetic and bureaucratic challenges. Acclaimed for his stunning compositions shooting Chen Kaige's Yellow Earth *(1984), he soon made a mark with* Red Sorghum *(1987), his directorial debut, followed by the not-to-be-missed trilogy,* Ju Dou *(1990),* Raise the Red Lantern *(1991), and* The Story of Qiu Ju *(1992). These early masterpieces, set in the first half of the 20th century, were strongly centered on China, the land and its people from a sensual, nuanced perspective of gender and generation far removed from social realism. (It took them a while to woo the censors.) With* Hero, *set in 212* B.C., *Zhang delves into ancient China with a fictional tale about Nameless, a loyal low-level functionary who eliminates three potential assassins of the ranking Emperor Qin with his invincible swordsmanship. These feats grant him a close audience with the Emperor. In differently colored flashbacks, three versions of his exploits are recounted.*

At a ten-pace distance, disabling the brutal tyrant would be a cinch. Yet, uncon-ventionally in martial arts terms, Nameless spares him. Succumbing to the yells of the crowd to execute him—much as Pontius Pilate was to do in 33 B.C.—Qin doesn't return the favor and has Nameless executed. He is nevertheless buried as a hero.

How to read the official endorsement of Hero *as China's next Oscar nomination? As an acknowledgment of its box office success, or as a surge of national pride in the highest-budgeted Chinese film ever made? After all, however fictitiously,* Hero *draws on deep history: the birth of China as a nation.*

Memorable for its finely-judged performances, superlative sound design and stylized visual compositions, shot by renowned Australian cinematographer Chris Doyle, this is a martial arts film that contrasts orderly military formations in wide shot with lyrical close-ups. A volley of arrows fills the skies like a swarm of bees or plague of locusts rather than the tools of warfare. Lingering shots of gleaming metal, the sonorous hiss clang and echo of a sword being unsheathed or falling to the ground evoke harmonics and reverb rather than unsightly atrocities—torn limbs and mem-branes or screams of pain.

Unlike Crouching Tiger's *didactic exposition,* Hero's *script unfurls coils of in-trigue, betrayal and revenge as agile and tortuous as the swordplay itself. Wry, spare dialogue enables Tony Leung, Maggie Cheung, Jet Li and Chen Dao Ming as the Emperor to rely on glancing looks to telegraph a gauntlet of emotions. Whether your heart aches from a surfeit of beauty, you'll have to decide for yourselves.*

Liza Béar interviewed Zhang Yimou in New York in 2004.

Liza Béar: When we last talked four years ago you'd just made *Not One Less*, about a 13-year-old teacher substitute in an impoverished rural school who saves a runaway student. What made you go in a very different direction?

Zhang Yimou: I've been reading martial arts novels since I was a child.

LB: [noticing book cover on table] In fact you're reading one now.

ZY: [laughter] When I graduated from school, young people all wanted to shoot art films. Nothing commercial. But during the last 7–8 years, the market for Chinese films is shrinking. Because the Hollywood films just came into China, and influenced . . .

LB: Isn't there a quota on imports of Hollywood films?

ZY: The problem is that Hollywood is competition for Chinese art films. So I thought I should make a film with box office promise, that refers to Chinese culture, but also contains an art element. That's why everything is in one film. I have to thank *Crouching Tiger Hidden Dragon*, because Ang Lee did something new for martial arts. To shoot *Hero* we needed a lot of money. Ang Lee created some space [for other filmmakers] to experiment. Both Ang Lee and I used an art film style in a martial arts movie.

LB: What is the philosophy behind *Hero*?

ZY: There's a writer in China [who] wrote martial arts novels. He said the best fighter in Chinese history will fight for the country and for the people. It's a very old saying in ancient China, from several thousand years ago, by the martial arts people, the best ones. But after the Cultural Revolution, things became more politicized.

LB: Jet Li has the chance to assassinate the King, and he doesn't. So maybe there's a different concept of a hero in the film?

ZY: *Hero* follows the ancient tradition. The number one fighter in the country would care for the people first. Jet Li understands that if he doesn't kill the Emperor, it's better for the people, because the war will end. The number one martial arts fighter decided not to kill the king, for the sake of peace. In this movie, my idea was to convey the message of peace.

LB: So your interest in the story, which you co-wrote, was in a strange way to make a pacifist film. Because the mood of the film seems not very warlike— long close-ups, the focus on visual structure, to suggest that beyond killing, there's another level of being, like in Taoism.

ZY: Well, trust is part of the martial arts tradition, like for example, between Tony Leung and Jet Li, and also at the end of the movie between Jet Li and the Emperor, they build up the trust between them.

LB: To go back to the question of limits on Hollywood imports.

ZY: When China joined the WTO, the rule was that the first year, 20 foreign movies could be imported to China. The second year, it was 30. Right now it seems like 40 foreign films can get into China. Most of them are Hollywood commercial movies. For example, in mid-June, *Troy* will be released in China, almost the same day as in Hong Kong. The young people in China love watching Hollywood movies. So do the young people in Hong Kong, Taiwan and Japan. I and other Chinese directors want the government to take action about this. Because the foreign films have a cultural impact, and that creates a problem for the Chinese films. The government cannot ban all foreign films from coming in because there's already a contract in existence. But what they can do is to limit the release date—so as to retain the golden release period for the Chinese films. It's necessary for the Chinese government to have a policy to prevent what happened to Hong Kong and Taiwan and Japan. They need to have a look at other countries and see what [Hollywood] films have done to them before they decide what can be done to protect Chinese film. But these controlled release date arrangements will be helpful.

LB: How exactly will that work?

ZY: The government will give the first 15 to 20 days [after release] as a golden period for Chinese movies. But there's still a problem. Because Chinese movies don't have such a high box office, sometimes the theater managers will get

Hollywood movies to replace them after only three days, in spite of the regulations. The ruling isn't a total guarantee.

LB: How easy or difficult was it for you, directing the swordplay and so on?

ZY: I discussed the action sequences with Tony Ching, the action director, while I was writing the story and also on set. We would decide what the martial arts should look like. But when it came to the moment of directing, I would let Tony Ching execute. Normally, what you see as two minutes on the screen took us 10 to 15 days to shoot. When Tony thought of some important changes for the direction, he would come back to me and discuss them first. While Tony was directing the action, my job was to sit and watch the monitor, and I looked like an assistant director. It might take four hours to shoot one shot.

LB: How did you come up with the color changes in the film: red, white, blue and green?

ZY: *Hero* is not a traditional martial arts movie. It's very structurally presented. I like Rashomon, and thought I could use different colors to represent different parts in the movie.

LB: Why those particular colors, red, white and blue?

ZY: There's no particular meaning to each color. I just needed the colors to represent . . .

LB: Points of view.

ZY: Yes, yes. Each color represents a different period and different [way of telling the] story . . .

LB: What was it like working with Tony Leung and Maggie Cheung on the set?

ZY: *Hero* is a director's movie, and so the actors don't have much space to maneuver in, which is a pity because they are really great actors. Because the movie is so tightly structured, their acting choices are limited. Both Tony Leung and Maggie Cheung could each carry a 2-hour movie. They need to play something from the heart.

LB: Exactly when and how did Quentin Tarantino get involved with this project?

ZY: Miramax [told] me that they wanted to put a credit for Tarantino at the head of the movie, kind of with Quentin Tarantino's recommendation. I feel very happy about that because he and I are old and good friends, and Tarantino loves Chinese movies. Then in Cannes I saw Tarantino at the premiere and at the after party for *House of the Flying Daggers*. I [learned] that Miramax had asked Tarantino to make some adjustments to the film. But Tarantino loved *Hero* so much, he didn't really want to change it, he wanted to protect the film as it was. But I think Tarantino gave his recommendation [in order] to help with the distribution.

Originally published on *indiewire.com*.

YACEF SÂADI

The Battle of Algiers

You can kill someone, but to educate him that's something else. And during the war we destroyed. There was an enemy and we killed him. Creating something is very difficult.

Yacef Sâadi, 2004

It's rare that a revolutionary leader becomes a film producer, and even more rare that a fiction film becomes the gold standard of cinema verité filmmaking. The Battle of Algiers *(1965), which recreates a key phase from 1954 to 1957 of the Algerians' fight against the French colonialists, is unique. Its meticulously realized authenticity results from having been shot in the Casbah, exactly where the events took place; and also from the collaboration of Italian resistance fighter and new realist director Gillo Pontecorvo with coproducer Yacef Sâadi, a former Front de Libération National (FLN) chief on whose experiences the film is directly based. Apart from the French paratrooper Colonel Mathieu (Jean Martin), the sterling cast is made up Algerian non professionals headed by Ali La Pointe (Brahim Haggiag) whose fiery intensity is the film's animus. With remarkable evenhandedness and not a trace of moralizing, the film brilliantly articulates the escalating logic of attacks, mutual bombings, torture, and assassination that form the essence of guerrilla warfare and the misguided attempts to suppress it. "Not everything has been said," Yacef Sâadi says. But last week, I spoke with Yacef Sâadi, who got both the insurrection and the film started. The film opened at New York's Film Forum.*

Liza Béar: What was harder, producing the film version of *The Battle of Algiers* or trying to lead a successful revolution?

Yacef Sâadi: First of all [before I answer the question] let me say that during this fight for independence, I was arrested and betrayed by one of my lieutenants, which also happens to very important people. It's always a relative or someone close who denounces you. I was condemned to death but in 1958, when [the

The Battle of Algiers (1966 Algeria/Italy), aka *La Battaglia di Algeri,* directed by Gillo Pontecorvo, produced by Yacef Sâadi. Shown center with outstretched arm: Brahim Haggiag as Ali La Pointe. © Rizzoli. Courtesy Rizzoli/Photofest.

French General] De Gaulle came to power, my death sentence was commuted to life imprisonment and I was transferred from a prison in Algeria to one in France. With plenty of time to reflect in my cell I wanted to write down the most important events of the war . . . I couldn't have done that in Algeria, where there were still 400,000 *pied-noirs* (French colonists). Some of them were prison guards who wouldn't allow you to do anything. But as a leader and former colonel in the FLN in a French prison I benefited from the new political regime in France.

LB: Let's backtrack: You were born in Algiers in 1928. What did your parents do?

YS: My parents were illiterate Berbers from the vast rural province of Kabylie. My father came to the city very young to make a living doing odd jobs, polishing boots, carrying bags. Then he opened a store and bought a house. But I was able to go to school until 1942 when the Allies landed [in Morocco and Algeria]. That's when my education came to a halt because my school was converted into military barracks for the Allies. At the time the Casbah—where I was born—was a two-kilometer-square section of Algiers with 80,000 inhabitants. You won't find this degree of overcrowding even in China. The Casbah was built on a hill like a citadel with lots of entrances and exits which was a big help during the fighting. It served as a *maquis,* a place we could hide like in the French Resistance. So, since the Allied soldiers had taken over our school the kids hung out on the street. To survive we sold chewing gum from the U.S. Army. We called it "le bizness." As we wised up we realized that the 80,000 people in the Casbah represented a kind of apartheid.

LB: At what point did you try to change things?

YS: I was one of the first to fire a gun in 1954.

LB: But before firing the first shot?

YS: At 17 I was a member of PPA (Algerian People's Party) which became the MPLTD (Movement for Triumph of Democracy) and did a lot of activist work. My parents supported me. The entire population of the Casbah wanted an end to social injustice. So we were preparing for an armed insurrection.

LB: That's where the film starts, [in 1954] but I want to know how you prepared for that moment.

YS: Before that we had a clandestine training organization, for instance we threw rocks as practice for throwing grenades. We were preparing to liberate ourselves from the French. Now, why.

LB: Yes, why?

YS: During the Second World War the Society of Nations favored decolonization. But in practice that wasn't happening. In 1947 the French had trouble in Madagascar. Then they lost Indochina. After that Morocco and Tunisia became independent. There'd already been serious uprisings in Algeria discounted by the French. While people were celebrating victory over the Nazis, the French killed more than 45,000 in Constantine. We were just waiting our turn. So we organized a small team, which set off a series of actions throughout Algeria.

LB: When did you meet Ali La Pointe? [The hero of the film.]

YS: I didn't meet him until 1955. He was condemned to death for having fired an unloaded gun at a French policeman. In prison he was educated by the political prisoners awaiting the guillotine. They'd say to him, "You can't read or write, you're the first victim of colonialism." He was so politicized that he escaped from prison. He hid in the Casbah and was looking to join the movement. Through a contact he reached me.

LB: Did you become friends?

YS: He became my deputy. Though illiterate he had a ferocious intelligence. [Note: the FLN communicated through written messages]

LB: People in the U.S. who are seeing the film for the first time may be surprised to find that there were children and women fighting amongst the FLN.

YS: In a word, evolution within the revolution. Normally women took the back seat. But when war broke out, we needed them. They fed us. They were look-outs on the terraces [of the Casbah]. The women were indispensable and totally implicated [in the action]. Among the women who gave me cover were law students who threw off the *yashmak*. They wanted to participate directly in the struggle—plant bombs, hide weapons, do liaison work. They were exactly like the men. Sometimes better. A woman who plants a bomb is better than a man who does nothing or just hands out flyers. They played a key role [getting past checkpoints where a man would have been searched]. Of course, there were some traditional women. Even now, 80 percent of Algerian women don't cover their faces, except in the past few years these fundamentalists who pretend to be Muslims make demands on women.

LB: How did you meet Pontecorvo, the director of the film?

YS: He's a genius who transferred what I wrote into cinematic language.

LB: But how did you meet him?

YS: When I got out of jail after independence my memoirs were published in France. But the French weren't interested in making a film.

LB: Understandably.

YS: At the time I was aware of Italian neorealist cinema. Pontecorvo had made a film called *Kapo*, about a girl in a Nazi concentration camp, which interested me. I already had the support of the new Algerian government. They said, "If you need anything we're there for you." I called my production Casbah Films because I was born in the Casbah. We've co-produced several films including an adaptation of *The Stranger* by Albert Camus and one about an executioner, the guy who cuts heads. When I finally met Pontecorvo in Rome he already wanted to make a film called *Para* from the point of view of a French paratrooper in Algiers with Paul Newman. I said, "Look, I lived there, I was a colonel, I know everything and I wrote this." Pontecorvo read it and said, "Let's call a screen-writer, Solinas." Making the film became an immediate priority for them.

LB: Pontecorvo had fought in the Italian resistance and was a member of the Communist Party.

YS: For a while.

LB: Once on location, you knew the terrain. As a colonel in the FLN "knowing the terrain" meant that you could be efficient. But in terms of shooting the film, your knowledge enabled Pontecorvo to make the best directorial choices.

YS: Yes, I was his facilitator.

LB: Were you there elbow to elbow during the production?

YS: Yes absolutely. Pontecorvo wanted to make a "choral" film. I told him it's because of the people that we got independence. Pontecorvo wanted me to be in the film as an FLN leader. But I hesitated.

LB: Why?

YS: Because I had played that part for real. For real I had killed. It was difficult to act the part. Then I accepted. I told myself [that by being in the film] I would then be able to guide Pontecorvo, warn him when something didn't ring true. All the events in the film, we shot them in the exact place where it had happened.

LB: For example?

YS: My arrest in the hide-out. All the details were recreated. The bombs (at the Milk Bar, the Cafeteria, and the airport lounge) were exploded in the same locations. We chose women who looked a bit European so that they could get into those places. Where Ali La Pointe died behind the false tiled wall, we rebuilt exactly the same house.

LB: Some of Ben Mhidi's key lines in the film—[paraphrasing] "It's hard to start a revolution . . . "

YS: " . . . it's harder to win it . . ." Yes, those were my lines. It doesn't matter. I give them to everybody!

LB: " . . . but the hardest is after you've won."

YS: Well, that's what's happening in Algeria right now. Ben Mhidi was assassinated by [French General] Aussaresses. He shot him, then hung him to make it look like a suicide. I gave Ben Mhidi those lines because when we spoke in real life, he would say he didn't want to be there after independence because there would be a power struggle. Algeria is unhappy because everyone wants to lead. He told me, "I hope I'm killed before independence."

LB: He really said that?

YS: I swear, just like you speaking to me now. There were people who were arrested who talked. They confessed. Under torture obviously. Ben Mhidi would say, I want to know why people talk. Finally we figured: someone who can bear 50 kilos, if you give him 100 kilos, he collapses.

LB: Were you tortured by the French?

YS: No.

LB: Never?

YS: A woman saved me.

LB: What woman?

YS: When I was arrested, I had discussions with her—I write about it in my book.

LB: Is it hard to think about all this now?

YS: Euh . . . I made a tabula rasa. I wiped the slate clean, but I haven't forgotten. I was wounded here (points to scar), but the boy next to me, he died. So I always remember.

LB: What are you doing in life right now?

YS: For the past four years I've been a senator in Algiers. I have another three to go.

LB: To go back to my first question. Is it harder to make a film or to win a revolution?

YS: It's harder to make a good film . . . You can kill someone, but to educate him that's something else. And during the war we destroyed. There was an enemy and we killed him. Creating something is very difficult.

Originally published on *indiewire.com.*

APPENDIX 1
Filmmakers by Continent and Country of Origin

AFRICA

Ousmane Sembène (Senegal)

LATIN AMERICA

Fabián Bielinsky (Argentina)
Alejandro González Iñárritu (Mexico)
Juan Carlos Cremata (Cuba)
Fernanda Montenegro (Brazil)

NORTH AMERICA

Sherman Alexie (United States)
Denys Arcand (Canada)
Miguel Arteta (United States)
Atom Egoyan, Arsinée Khanjian (Canada)
Abel Ferrara (United States)
Milos Forman (United States)
Nicole Holofcener (United States)
Jim Jarmusch (United States)

ASIA

Wong Kar-wai (Hong Kong)
Takeshi Kitano (Japan)
Alan Mak and Andrew Lau (Hong Kong)
Tsai Ming-liang (Taiwan)
Hayao Miyazaki (Japan)

Gleb Panfilov (former USSR)
Masayuki Suo (Japan)
Wayne Wang (Hong Kong)
Wang Xiaoshuai (China)
Zhang Yimou (China)

AUSTRALIA

Gillian Armstrong
Shirley Barrett
Judy Davis

EASTERN EUROPE

Lucian Pintilié (Romania)
Jan Sverak (Czechoslovakia)

WESTERN EUROPE

Chantal Akerman (Belgium)
Alain Berliner (Belgium)
Catherine Breillat (France)
Laurent Cantet (France)
Karim Dridi (France)
Bruno Dumont (France)
Marleen Gorris (Netherlands)
Rupert Graves (United Kingdom)
John Hurt (United Kingdom)
Cédric Klapisch (France)
Patrice Leconte (France)

Chris Menges (United Kingdom)
Manoel de Oliveira (Portugal)
François Ozon (France)
Jacques Rivette (France)
Brigitte Rouan (France-Algeria)
Barbet Schroeder (France-Colombia)
Shawn Slovo (United Kingdom)
Agnès Varda (France)
Michael Winterbottom (United Kingdom)

MIDDLE EAST

Ra'anan Alexandrowicz (Israel)
Abbas Kiarostami (Iran)
Mohsen Makhmalbaf (Iran)
Samira Makhmalbaf (Iran)
Jafar Panahi (Iran)
Elia Suleiman (Palestine)

APPENDIX 2

First Feature Films

Ra'anan Alexandrowicz, *James' Journey to Jerusalem*   254
Sherman Alexie, *Smoke Signals*   157
Miguel Arteta, *Star Maps*   128
Shirley Barrett, *Love Serenade*   134
Alain Berliner, *Ma Vie en Rose*   144
Fabián Bielinsky, *Nine Queens*   237
Juan Carlos Cremata, *Nada*   240
Alejandro González Iñárritu, *Amores Perros*   211
Nicole Holofcener, *Walking and Talking*   92
Cédric Klapisch, *Chacun Cherche Son Chat*   125
Samira Makhmalbaf, *The Apple*   168
Chris Menges, *A World Apart*   19
François Ozon, *Criminal Lovers*   190
Jafar Panahi, *The White Balloon*   79
Benjamin Ross, *The Young Poisoner's Handbook*   89
Brigitte Rouan, *Outremer*   39
Shawn Slovo, *A World Apart*   10
Masayuki Suo, *Shall We Dance?*   131

INDEX

About the Author

LIZA BÉAR is a New York–based writer, filmmaker, and activist. In the seventies she cofounded and edited the legendary conceptual art magazine *Avalanche*. In 1990 she received a New York Foundation for the Arts fellowship in creative nonfiction, and in 1994 an Edward Albee Writing Fellowship. She has taught at the film schools of Columbia and New York University, and her film interviews have appeared in *Newsday*, the New York *Daily News, Ms., Elle, Salon.com*, the *Boston Globe*, and other large-circulation metro dailies. She is a contributing editor at *Bomb*.